W9-CRR-222

United States
of
America

WORLD BIBLIOGRAPHICAL SERIES

General Editors:
Robert L. Collison (Editor-in-chief)
Sheila R. Herstein
Louis J. Reith
Hans H. Wellisch

VOLUMES IN THE SERIES

VOLUME 16

United States
of
America

Sheila R. Herstein
Naomi C. Robbins
Compilers

CLIO PRESS
OXFORD, ENGLAND · SANTA BARBARA, CALIFORNIA

British Library Cataloguing in Publication Data

Herstein, Sheila
United States of America. – (World bibliographical series; 16)
1. United States – Bibliography
I. Title II. Robbins, Naomi III. Series
016.973   Z1201

ISBN 0-903450-29-1

Clio Press Ltd.,
Woodside House, Hinksey Hill,
Oxford OX1 5BE, England.
Providing the services of the European
Bibliographical Centre and the American
Bibliographical Center.

American Bibliographical Center-Clio Press,
Riviera Campus, 2040 Alameda Padre Serra,
Santa Barbara, Ca. 93103, U.S.A.

Designed by Bernard Crossland
Computer typeset by Peter Peregrinus Ltd.
Printed in Great Britain
by the Camelot Press, Southampton

THE WORLD BIBLIOGRAPHICAL SERIES

This series will eventually cover every country in the world, each in a separate volume comprising annotated entries on works dealing with its history, geography, economy and politics; and with its people, their culture, customs, religion and social organization. Attention will also be paid to current living conditions — housing, education, newspapers, clothing, etc. — that are all too often ignored in standard bibliographies; and to those particular aspects relevant to individual countries. Each volume seeks to achieve, by use of careful selectivity and critical assessment of the literature, an expression of the country and an appreciation of its nature and national aspirations, to guide the reader towards an understanding of its importance. The keynote of the series is to provide, in a uniform format, an interpretation of each country that will express its culture, its place in the world, and the qualities and background that make it unique.

SERIES EDITORS

Robert L. Collison (Editor-in-chief) is Professor Emeritus, Library and Information Studies, University of California, Los Angeles, and is currently the President of the Society of Indexers. Following the war, he served as Reference Librarian for the City of Westminster and later became Librarian to the BBC. During his fifty years as a professional librarian in England and the USA, he has written more than twenty works on bibliography, librarianship, indexing and related subjects.

Sheila R. Herstein is Reference Librarian and Library Instruction Coordinator at the City College of the City University of New York. She has extensive bibliographic experience and recently described her innovations in the field of bibliographic instruction in 'Team teaching and bibliographic instruction', *The Bookmark*, Autumn 1979. In addition, Doctor Herstein co-authored a basic annotated bibliography in history for Funk & Wagnalls *New encyclopedia*, and for several years reviewed books for *Library Journal*.

Louis J. Reith is librarian with the Franciscan Institute, St. Bonaventure University, New York. He received his PhD from Stanford University, California, and later studied at Eberhard-Karls-Universität, Tübingen. In addition to his activities as a librarian, Dr. Reith is a specialist on 16th century German history and the Reformation and has published many articles and papers in both German and English. He was also editor of the *American Society for Reformation Research Newsletter*.

Hans H. Wellisch is Associate Professor at the College of Library and Information Services, University of Maryland, and a member of the American Society of Indexers and the International Federation for Documentation. He is the author of numerous articles and several books on indexing and abstracting, and has most recently published *Indexing and abstracting: an international bibliography*. He also contributes frequently to *Journal of the American Society for Information Science, Library Quarterly*, and *The Indexer*.

Contents

Contents

Contents

Introduction

The United States of America is a country of more than 225 million people. It stretches from the Atlantic Ocean to the Pacific, covering an area of more than 3 million square miles. The fifty states that comprise the nation are characterized by nothing so much as their diversity. Diversity of climate, ethnic groups, language, music, culture and tradition. Yet the variety which is uniquely American is overlaid by a political and philosophical unity that has endured and evolved in the 200 years of the nation's history.

This bibliography attempts to lead the interested reader to sources on every aspect of American life. Our purpose has been to compile a basic core collection for the serious non-specialist reader who wishes to learn more about the United States. Great efforts have been expended to ensure that a balance is maintained between older works of enduring value and newly published material. No work has been included simply because it is of recent origin. Similarly, no volume has been excluded on the basis of an arbitrary decision as to age.

The literature of the United States is enormous and we have looked at thousands of volumes, selecting carefully in an attempt to provide a final product that will give the reader a broad framework for studying the country in all its complexity. We hope that our choices represent a wide variety of political and social views.

The literature of the United States is rich with biographical works on the thousands of men and women who have contributed to every facet of the nation's growth. For reasons of space we have consciously excluded all biographical works and have chosen instead to include survey volumes in every field whose bibliographical apparatus will lead the reader to biographical material when desired.

It is also important to note that because the United States is essentially a nation of immigrants it would be impossible to give individual bibliographical representation to every racial and ethnic element within the population. Therefore the Nationalities and Minorities section attempts to alert the reader to the richness of the population, to survey

Introduction

the highlights of the immigrant experience and to point out the most important works on minorities of special interest. The term 'minorities' is used in its contemporary sense to include women, whose special problems and role within the nation's history are generating a literature of increasing scope and depth.

The annotations are intended to describe each work and to place it within the context of the general literature. There must be errors and omissions in a work of this scope and for these we apologize. We have tried to create a listing which can be used to guide a reading programme and have aimed at stimulating the reader to go from this bibliography to the works described.

We are grateful to all those who have helped us in the compilation of this book, particularly the many librarians in New York and New Jersey who have allowed us to review materials in their collections. Special thanks are due to Murray and Steven Robbins and Clara Herstein for their patience and support throughout this project.

The Country and Its People

1 **Alistair Cooke's America.**
Alistair Cooke. New York: Knopf, 1974. 400p.
This superbly illustrated survey 'in pursuit of the American essence' is based on the television series which took the noted journalist and commentator all across the United States. A well-written personal exploration of the country and its people, the text is amply supplemented by paintings, photographs, drawings and cartoons.

2 **America as a civilization: life and thought in the United States today.**
Max Lerner. New York: Simon & Schuster, 1957. 1,036p. bibliog.
Although somewhat dated in the 'today' Lerner attempted to capture, this monumental study is still a worthy introduction to modern American society. There are particularly interesting chapters on 'The arts and popular culture' and 'Class and status in America'. Lerner used a wealth of information to create a composite portrait of America in the 1950s that is far richer than the ordinary narrative. Well written for the general reader.

3 **The American conscience.**
Roger Burlingame. New York: Knopf, 1957. 420p. bibliog.
Well-researched popular survey of American moral attitudes. The author identifies a pervasive puritanism in American society, 'a peculiar American compulsion to assign moral values to every historical event, economic theory, or social trend'. Useful introduction to the literature of the American national character.

The Country and Its People

4 **The American image: photographs from the National Archives, 1860-1960.**
National Archives Trust Fund Board. New York: Pantheon, 1979. 189p.
An introductory essay by Alan Trachtenberg, 'Photographs as symbolic history', has been combined with a carefully indexed collection of 250 photographs selected from the millions compiled by government agencies for their historical value. The volume includes sections on the Civil War, the First World War, a survey of coal mines and a number of other topical subdivisions. A splendid pictorial introduction to American history.

5 **The American mind: an interpretation of American thought and character since the 1880's.**
Henry Steele Commager. New Haven, Connecticut: Yale University Press, 1950. 485p. bibliog.
Continues the analysis begun in Vernon Parrington's *Main currents in American thought* (q.v.). The 1880s are a watershed in American thought, according to Commager, who gives prominence to figures such as William James. This is a detailed, sharply analytical survey of the social thought that shaped 20th century American life.

6 **The American South: portrait of a culture.**
Edited by Louis D. Rubin. Baton Rouge, Louisiana: Louisiana State University Press, 1980. 379p. (Southern Literary Studies).
Originally *Voice of America* programmes on the South, these twenty-one essays and two conversations cover a variety of subjects, including the role of country music and the stock car in Southern life. There is a strong emphasis on literary developments in the region. Designed for the 'informed non-specialist' this is a good introduction to the region.

7 **The Americans.**
Daniel J. Boorstin. New York: Random House, 1958-73. 3 vols.
This trilogy explores the experience of American settlement and development in terms of the creation of a unique American character. The final volume emphasizes the democratization of that national character over the past hundred years and the importance of the growth of technology on the quality of life. Vol. I: *The colonial experience*; vol. II: *The national experience*; vol. III: *The democratic experience*.

8 **Anti-intellectualism in American life.**
Richard Hofstadter. New York: Knopf, 1969. 434p. bibliog.
Winner of a Pulitzer prize, this work is not a formal history of a single idea, but rather an exploration of various features of the American character. Hofstadter examines anti-intellectuals throughout United States history, but also defines the intellectual and what influence these individuals can have in a democratic society.

9 As others see us: the United States through foreign eyes.
Edited by Franz M. Joseph. Princeton, New Jersey: Princeton
University Press, 1959. 360p.
Essays by twenty foreign scholars resulting from a project of the American
European Foundation. Each author conveys a personal impression of the United
States and tries to include a synthesis of the image of America held in his
country. This attempt to construct the national character from foreign viewpoints
is fascinating and includes essays by Raymond Aron and Denis Brogan.

**10 Assimilation in American life: the role of race, religion and
national origins.**
Milton M. Gordon. New York: Oxford University Press,
1964. 276p. bibliog.
This examination of American society concludes that America is not the 'melting
pot' that has often been discussed, but rather a culturally pluralistic society. The
nation is said to consist of a variety of individual 'subsocieties' which maintain
their identities while adjusting to the 'core' of Anglo-Saxon Protestant middle
class values which provides the societal framework. The reader should consult
Polenberg's *One nation divisible* (q.v.) for a re-examination and affirmation of
this thesis.

11 The growth of American thought.
Merle Eugene Curti. New York: Harper & Row, 1964. 3rd
ed. 939p. bibliog.
A noted intellectual historian, Curti has placed the development of American
thought within a social framework. A classic work, this third edition should be
read by every student of the American experience.

12 Human nature in American thought: a history.
Merle Eugene Curti. Madison, Wisconsin: University of
Wisconsin Press, 1980. 453p. bibliog.
The dean of American intellectual historians adds to his already impressive
publication list an intriguing study of human nature. He considers the intellectual
ideas the colonists brought with them and the changes the new country caused.
He traces recurring themes in American history - democracy, patriotism, education, family and race relations. The formation and development of an American
character based on hope in the future and optimism is discussed as are major
events and themes such as puritanism, transcendentalism and Freudian thought. A
challenging and valuable contribution to the study of the American character.

13 The lonely crowd: a study of the changing American character.
David Riesman. New Haven, Connecticut: Yale University
Press, 1961. abridged ed. 315p. bibliog.
This classic study of American character types, first published in 1951, has
sparked discussion and review ever since. The author defined the population in
terms of 'inner-directed', 'other-directed' and 'autonomous' individuals. These
types derived from the changing population, society and technology that
surrounded them. Essential for every reader interested in the development of the
modern American character.

14 **O strange new world: American culture: the formative years.**
Howard Mumford Jones.   New York: Viking Press, 1964.
464p. bibliog.

Awarded a Pulitzer prize in 1965, this work is a study of the effect of Old World ways on the New. Beginning with Columbus' first report from the *Nina* in 1493, the author examines events through the 1840s, tracing the impact of European influence on American culture. Contradictions in terms of values, habits and physical surroundings led to modification, rejection, assimilation and eventually to the creation of a peculiarly American culture.

15 **One nation divisible: class, race, and ethnicity in the United
States since 1938.**
Richard Polenberg.   New York: Viking Press, 1980. 363p.
bibliog.

Well-written examination of American society since 1938. The issues of class, race and ethnicity are considered against the background of the Second World War, the cold war, Vietnam and Watergate. The author concludes that despite some modifications, class, ethnicity and race continue to divide American society. Useful interpretive volume for all levels.

16 **People of plenty: economic abundance and the American
character.**
David M. Potter.   Chicago: University of Chicago Press,
1954. 245p.

This work grew out of the Charles R. Walgreen Foundation lectures at the University of Chicago. The author's premise is that economic abundance has had a strong psychological impact on the national character. A well-written concise analysis striking a theme that has been re-echoed in later studies seeking the essence of America.

Geography

General

17 **Aridity and man: the challenge of the arid lands in the United States.**
Edited by Carle Hodge. Washington, DC: Association for the Advancement of Science, 1963. 584p. maps. (American Association for the Advancement of Science, Publication no. 74).
The result of a conference held by the Committee on Desert and Arid Zones Research of the American Association for the Advancement of Science, this is a basic collection of essays on America's arid lands, the problems of the present and the potential for improvement of existing conditions.

18 **Face of North America.**
Peter Farb. New York: Harper & Row, 1963. 316p. bibliog.
This natural history of the continent is an introduction to the variety of landforms that define and link its regions. The emphasis is on change, the geological and ecological development that results in the cycle of land formation. Each section deals with a broad landform. There are many helpful drawings and photographs as well as a useful appendix listing 'outstanding natural areas of North America, by state and province'.

19 **Physiography of eastern United States.**
Nevin M. Fenneman. New York, London: McGraw-Hill, 1938. 714p. maps.
A good basic work on physical geography, geology, climate and vegetation of the eastern portion of the United States. It remains a staple for the modern reader.

20 **Physiography of the United States.**
Charles B. Hunt. San Francisco: W. H. Freeman, 1967.
480p. maps.

An overview of the natural features and resources of the United States. The author describes physical geography, geology, climate, vegetation, etc., and discusses the variety of resources available and the need for conservation and management of these resources.

21 **Physiography of western United States.**
Nevin M. Fenneman. New York, London: McGraw-Hill,
1931. 534p. maps.

A companion to the author's later work *Physiography of eastern United States* (q.v.), this is a useful basic physical geography for the western part of the country. Both volumes remain useful studies today.

Maps and atlases

22 **Atlas of the historical geography of the United States.**
Charles Oscar Paullin. Washington, DC: Carnegie
Institution of Washington and the American Geographical
Society of New York, 1932. 162p. 688 maps. (Carnegie
Institution of Washington Publication no. 401).

A basic work consisting of a careful selection of maps, cartograms and reproductions of early maps on many different scales, illustrating the natural environment of the USA and its demographic, economic, political and military history. The text explains the maps and lists the sources from which they were compiled.

23 **Climatic atlas of the United States.**
Stephen Sargent Visher. Cambridge, Massachusetts:
Harvard University Press, 1954. 403p. 1,031 maps. diags.

A basic atlas source for the climate of the United States. It contains a finely detailed collection of maps and diagrams of the highest quality.

24 **Commercial Atlas and Marketing Guide.**
Chicago: Rand McNally, 1876/77- . annual. maps.

This standard volume is revised annually. It is the most widely known and used atlas emphasizing economically oriented geographical information on the USA. It provides information and maps of many countries in addition to extensive American coverage.

25 **A comparative atlas of America's great cities: twenty metropolitan regions.**
John S. Adams, research director, and Ronald Abler, chief cartographer. Minneapolis, Minnesota: University of Minnesota Press, 1976. 503p. maps. (Association of American Geographers. Comparative Metropolitan Analysis Project, vol. 3).

26 **Contemporary metropolitan America.**
Edited by John S. Adams. Cambridge, Massachusetts: Ballinger, 1976. 4 vols. maps. (Association of American Geographers. Comparative Metropolitan Analysis Project, vol. 1).

27 **Urban policymaking and metropolitan dynamics: a comparative geographical analysis.**
Edited by John S. Adams. Cambridge, Massachusetts: Ballinger, 1976. 576p. maps. (Association of American Geographers. Comparative Metropolitan Analysis Project, vol. 2).
This title and the two preceding entries provide a landmark contribution to students of urban problems and geography in general. The four books of volume 1 explore conditions in twenty major American cities at the end of the 1960s and examine the evolution of those cities. The second volume considers the national legislative programmes designed to deal with urban problems in relation to those areas and assesses the overall effort. Volume 3 is an atlas of information never before available on metropolitan areas. These three titles comprise an essential set for everyone studying the American city.

28 **The national atlas of the United States of America.**
Edited by A. C. Gerlach. Washington, DC: US Government Printing Office, 1970. 417p. maps.
Produced under the auspices of the US Geological Survey, this is a collection of 765 maps, including general reference maps for purely locational information and various subject maps on a variety of physical, historical, economic and cultural topics. There is an index to map subjects plus an alphabetical index of place-names and physical and cultural features. This is an unsurpassed staple for the atlas collection on the United States.

29 **Township atlas of the United States.**
John L. Andriot. McLean, Virginia: Andriot Associates, 1979. 1,184p. maps.
A series of maps showing states, counties, townships, census county divisions and other minor civil divisions for all fifty states. Broader in scope than the earlier 1977 edition, which covered only twenty-two states. There are good indexes for populated places, townships and counties.

30 **United States and Canada.**
Oxford, England: Clarendon Press, 1967. 35p. 128 plates.
(col. maps).

Prepared by the cartographic department of the Clarendon Press under the supervision of advisory editors John D. Chapman and John C. Sherman, this is a quality atlas examining economic conditions in both the United States and Canada. It remains a useful cartographic tool.

31 **The West Point atlas of American wars.**
Edited by Vincent J. Espositor. New York: Praeger, 1959. 2 vols.

Prepared by the Department of Military Art and Engineering of the US Military Academy, West Point, this is a fine two-volume atlas of military activities from America's beginnings. A must for anyone interested in military history.

Exploration and travel

32 **Discovering America, 1700-1875.**
Henry Savage, Jr. New York: Harper & Row, 1979. 394p. maps. bibliog. (New American Nation Series).

Gracefully written, carefully researched account of the explorers and naturalists who, through books and paintings and maps, first revealed to the public the wonders of North America - its geography, its pristine fauna and flora and its native people. Savage is concerned as much with scientific discovery as with geographic discovery. This work should appeal to scholar and general reader alike.

33 **The European discovery of America.**
Samuel Eliot Morison. New York: Oxford University Press, 1971-74. 2 vols. maps.

A superb account by a noted historian who made extensive use of primary sources. This work should be read by everyone interested in the exploration of the United States. Vol. 1: *The northern voyages: AD500-1600*; vol. 2: *The southern voyages: AD1492-1616.*

34 **North America from earliest discovery to first settlements: the Norse voyages to 1612.**
David B. Quinn. New York: Harper & Row, 1977. 621p. 56 maps. bibliog. (New American Nation Series).

A noted scholar on European explorations of America, Quinn has written a clear, scholarly treatment of this subject. The maps are excellent, and the fine bibliographical essay makes this work a must for every level of reader.

35 **The Old World and the New, 1492-1650.**
J. H. Elliott. New York: Cambridge University Press, 1970.
128p.
Originally delivered as lectures at Queen's University, Belfast, this is a brief, beautifully written study by a British historian. It analyses European attitudes toward the New World during the period of exploration and discusses the economic, political and cultural ramifications of the opening of that world.

36 **Original journals of the Lewis and Clark expedition.
1804-1806.**
Edited by Reuben Gold Thwaites. New York: Arno Press,
1969. 8 vols. maps.
This complete edition of the *Journals* (a reprint of the 1904-05 edition) contains enormous detail regarding the exploration carried out by President Jefferson's secretary Meriwether Lewis and others. There are useful editorial notes and a helpful introduction by Bernard Devote who edited an abridged version of the *Journals* published by Houghton Mifflin in 1953. This is an important primary source.

37 **Sixteenth-century North America: the land and the people as seen by the Europeans.**
Carl Ortwin Sauer. Berkeley, California: University of
California Press, 1971. 331p. maps.
A noted geographer examines the European reactions to the New World in the era before the beginning of colonial settlement. This volume is based to a large degree on original accounts by European explorers.

38 **Society in America.**
Harriet Martineau. New York: AMS Press, 1966. 3 vols.
This noted English author travelled for two years in the USA between 1834 and 1836. Her journey extended west to Chicago and south to New Orleans. These three volumes, reprinted from the 1837 edition, are a detailed account of her experiences and an enthusiastic appraisal of American society.

39 **This was America: true accounts of people and places, manners and customs as recorded by European travellers to the western shore in the eighteenth, nineteenth and twentieth centuries.**
Edited by Oscar Handlin. Cambridge, Massachusetts:
Harvard University Press, 1949. 602p. maps.
An excellent collection of excerpts from travel accounts by foreign visitors throughout American history. Selected by the well-known historian Oscar Handlin, who has provided explanatory comment, they provide a readable, vivid look at the developing nation through European eyes.

40 **Tocqueville in America.**
George Wilson Pierson, abridged by Dudley C.
Lunt. Gloucester, Massachusetts: Peter Smith, 1969. 506p.

Based on Pierson's *Tocqueville & Beaumont in America*, 1938, this reprint of the 1959 abridged adition is a useful source on the journey of Alexis de Tocqueville through America in the 1830s. It was this journey which inspired Tocqueville's classic *Democracy in America*, an extraordinary analysis of American society and its democratic political system.

41 **Travels in the old South.**
Edited by Thomas D. Clark. Norman, Oklahoma: University of Oklahoma Press, 1956-59. 3 vols.

This extraordinary annotated bibliography of travel accounts is an essential reference tool. It can be used with a microcard edition of the travels or as a guide to the many published editions available. Vol. 1: *The formative years, 1527-1783*; vol. 2: *The expanding South, 1750-1825*; vol. 3: *The antebellum South, 1825-1860*.

42 **Travels in the new South.**
Edited by Thomas D. Clark. Norman, Oklahoma: University of Oklahoma Press, 1962. 2 vols.

This continues the superb annotated bibliography *Travels in the old South* (see the preceding item). Here more than 2,000 annotated entries are chronologically arranged. Vol. 1: *The postwar South, 1865-1900*; vol. 2: *The twentieth century South, 1900-1955*. The years 1860-65 are omitted because of the existence of Ellis Merton Coulter's *Travels in the Confederate states* (1948), a fine annotated bibliography which completes the series.

Travel guides

43 **Adventure travel USA.**
Edited by Pat Dickerman. New York: Adventure Guides, 1976. 221p.

A guidebook to thousands of adventure excursions such as backpacking, canoe trips, ski-touring and mountaineering. This work was previously published under the title *Adventure trip guide* and continues to be updated periodically.

44 **Amazing America.**
Jane Stern, Michael Stern. New York: Random House, 1978. 463p.

A guidebook to Americana, arranged by geographical areas of the country and then by state. There are concise descriptions of local museums, unusual art, special tours, annual festivals, etc.

45 American guide series.
Compiled and written by the Federal Writers' Project and the Writers' Program. New York: Hastings House, 1939-56. reprints.

This series was produced between 1936 and 1943 as a way of keeping writers and artists employed during the Depression; the 155 volumes in the series have been gradually reissued during the intervening years because of their enduring value. They are beautifully written and extensively detailed. All are illustrated with photographs and maps. They provide a unique source for the traveller or arm-chair explorer and include volumes on American cities, states and territories.

46 Back to nature in canoes: a guide to American waters.
Rainer Esslen. Frenchtown, New Jersey: Columbia, 1976. 345p. maps. bibliog.

A useful handbook for campers and canoeists describing in detail the myriad waterways in the USA - and some in Canada which are suitable for canoeing. The work includes information on places to buy supplies, obstacles and hazards, scenery, canoe liveries available, points to enter and leave the water, portages and much more.

47 Fodor's USA.
Eugene Fodor. New York: David McKay, 1953– . annual. maps.

A standard travel guide, this annual gives up-to-date information on all states. It includes pertinent data on sightseeing, accommodation, restaurants, transportation, climate, etc. Eugene Fodor has created a well-known series of travel guides which cover many areas of the world.

48 Guide to backpacking in the U.S.
Eric Meres. New York: Macmillan, 1977. 248p. maps. bibliog.

A detailed and useful guide to backpacking for the vacation planner.

49 Mini-vacations, USA.
Karen Case. Chicago: Follett, 1976. 216p. bibliog.

This work is designed to provide ideas for short vacations within the USA. Directions to and descriptions of inns, restaurants, museums, parks, biking and hiking trails are abundant.

50 National wonders of America.
Edited by Beverly da Casta. New York: American Heritage, 1972. 319p. maps.

Prepared by the editors of *American Heritage* magazine, this compact guidebook is arranged alphabetically by state. It describes a variety of natural wonders to be seen within each state and includes all national forests, the physical features of National Park Service properties, as well as a number of privately owned sites which are open to the public. It contains information on hours and admission fees that may be out-of-date, but can easily be updated.

51 **The new America's wonderland: our national parks.**
Washington, DC: National Geographic Society, 1975. 3rd ed.
464p. maps. (World in Color Library).

A successor to the society's earlier *America's wonderland*, this beautifully illustrated volume describes the national park system, discusses environmental problems, provides information on planning vacations at the parks, and tells of new
services provided at the time of publication. The magnificent photographs are
particularly inspiring.

52 **The Random House guide to natural areas of the eastern
United States.**
John Perry, Jane G. Perry. New York: Random House,
1980. 835p. maps.

This 'field guide for people who enjoy the outdoors' describes 800 areas in fifteen
seaboard states and Vermont and West Virginia. It includes national parks and
wildlife preserves. Arranged by state with site lists within each state and useful
information on fishing, swimming and hiking as well as canoeing and backpacking, this is a must for the wanderer in the eastern USA.

53 **Scenic wonders of America.**
New York: Readers Digest Association, 1973. 575p. maps.

A lavishly illustrated volume describing the editor's choices of the fifty most
outstanding scenic places in America. Such sites as Maine's Acadia National
Park, the Florida Everglades and New York's Niagara Falls are explored and
enjoyed.

54 **Traveling weatherwise in the U.S.A.**
Edward Powers, James Witt. New York: Dodd, Mead,
1972. 299p. 150 weather maps, charts and tables.

A book for the layman, providing weather characteristics of all parts of the USA,
designed to help plan vacation, business travel or retirement locations.

55 **Traveling with children in the USA: a guide to pleasure,
adventure, discovery.**
Leila Hadley. New York: William Morrow, 1977. 480p.
(Americans Discover America Series).

A useful guidebook for families vacationing with children. Arranged alphabetically by state, the lists of places to visit include information on addresses, hours
open and whether admission is free, or if the charge is under or over one dollar.

56 **Walking: a guide to beautiful walks and trails in America.**
Jean Calder. New York: William Morrow, 1977. 340p.
(Americans Discover America Series).

A useful guide to walking trails, meant to be used with good highway maps or
park and forest maps obtained from sources indicated in the guide. Trails are
rated by difficulty in walking them, admissions are listed if charged and addresses
for further information are provided.

Archaeology and Prehistory

57 **Camera, spade and pen: an inside view of Southwestern archaeology.**
Marc Gaede. Tucson, Arizona: University of Arizona Press, 1980. 160p.
Beautifully illustrated introduction to the prehistoric archaeological sites of the American Southwest. Fourteen sites or localities are studied in detail.

58 **Chronologies in New World archaeology.**
Edited by R. E. Taylor, Clement W. Meighan. New York: Academic Press, 1978. 587p. maps. bibliog. (Studies in Archaeology Series).
Excellent reference tool on the prehistory of the New World. The summary chapter by noted scholar Gordon R. Willey, good chronological charts, area culture histories and detailed bibliographies enhance the value of the work. The regions detailed include the arctic and subarctic (Anderson), the eastern USA (Griffin), the plains (Caldwell & Henning), and California (Meighan).

59 **Discovering man's past in the Americas.**
George E. Stuart. Washington, DC: National Geographic Society, 1969. 211p. maps.
Well-illustrated readable survey of the archaeology of the Americas. This treatment is both chronological and regional and deals with the United States within the broader context of the Americas.

60 **Hidden America.**
Roland Wells Robbins, Evan Jones. New York: Knopf,
1959. 263p. maps. bibliog.
Straightforward informative guide to sites and artifacts that might be uncovered
in almost every American backyard. Aimed at the aspiring amateur archaeologist.

61 **A history of American archaeology.**
Gordon Randolph Willey, Jeremy Sabloff. San Francisco:
W. H. Freeman, 1974. 252p. bibliog.
Concise introductory survey of the archaeology of the Americas. Includes North,
Middle and South America and explains archaeological activities since 1492.

62 **In small things forgotten: the archaeology of early American
life.**
James J. F. Deetz. New York: Anchor and Doubleday,
1977. 184p.
Basic introduction to historical archaeology in America, emphasizing the New
England area. Discusses the connections between written documents and archaeological findings and examines methods of dating pottery, gravestones and house
construction.

63 **The moundbuilders of ancient America: the archaeology of a
myth.**
Robert Silverberg. New York: Graphic Society, 1968. 369p.
maps.
Useful attempt to deal with the need for a history of American archaeology. A
well-written survey of the long-standing theory that earth mounds scattered over
the eastern United States are the remains of an extinct gifted race. The mounds
still spread over valleys from the Ohio river to Wisconsin and Illinois and to
Alabama and Florida.

64 **Prehistoric man in the New World.**
William Marsh Rice University. Chicago: University of
Chicago Press, 1964. 633p. bibliog.
A series of papers resulting from a conference at Rice University in November,
1962. They include Erik Reed's 'The greater southwest', Waldo Wedel's 'The
Great Plains', Robert Heizer's 'The western coast of North America', James
Griffin's 'The northeast woodlands area', and William Sears' 'The southeast
United States'.

65 **Prehistoric man on the Great Plains.**
Waldo R. Wedel. Norman, Oklahoma: University of
Oklahoma Press, 1961. 355p. bibliog.
This summary of discoveries made in the thirty years between 1935-65 is aimed
at both scholars and general readers. It introduces the tools of the archaeologist,
presents surveys of the prehistory of the various sub-areas within the Great
Plains, as well as analysing the evidence of prehistoric man's occupation of that
area uncovered since 1935.

66 **Prehistory of the far west: homes of vanished peoples.**
Luther Sheeleigh Cressman. Salt Lake City, Utah:
University of Utah Press, 1977. 248p. maps. bibliog.

A survey by a noted authority of the prehistory of western North America from the continental divide to the Pacific ocean. Good bibliography and numerous maps and charts. The study reviews the geography of the area and discusses the earliest evidence for the initial peopling of the New World.

67 **Public archaeology.**
Charles R. McGimsey. New York: Seminar Press, 1972.
265p.

Useful reference tool and guide to public programmes and laws for the preservation of artifacts and sites in the United States. The work is aimed at raising the awareness of citizens and public officials as well as professional archaeologists toward the archaeological heritage of states and localities. More than two-thirds of the book lists state-by-state information on programmes and local legislation.

History

Reference works

68 Album of American history.
Edited by James Truslow Adams. New York: Charles
Scribner's Sons, 1960-69. 6 vols.
A standard pictorial history of America. Vol. 1: colonial period; vol. 2: 1783-
1853; vol. 3: 1853-93; vol. 4: end of an era; vol. 5: 1917-53; vol. 6: 1953-68 and
general index. Brief introductions link the pictures, which are extremely useful for
details of dress and everyday living.

69 America: History and Life.
Santa Barbara, California: ABC Clio, 1964- . five year
indexes: 1964/65-68/69; 1969/70-72/73.
This valuable bibliographical service abstracts articles on the history of the
United States and Canada published throughout the world and articles dealing
with current American life and times. It surveys some 2,200 serial publications,
including annuals and Festschriften. Numbers 1-3 of each volume contain
abstracts, the fourth quarterly issue is the annual index. Beginning in 1974 the
abstract was issued in four parts: A: article abstracts and citations; B: book
reviews; C: American history bibliography; D: annual index.

70 Atlas of American history.
Kenneth T. Jackson. New York: Charles Scribner's Sons,
1978. rev. ed. 294p. maps.
This revision of the 1943 work which carried James Truslow Adams' name on its
title page was designed as a supplement to the *Dictionary of American history*
(q.v.). It contains 198 maps; 51 are new, the others have been updated. They are
arranged chronologically and show the growth, expansion and military history,
etc., of the United States. Most of the new maps relate to 20th century developments and to topics of current interest such as the women's movement, race riots,
etc. There is an alphabetical index of the places mentioned on the maps.

71 **Biographical directory of the governors of the United States, 1789-1978.**
Edited by Robert Sobel, John Raimo. Westport, Connecticut: Meckler, 1978. 4 vols.
A valuable reference for data on all governors. It is organized in chronological order by state. There is an introductory essay and index of governors' names which reappears in each of the four volumes. It will be revised in 1982 to bring it up to date.

72 **Dictionary of American communal and utopian history.**
Robert S. Fogarty. Westport, Connecticut: Greenwood Press, 1980. 271p. bibliog.
Excellent comprehensive treatment of the subject of communitarianism in the United States. There is a biographical section including sketches of 152 leaders in the search for alternative life-styles. There are examinations of fifty-eight colonies including the Shaker communities of the late 18th century and the People's Temple of the late 1970s. A good introduction and an appendix which includes an annotated listing of utopian societies in the USA between 1789 and 1919 plus an excellent bibliographical essay make this a first-rate volume for every level.

73 **Dictionary of American history.**
James Truslow Adams. New York: Charles Scribner's Sons, 1978. rev. ed. 8 vols.
More than 800 authors prepared 7,200 new or revised entries for this new edition of Adams' classic work, first published in 1940. There is a superb analytic index of every item of information in the *Dictionary* under every possible heading. This is a basic reference source for all aspects of the nation's history.

74 **Documents of American history.**
Edited by Henry Steele Commager. New York: Appleton-Century-Crofts, 1973. 9th ed. 838p. bibliog.
A compilation of fundamental sources for the study of American history from the age of discovery to contemporary times. The author has limited his selection 'to documents of an official and quasi-official character'. The documents include presidential speeches and letters, Supreme Court cases, laws, treaties, etc. There are illuminating if concise accompanying notes and helpful bibliographical notes.

75 **Encyclopedia of American facts and dates.**
Edited by Gordon Carruth (and others). New York: Thomas Y. Crowell, 1979. 7th ed. 1,015p.
This standard reference tool was last revised in 1972 and now includes events through to 1977. The material on 1970-77 is included in a supplement of the 1970s which has its own twenty-five page index. The supplement is particularly useful for chronological coverage of Vietnam and Watergate.

76 **Encyclopedia of American history.**
  Richard B. Morris.   New York: Harper & Row, 1976.
  bicentennial ed. 1,245p.

A volume of essential facts about American life and institutions, this tool is organized both chronologically and topically. The text is designed to be read as a narrative, but dates, events, and achievements stand out. Part 1: basic chronology; part 2: topical chronology; part 3: biographical section. Part 1 includes major political and military events. Part 2 emphasizes the non-political aspects of American life.

77 **The encyclopedia of Southern history.**
  Edited by David C. Roller, Robert W. Twyman.   Baton
  Rouge, Louisiana: Louisiana State University Press, 1979.
  1,421p. maps. bibliog.

This fine reference tool is the cooperative effort of 1,100 scholars who have contributed more than 2,900 signed articles on every phase of the South's history and culture. It immediately became the standard reference work in the field and because of the historiographical articles and the bibliographies following most entries it is an aid to research. Biographies are included, as are lengthy treatments of each Southern state. There has been a strong effort to balance political, economic and military with social and cultural topics and to include women, blacks and Indians.

78 **Facts about the presidents.**
  Compiled by Joseph Nathan Kane.   New York: H. W.
  Wilson, 1974. 416p. Suppl., 1978. 19p.

Invaluable ready reference tool on presidential lives, backgrounds and administrations. Well-illustrated and carefully indexed, this is a compact first source on the nation's chief executives. The supplement updates the work to 1977.

79 **Great events from history: American series.**
  Edited by Frank N. Magill.   Englewood Cliffs, New Jersey:
  Salem Press, 1975. 3 vols.

The arrangement of these volumes is chronological, beginning with the arrival of the Indians and ending with the first manned lunar landing in 1969. Approximately 336 events are studied in detail. The articles consist of four sections each: 1: quick reference material; 2: a summary of the event, a journalistic account; 3: pertinent literature, a bibliographical essay reviewing works about the event; 4: additional recommended reading. There are more than sixty contributors to this useful set.

80 **Handbook of American popular culture.**
  M. Thomas Inge.   Westport, Connecticut: Greenwood Press,
  1979. 404p.

This first of two projected volumes begins coverage of the vast area of American popular culture. It includes material on newspapers and pulps, stage and film, cars and sports.

81 **Harvard guide to American history.**
Edited by Frank Freidel.   Cambridge, Massachusetts:
Belknap Press of Harvard University Press, 1974. rev. ed. 2
vols.
The basic bibliography for American history. This revision updates the first edition of 1954, which succeeded the 1912 *Guide to the study and reading of
American history* by Channing, Hart and Turner. About one-third of the entries
are new to this edition. Covering the whole range of American history, it cites
books and periodicals. The arrangement is substantially topical. Entries in volume
1 are arranged by topic, the first few chapters essentially for reference and
dealing with historical method and materials. Volume 2 is chronological, then
topical within historical period. There is a detailed table of contents and separate
name and subject indexes. The terminal date for books and periodicals cited is
1970, with a few exceptions. An absolute must for all levels of research.

82 **New American world: a documentary history of North
America to 1612.**
Edited by David B. Quinn.   New York: Arno Press, 1979. 5
vols. maps.
A collection of 851 primary documents and 147 maps in five volumes of over
2,900 pages. This extremely complete collection of source materials on the discovery, exploration and early colonization of North America is invaluable. It
includes material on the first European contacts with North America and the
customs of the Amerindians.

83 **The reader's encyclopedia of the American West.**
Edited by Howard R. Lamar.   New York: Thomas Y.
Crowell, 1978. 1,306p. maps. bibliog.
Representing the work of over 200 contributors, this is an excellent basic refer-
ence work. The signed articles vary in length and many include lists of sources.
The book covers the history of the area from Indian days to the present.

84 **Yesterday and today: a dictionary of recent American history -
1945 to the present.**
Stanley Hochman.   New York: McGraw-Hill, 1979. 407p.
Nine hundred articles cover a variety of political and social topics from hula
hoops to zero population growth. Good cross-referencing makes this an excellent
ready reference tool.

19

General

85 A concise history of the American republic.
Samuel Eliot Morison, Henry Steele Commager, William E.
Leuchtenburg. New York: Oxford University Press, 1977.
870p. 30 maps. bibliog.
A balanced, lively and thorough abridged version of the classic survey of American history, *The growth of the American republic* (q.v.).

86 The great republic: a history of the American people.
Bernard Bailyn (and others). Lexington, Kentucky:
Lexington and D. C. Heath, 1981. 2nd ed. 1,008p. maps.
bibliog.
An excellent survey of American history with fine illustrations. Each section is individually written by one of the co-authors, but the whole is well integrated. There is good treatment of social and cultural developments and an emphasis on the pre-1865 period, which is particularly helpful and unusual in a survey of this type.

87 The growth of the American republic.
Samuel Eliot Morison, Henry Steele Commager, William E.
Leuchtenburg. New York: Oxford University Press, 1980.
7th ed. 2 vols. 54 maps. bibliog.
This classic history has been revised and expanded in the same fine narrative style that has won the work so many admirers during the past half century. Extended coverage in the seventh edition includes major social, political and economic events and trends of the last decade.

88 Out of our past: the forces that shaped modern America.
Carl N. Degler. New York: Harper & Row, 1970. rev. ed.
566p.
This survey of American history selectively examines the nation's past, concentrating on developments that contributed to the evolution of the modern American lifestyle. A useful method for introducing readers to the American experience.

89 A people's history of the United States.
Howard Zinn. New York: Harper & Row, 1978. 614p.
bibliog.
A moving history of the American people from the point of view of those exploited politically and economically, those segments of society generally ignored by history. The work covers United States history through the 1970s. There is an effective use of quotes and extensive use of letters, documents and other primary source materials. Blacks, women, Indians and other minorities tell their stories in their own words.

90 **Problems in American civilization.**
Boston, Massachusetts: D. C. Heath, 1949- .
The more than forty-five volumes in this series are constantly revised, additional volumes being added as new subjects gain prominence. Selected readings are accompanied by introductory text and good bibliographical essays. This series provides an excellent historiographical introduction to the reader in a variety of areas as diverse as *The causes of the American Revolution* and *The debate over thermonuclear strategy.*

91 **The rise of American civilization.**
Charles A. Beard, Mary Beard. New York: Macmillan, 1949. rev. & enl. ed. 2 vols. in one.
A comprehensive text by two prominent historians. The work surveys economic, political, intellectual and social forces in American history. Its clarity and the reputation of its authors continue to make this a valuable, if somewhat dated, work.

92 **States and the nation series.**
New York: Norton, 1976-79. 51 vols.
The entire set of fifty-one books (on each of the fifty states and the District of Columbia) was underwritten by the National Endowment for the Humanities as a bicentennial contribution. The American Association for State and History administered the project. An effort was made to choose authors representing a variety of backgrounds. The books have a common format. Each has a handsome pictorial essay, and the texts average about 200 pages, containing a minimum of footnotes and concluding with brief, suggestive bibliographical essays. On the whole the volumes are factually accurate. These well-written accounts offer a wide variety of organizational approaches and serve as a reminder that the United States is a collection of states, a fact often ignored in general surveys of the nation's history.

General and special topics

93 **From Main Street to State Street: town, city, and community in America.**
Park D. Goist. Port Washington, New York: Kennikat Press, 1977. 180p. bibliog. (Interdisciplinary Urban Series).
An examination of the several meanings associated with the terms 'town', 'city', and 'community' in America between 1890 and 1940. Part I discusses the town as portrayed by writers like Sherwood Anderson and Sinclair Lewis. Part II considers sociologists, journalists, social workers and planners like Jane Addams and Lewis Mumford in relation to the concept of the 'city'. This is a good interdisciplinary survey with a useful bibliography.

94 **Small town America: a narrative history, 1620 - the present.**
Richard R. Lingeman.   New York: Putnam, 1980. 574p.
bibliog.
A well-written overview of the history of the small town experience. It includes
anecdotes and descriptions and an interesting analysis of the small town myth and
its place in American fiction.

95 **The compact history of the United States Air Force.**
Caroll V. Glines.   New York: Hawthorn, 1963. 339p.

96 **The compact history of the United States Army.**
Richard Ernest Dupuy.   New York: Hawthorn, 1961. 318p.
bibliog.

97 **The compact history of the United States Marine Corps.**
Philip N. Pierce, Frank O. Hough.   New York: Hawthorn,
1964. rev. ed. 334p. bibliog.

98 **The compact history of the United States Navy.**
Hartley E. Howe.   New York: Hawthorn, 1962. rev. ed.
350p.
The four entries listed above are useful narratives at a popular level. Written by
experts on military history they provide concise introductions to the armed
services.

99 **The U.S. Naval Academy.**
Jack Sweetman.   Annapolis, Maryland: Naval Institute
Press, 1979. 280p.
A well-written history of one of the military academies. From the days of duell-
ing and mutiny to the entrance of female midshipmen, the story of Annapolis
unfolds in a lucid vivid narrative.

100 **The U.S. Navy: an illustrated history.**
Nathan Miller.   New York: American Heritage and Naval
Institute Press, 1977. 414p. maps. bibliog.
A superb one-volume history. Beautifully illustrated, well-indexed and clearly
written, this is a scholarly work, comprehensive and uncomplicated.

101 **America revised.**
Frances Fitzgerald.   Boston, Massachusetts: Little, Brown,
1979. 240p.
This analysis of American history textbooks from Noah Webster to the present
asserts that the tailoring of the content and form of those works to suit pedagogi-
cal fads and political interest groups has left no clear idea of the American
experience of American ideals. First published in a series of articles in the *New
Yorker*, this beautifully written condemnation of the mediocrity, dullness and lack

of analysis which has prevailed in American history texts should be read by every level. The author, a noted journalist and historian, has left no doubt that American history textbooks need drastic change.

102 The peace reform in American history.
Charles DeBenedetti. Bloomington, Indiana: University of Indiana Press, 1980. 245p. bibliog.
This is the first comprehensive narrative on United States' peace movements since Merle Curti's *Peace or war* (1936). This clear chronological account carries the issue from the colonial years to the Vietnam War. There are good footnotes and a useful detailed index.

Colonial period

103 The bold and magnificent dream: America's founding years, 1492-1815.
Bruce Catton, William B. Catton. New York: Doubleday, 1978. 495p. map. bibliog. (Doubleday Basic History of the United States).
This first of two volumes to survey American history is a narrative with some analysis. It contains a multitude of interesting personal vignettes. This is a good basic introduction.

104 History of the United States of America, from the discovery of the continent.
George Bancroft. New York: Appleton-Century-Crofts, 1891-92. rev. ed. Reprinted, Port Washington, New York: Kennikat Press, 1967. 6 vols.
Extending to the adoption of the Constitution, this classic of 19th century American historical writing is always useful. Bancroft, a Unitarian minister who served as a diplomat and politician, was a noted historian. Vol. 1: United States of America as colonies; vol. 2: history of the colonization of the United States of America; vols. 3-5: the American Revolution; vol. 6: the formation of the American Constitution.

105 Founding the American colonies, 1583-1660.
John E. Pomfret. New York: Harper & Row, 1970. 397p. maps. bibliog. (New American Nation Series).
This is a detailed examination of the early period of American colonization. It is a useful addition to a classic series.

106 **The great discoveries and the first colonial empires.**
Charles E. Nowell.   Ithaca, New York: Cornell University
Press, 1954. 164p. maps. bibliog.

A brief factual introduction to European explorations and the early colonial
empires of Portugal, Spain, France, Holland and England, this work remains
useful for the non-specialist.

107 **The cultural life of the American colonies, 1607-1703.**
Louis B. Wright.   New York: Harper & Row, 1957. 304p.
bibliog. (New American Nation Series).

This volume in the noted New American Nation Series covers the colonial period
in terms of its cultural life. There is a clear presentation of developments in
education, science, books, libraries, the press and communications. Aimed at both
the general reader and the scholar this remains an excellent synthesis with a
superb bibliographical essay.

108 **The first frontier: the Indian wars and America's origins,
1607-1776.**
David Horowitz.   New York: Simon & Schuster, 1978.
251p.

Fast-paced readable account of the first 150 years of American history, beginning
with the Pilgrims' arrival at Plymouth and culminating with independence. A
largely narrative history, it is detailed and factually accurate, although it lacks
documentation. This is a good summary of recent scholarship on Indian-white
relations during the period.

109 **The formative years, 1607-1763.**
Clarence Lester Ver Steeg.   New York: Hill & Wang,
1964. 342p. 2 maps. bibliog. (Making of America).

This basic introduction to early American history examines the process which
transformed 'transplanted Englishmen' into 'provincial Americans'. An excellent
bibliographical essay supplements the text.

110 **Colonies in transition, 1660-1713.**
Wesley Frank Craven.   New York: Harper & Row, 1968.
363p. maps. bibliog. (New American Nation Series).

A good narrative survey of the later colonial period. It should be read with
Pomfret's *Founding the American colonies, 1583-1660* (q.v.), the volume in the
New American Nation Series which covers the initial period of colonization.

111 **Foundations of colonial America.**
Edited by Keith W. Kavenaugh.   New York: Chelsea
House and R. R. Bowker, 1973. 3 vols.

Each volume contains charters and public documents of the colonies, including
material on politics, religion and trade. There is brief introductory material to
supplement the documents. Vol. 1: northern colonies; vol. 2: middle Atlantic
colonies; vol. 3: southern colonies. This is a useful compilation of primary source
materials.

112 **America at 1750: a social portrait.**
Richard Hofstadter. New York: Knopf, 1971. 322p.
bibliog.
Part of a three-volume work which Hofstadter was writing when he died, this is a useful exploration of American colonial society. Topics such as slavery and class structure are of particular interest. Suitable for all levels.

113 **The spirit of '76: the growth of American patriotism before independence.**
Carl Bridenbaugh. New York: Oxford University Press, 1975. 162p.
Designed for the non-specialist, this inquiry into the origins of the American spirit raises many questions. It will stimulate spirited discussion since its author contends that ideas of nationalism in America were growing for almost as many years before the revolution as have passed since. It is a provocative, gracefully written study.

Revolution

114 **The age of the democratic revolution: a political history of Europe and America, 1760-1800.**
R. R. Palmer. Princeton, New Jersey: Princeton University Press, 1959-64. 2 vols. maps. bibliog.
A fine analysis of the revolutionary period which places the American War for Independence within the context of European development. Essential for the serious student.

115 **The birth of the republic, 1763-1789.**
Edmund S. Morgan. Chicago: University of Chicago Press, 1956. 176p. bibliog. (Chicago History of American Civilization).
Useful concise introduction to the period. A readable survey for the non-specialist.

116 **The coming of the revolution, 1763-1775.**
Lawrence Henry Gipson. New York: Harper & Row, 1954. 287p. maps. bibliog. (New American Nation Series).
The author of the encyclopaedic fifteen-volume *British Empire before the American Revolution* (1936-1970), provides a basic interpretation of the origins of the American War for Independence in this study. Part of the classic Harper New American Nation Series, the volume remains a staple for the reader seeking a detailed introduction to the prerevolutionary period.

History. Revolution

117 **Empire or independence, 1760-1776: a British-American dialogue on the coming of the American Revolution.**
Ian R. Christie, Benjamin W. Labaree. New York: Norton, 1976. 332p.
The authors, well-known historians in their respective lands, have produced a well-written introduction to the issues that resulted in the American Revolution. Their dual perspectives give an added dimension to their clear, concise narrative. Their premise is that the American Revolution was less a result of economic determinism or a clash of political ideas than of suspicion and fear that led to a conflict neither side had anticipated or desired.

118 **Encyclopedia of the American Revolution.**
Mark Mayo Boatner. New York: David McKay, 1966. 1,287p. maps. bibliog.
As in Boatner's *Civil War dictionary* (q.v.), biographical sketches predominate here. There are entries for battles and other specific events in addition to more general 'covering' articles which provide background and an overview. Some articles include bibliographical references. There is an additional general bibliography and an index to the maps. The 'bicentennial' edition published in 1974 (1,290p.) is a reprint with few changes from the 1966 publication.

119 **A history of the American Revolution.**
John R. Alden. New York: Knopf, 1969. 564p. maps. bibliog.
The author of the New American Nation Series volume, *The American Revolution, 1775-1783* (1954), Alden has produced a broader study in this volume. It includes more social and political history to supplement the detailed military analysis which characterized the earlier work.

120 **A new age now begins: a people's history of the American Revolution.**
Page Smith. New York: McGraw-Hill, 1976. 2 vols. bibliog.
A well-written detailed examination of the American Revolution concluding that it is still a potentially vital force in the life of the nation. The first part of the work is social history, the remaining nine parts are primarily political and military. This is a superb introduction for all readers.

121 **The peacemakers: the Great Powers and American independence.**
Richard B. Morris. New York: Harper & Row, 1965. 572p. bibliog.
This is a definitive account of the negotiations which resulted in the Peace of Paris in 1783 and ended the Revolutionary War. This diplomatic study provides enlightening portraits of John Adams, John Jay and Benjamin Franklin.

122 **The philosophy of the American Revolution.**
Morton Gabriel White. New York: Oxford University
Press, 1978. 299p. bibliog.
This readable study is the result of a series of bicentennial lectures which were
delivered worldwide by the author. This volume's central theme is Jefferson and
the Declaration of Independence, considered in the context of 17th and 18th
century thought. The philosphies of John Adams, Alexander Hamilton and James
Wilson are also discussed.

123 **The press and the American Revolution.**
Edited by Bernard Bailyn, John B. Hench. Worcester,
Massachusetts: American Antiquarian Society, 1980. 383p.
A distinguished collection of essays on the role, activities and influence of Ameri-
can printers and journalists during the revolutionary period. Includes Richard
Buel's 'Freedom of the press in revolutionary America', and G. Thomas Tansell's
'Some statistics on American printing, 1764-1783' among the essays.

124 **The revolution remembered: eyewitness accounts of the War
for Independence.**
Edited by John C. Donn. Chicago: University of Chicago
Press, 1980. 446p.
A magnificent piece of oral history which vividly presents the events of the War
for Independence. Seventy-eight accounts, chosen from some 80,000 pension
applications in the National Archives, are presented. All are personal accounts or
depositions made by ordinary men and women who in their youth had participated in the revolutionary war and in old age were applying for pensions. They
describe a host of incidents, including Benedict Arnold's departure to join the
British and conversations with Washington and other notables. Fascinating reading for every level of study.

125 **Seedtime of the republic: the origin of the American tradition
of political liberty.**
Clinton Lawrence Rossiter. New York: Harcourt Brace,
1953. 572p.
A broad analysis of the evolution of American political liberty by a prominent
scholar. The contributions of six major figures are discussed: Thomas Hooker,
Roger Williams, John Wise, Jonathan Mayhew, Richard Bland and Benjamin
Franklin. The political, economic and religious forces contributing to the idea of
freedom are examined along with written tracts expressing ideas of liberty and
individual rights within a political framework.

126 **Sources and documents illustrating the American Revolution,
1764-1788 and the formation of the federal constitution.**
Edited by Samuel Eliot Morison. New York: Oxford
University Press, 1965. 2nd ed. 380p.
A good selection of sources and documents for the study of the revolution and the
framing of the American Constitution.

The young nation, 1789-1860

127 **The American quest, 1790-1860: an emerging nation in
search of identity, unity and modernity.**
Clinton Lawrence Rossiter. New York: Harcourt Brace
Jovanovich, 1971. 396p. bibliog. (The Founding of the
American Republic).

A good general introduction written in a simple style. It explores the American
search for nationhood and modernity.

128 **The growth of Southern civilization, 1790-1860.**
Clement Eaton. New York: Harper & Row, 1961. 370p.
bibliog. (New American Nation Series).

The diversity of Southern society and its evolution in the period before the Civil
War is examined in this detailed well-written survey. The volumes of the New
American Nation Series are basic references on the nation's history and this work
maintains the quality of that series.

129 **Rise of the West, 1754-1830.**
Francis S. Philbrick. New York: Harper & Row, 1966.
389p. maps. bibliog. (New American Nation Series).

A fine addition to the New American Nation Series. Philbrick's analysis generally de-emphasizes the West as a base of sectional conflict. For him, the West is
the source of American nationalism.

130 **The shaping of America: a people's history of the young
republic.**
Page Smith. New York: McGraw-Hill, 1980. 870p. maps.
bibliog.

This outstanding sequel to Smith's study of the American Revolution, *A new age
now begins* (q.v.), covers the period 1783-1824. It is a good mixture of the
political, intellectual and socio-cultural aspects of American history, and it brings
current historical research and reappraisal into focus. There is a vivid, human
quality to the narrative.

131 **The trans-Appalachian frontier: people, societies, and
institutions, 1775-1850.**
Malcolm J. Rohrbough. New York: Oxford University
Press, 1978. 444p. maps. bibliog.

An important contribution to frontier history which should be read with Philbrick's *Rise of the West, 1754-1850* (q.v.) and Turner's *Frontier in American
history* (q.v.). This study emphasizes the role of towns and county courts in
frontier history. It is divided into five sections which examine the development
and finally the closing of the frontier.

132 **The federalist era, 1789-1801.**
John Chester Miller. New York: Harper & Row, 1960.
304p. bibliog. (New American Nation Series).
A concise narrative examining the major political and diplomatic events during the administrations of George Washington and John Adams. Traces the origins of the American quest for national unity and the call for individual liberty, while exploring the emergence of the Federalist Party.

133 **The democratic republic, 1801-1815.**
Marshall Smelser. New York: Harper & Row, 1968. 383p.
maps. bibliog. (New American Nation Series).
An extensively researched, readable survey of the era of Jefferson and Madison. The narrative includes political and social developments. Like the rest of this series Smelser's work is useful for scholar and student alike.

134 **The War of 1812.**
Reginald Horsman. New York: Knopf, 1969. 286p. maps.
bibliog.
An analysis of the causes of the war is coupled with a comprehensive narrative of the military campaigns. A useful overview.

135 **The awakening of American nationalism, 1815-1828.**
George Dangerfield. New York: Harper & Row, 1965.
331p. bibliog. (New American Nation Series).
A lively study of the period which Dangerfield characterizes as a struggle between economic and democratic nationalism. The work includes treatments of the presidential elections and the presidencies of Monroe and John Quincy Adams as well as analyses of the Monroe Doctrine and the Panic of 1819. The study ends with Jackson's election as president in 1828.

136 **Liberty and union.**
David Herbert Donald. Boston, Massachusetts: Little,
Brown, 1978. 318p. 22 maps. bibliog.
A well-written and researched survey of American history between 1830 and 1890. Good illustrations and a wealth of statistical data supplement the narrative. The volume's emphasis is on one central problem - the reconciliation of the principle of majority rule with the guarantee of minority rights.

137 **The age of Jackson.**
Arthur M. Schlesinger, Jr. Boston, Massachusetts: Little,
Brown, 1953. 577p. bibliog.
This work received the Pulitzer prize in history in 1945. For Schlesinger, class conflict was the principal motivating force of the Jacksonian movement, which he defined as a 'second American phase of the enduring struggle between the business community and the rest of society'. Fine scholarship is enhanced by graceful presentation in this work.

138 **Antislavery reconsidered: new perspectives on the abolitionists.**
Edited by Lewis Perry, Michael Fellman. Baton Rouge, Louisiana: Louisiana State University Press, 1979. 348p.

A collection of fourteen original essays providing good coverage of current research in the anti-slavery field. The common theme of these essays is their view of abolition in the context of the larger society. The women's rights movement and the class struggle are issues considered in relation to abolitionism. The papers are consistently well written and researched.

139 **The crusade against slavery, 1830-1860.**
Louis Filler. New York: Harper & Row, 1960. 318p. bibliog. (New American Nation Series).

A comprehensive history of abolitionism. It illustrates the relationship of various reform movements to the anti-slavery campaign. This is an excellent overview, in keeping with all the volumes in this important series.

140 **The far western frontier, 1830-1860.**
Ray Allen Billington. New York: Harper & Row, 1956. 343p. bibliog. (New American Nation Series).

A detailed, lucid narrative describing the settlement of Texas, California, Utah, New Mexico and Oregon between 1830 and 1860. Billington's work on the frontier is well known. His general survey, *Westward expansion* (q.v.), should be read for a synthesis of frontier historiography.

141 **The frontier in American history.**
Frederick Jackson Turner, foreword by Ray Billington. New York: Holt, Rinehart & Winston, 1962. 375p. bibliog.

Frederick Jackson Turner (1861-1932), was convinced that the frontier experience contributed to the growth of a democratic way of life in America. This reprint of a 1920 work contains thirteen essays - including Turner's noted contribution of 1893, 'The significance of the frontier in American history' - and a useful foreword by Ray Billington. This is a classic volume in frontier history.

142 **The idea of a Southern nation: Southern nationalists and Southern nationalism, 1830-1860.**
John McCardell. New York: Norton, 1979. 394p. bibliog.

Winner of the Allan Nevins award of the Society of American Historians, this well-written work analyses the nature of the secessionist movement. A series of topical and biographical chapters focus on the period after 1830. The author distinguishes between sectionalism and nationalism and charts the evolution of the South toward nationalism and eventual secession.

143 **The Jacksonian era, 1828-1848.**
Glyndon G. Van Deusen. New York: Harper & Row,
1959. 291p. bibliog. (New American Nation Series).
This study emphasizes American politics from the election of Andrew Jackson
through to that of Zachary Taylor. The analysis is detailed, the presentation clear
and the text is supplemented by an extensive bibliographical essay.

144 **Manifest destiny and mission in American history.**
Frederick Merk. New York: Knopf, 1963. 265p. bibliog.
A careful exploration of the ideology, prevalent in the United States during the
years 1840-90, which generated a national spirit of manifest destiny. The extension of the continental limits of the United States was the prime interest of the
early advocates of the doctrine, which evolved into a defence of Caribbean and
international expansion and lost its initial emotional fervour.

145 **The peculiar institution: slavery in the anti-bellum South.**
Kenneth M. Stampp. New York: Vintage, 1964. 459p.
bibliog.
Stampp challenges the vision of a benign slavery in this classic work first
published in 1956. He examines all facets of Southern slavery and plantation life
and concludes that the abusive and brutal aspects of the system were sympto-
matic of its essentially evil nature.

146 **The turbulent era: riot and disorder in Jacksonian America.**
Michael Feldberg. New York: Oxford University Press,
1980. 136p. bibliog.
An analysis of urban disorder, a common occurrence during the Jacksonian
period. The volume is well indexed and contains a fine bibliographical essay.

147 **Westward expansion: a history of the American frontier.**
Ray Allen Billington. New York: Macmillan, 1967. 3rd ed.
933p. maps. bibliog.
A revised version of the 1960 edition, this general survey examines the succession
of frontiers in American development: the colonial, followed by the trans-
Appalachian and the trans-Mississippi. This is a synthesis of scholarship on the
meaning of the frontier in American history.

Civil War and reconstruction

148 **Biographical dictionary of the Confederacy.**
Jon L. Wakelyn. Westport, Connecticut: Greenwood Press,
1977. 601p. bibliog.
Introductory chapters examining Confederate leadership in general are followed
by sketches of soldiers, politicians, women, editors, clergymen and other Confeder-

ate leaders. Several appendixes categorize the biographies by principal occupations, religious affiliation, education, pre- and post-war political party affiliation and geographical mobility before and after the war.

149 **The centennial history of the Civil War.**
Bruce Catton. Garden City, New York: Doubleday, 1961-65. 3 vols. bibliog.
A well-written general history of the Civil War. Vol. 1: *The coming fury*; vol. 2: *Terrible swift sword*; vol. 3: *Never call retreat*. The first volume opens with the Democratic convention of 1860 and ends after the first Battle of Bull Run, the second volume ends in the fall of 1862, and the final volume concludes with the surrender at Appomatox and Lincoln's assassination. This is a useful overview for the general reader.

150 **The Civil War and reconstruction.**
James Randall, David Herbert Donald. Boston, Massachusetts: D. C. Heath, 1969. 2nd ed. 866p. maps. bibliog.
This comprehensive survey first appeared in 1937. Donald, a student of Randall's, began revising in 1961 to assimilate the scholarship of intervening years. In the 1961 edition he made major changes to the reconstruction sections. This revision is almost unchanged from that of 1961 except for additional bibliographical sources. The volume remains an excellent introduction to the period.

151 **The Civil War dictionary.**
Mark Mayo Boatner. New York: David McKay, 1959. 974p. maps.
This ready-reference tool includes articles on campaigns, battles, and laws, but biographical material predominates.

152 **Civil War in the making, 1815-1860.**
Avery O. Craven. Baton Rouge, Louisiana: Louisiana State University Press, 1959. 115p.
This brief examination of the causes of the war grew out of the Walter Lynwood Fleming lectures in Southern history at Louisiana State University. The author's *The growth of Southern nationalism, 1848-61* (1953), is a further exploration of the growing hostility between North and South.

153 **The Confederate nation, 1861-1865.**
Emory M. Thomas. New York: Harper & Row, 1979. 384p. maps. bibliog. (New American Nation Series).
A well-written, precise account of the Confederacy. It should become the standard study of the South's brief experiment with nationhood from antebellum dreaming of separation to secession to war and finally to defeat. An appendix contains the constitution of the Confederacy and there is also a fine annotated bibliography. This work replaces Clement Eaton's *A history of the Southern Confederacy* (1954) and Ellis Merton Coulter's *The Confederate states of America, 1861-1865* (1950) as the standard history of the Confederacy.

154 **Emancipation and equal rights: politics and constitutionalism in the Civil War era.**
Herman Belz. New York: Norton, 1978. 171p. bibliog. (Norton Essays in American History).

A concise interpretive study, well documented, which analyses political and constitutional history from the 1850s to the 1880s. It includes a good summary of the Confiscation Act of 1862 and the Reconstruction Act of 1867. The smooth clear style makes the mass of detail easy to absorb. This is an excellent synthesis of existing scholarship enhanced by the author's own research and analysis.

155 **Era of reconstruction, 1865-1877.**
Kenneth M. Stampp. New York: Knopf, 1965. 228p. bibliog.

This positive assessment of the reconstruction incorporates revisionist scholarship on the period. While recognizing the corruption of Republican political leaders, Stampp asserts that on balance their motives were worthy and their genuine accomplishments included adoption of the Fourteenth and Fifteenth Amendments to the Constitution. The responsibility for introducing segregation and discrimination is placed with the provisional governments established by Johnson in the South. This is a superb and classic example of revisionist views of the era.

156 **The imperiled union: essays on the background of the Civil War.**
Kenneth M. Stampp. New York: Oxford University Press, 1980. 320p.

This is a 'guided tour of the classic antebellum battlefields of historiography'. Twenty-five years ago Stampp opened a reassessment of slavery with his book *The peculiar institution* (q.v.) in which he challenged the view of slavery as benign and slaves as contented. Here he presents a summation of his views on the background of the Civil War. The work contains eight essays, two previously unpublished and four substantially revised. Stampp explores the American concept of a perpetual union, two historiographical controversies on the nature of slavery, the main elements of Republican Party thought in the antebellum period, and the causes of the Civil War. Essential for every level of inquiry.

157 **Ordeal of the union.**
Allan Nevins. New York: Charles Scribner's Sons, 1947-71. 8 vols. maps. bibliog.

This massive scholarly contribution covers the period from 1857 to 1865. The three portions of the work can stand independently: vols. 1-2, *The ordeal of the union*; vols. 3-4, *The emergence of Lincoln*; vols. 5-8, *The war for the union*. This is a detailed narration by a noted historian, a classic work on the period.

158 **Reconstruction: after the Civil War.**
John Hope Franklin. Chicago: University of Chicago Press, 1961. 258p. bibliog.

An examination of the economic and social effects of the reconstruction policy in the decade that followed the Civil War. The growth of the new South is viewed against the background of the broad national problem of industrialization. Franklin includes a discussion of the rise of the Ku Klux Klan. He concludes that reconstruction failed as much because of Northern agreement with Southern prejudice as because of Southern conditions themselves.

159 Reconstruction: ending of the Civil War.
Avery O. Craven. New York: Holt, Rinehart & Winston, 1969. 336p. bibliog.

A careful analysis of the conflicting presidential and congressional plans for reconstruction. Craven asserts that the failure of these plans resulted in American society's enduring racial problems. Craven's examination covers the period through to the presidency of U. S. Grant.

160 Retreat from reconstruction, 1869-1879.
William Gillette. Baton Rouge, Louisiana: Louisiana State University Press, 1980. 463p. bibliog.

Explores reconstruction after the passage of the reform measures of the 1860s. This chronological narrative describes the enforcement of the Fifteenth Amendment, the presidential election of 1872, Grant's reconstruction policies, the Civil Rights Act of 1875, the disputed election of 1876 and President Hayes' Southern policy. Gillette concludes that reconstruction 'was over almost as soon as it had begun'. A useful index and good bibliography supplement this new major work on the reconstruction.

The 'gilded age', 1877-1900

161 The age of excess: the United States from 1877 to 1914.
Ray Ginger. New York: Macmillan, 1965. 386p. bibliog.

A clear synthesis of the economic, political and social developments during the 'gilded age'. A useful introduction for the general reader.

162 The age of reform: from Bryan to F.D.R.
Richard Hofstadter. New York: Knopf, 1955. 330p.

A broad analytical examination of the populism of the 1890s and the Bryan campaign of 1896, the progressive movement from about 1900 to 1914, and the New Deal, with emphasis on the dynamic period of the 1930s. A superb synthesis of the history of the reform period, this work remains a standard for the modern reader.

163 The nation transformed.
Edited by Sigmund Diamond. New York: G. Braziller, 1963. 528p. bibliog.

A selection of contemporary writings on the 'gilded age', emphasizing the developments contributing to the creation of an industrial society. This anthology includes a variety of primary sources carefully chosen to illustrate the attitudes of every segment of society. Excellent source for contemporary opinions.

164 The new commonwealth, 1877-1890.
John Arthur Garraty. New York: Harper & Row, 1968. 364p. bibliog. (New American Nation Series).

A good general survey in this major historical series. The work assesses the period in terms of the transition from *laissez-faire* individualism to the collective approach to problem-solving. It includes political, economic and social history and is an excellent source for student and scholar alike.

165 The origins of the new South, 1877-1913.
C. Vann Woodward. Baton Rouge, Louisiana: Louisiana State University Press, 1951. 557p. bibliog. (History of the South).

The author, a noted historian of the region, contributed this study to the multi-volume *History of the South.* It remains a classic, thoughtfully examining the changing South from the end of the reconstruction to the opening of the First World War.

166 Politics, reform and expansion, 1890-1900.
Harold V. Faulkner. New York: Harper & Row, 1959. 312p. bibliog. (New American Nation Series).

A comprehensive political, economic and social history of the decade. It explores the consequences of the national shift from a rural and agricultural to an urban and industrial society, as well as the change from an isolationist to an interventionist world view. Faulkner concludes that the 1890s were a watershed in American history. The modern reader remains well served by this contribution to the New American Nation Series.

167 Populism: the critical issues.
Edited by Sheldon Hackney. Boston, Massachusetts: Little, Brown, 1971. 190p. bibliog.

A well-chosen group of essays on populism by noted scholars, including Richard Hofstadter, C. Vann Woodward and others. This is a good introduction to the literature for the beginner.

168 Rendezvous with destiny: a history of modern American reform.
Eric F. Goldman. New York: Knopf, 1952. 503p. bibliog.

Winner of the 1952 Bancroft prize for distinguished American history, this is a provocative, well-written and richly documented survey of American reform from the late 1860s through the Fair Deal of the Truman years. It emphasizes progressivism and the New Deal. An entertaining and thoughtful volume for every level of reader.

169 The response to industrialism, 1885-1914.
Samuel P. Hayes. Chicago: University of Chicago Press, 1957. 210p. (Chicago History of American Civilization).

This is a readable, extensively researched survey of a period of great economic change in America. It discusses the populists, progressives and socialists in terms of the national effort to adjust to industrialization. It remains a standard study of the period.

170 **The tarnished dream: the basis of American anti-Semitism.**
Michael N. Dobkowski. Westport, Connecticut: Greenwood Press, 1979. 291p. bibliog. (Contributions in American History).

A valuable study. Not since the 1950s have American historians engaged in serious analysis of the roots of anti-Semitism in the USA. Dobkowski explores the question more broadly and deeply than Handlin, Hofstadter and Higham did a generation ago. Like them he focuses on the 'gilded age' and the progressive era, but unlike them he demonstrates the pervasiveness of anti-Semitism in American society.

171 **Years of decision: American politics in the 1890s.**
R. Hal Williams. New York: John Wiley & Sons, 1978. 219p. bibliog. (Critical Episodes in American Politics).

A well-researched, lucid narrative on the 1890s in America. Examines a variety of issues such as tariffs, the inherited Civil War issues, monetary and foreign policy and ethical and religious questions. It concludes with an analysis of McKinley's politics in 1900-01, viewed as a harbinger of the transition to progressivism.

Twentieth century

1900-1929

172 **The emergence of the new South, 1913-1945.**
George B. Tindall. Baton Rouge, Louisiana: Louisiana State University Press, 1967. 822p. bibliog. (History of the South).

A contribution to the multi-volume *History of the South*, Tindall's work emphasizes the changing economic conditions in the region throughout the period. Social and cultural changes are also considered in this extensive and detailed study.

173 **The era of Theodore Roosevelt and the birth of modern America, 1900-1912.**
George E. Mowry. New York: Harper & Row, 1958. 330p. bibliog. (New American Nation Series).

A good general survey exploring the origins and nature of progressivism and examining the presidencies of Roosevelt and Taft. Roosevelt's role is re-evaluated and he is assessed as the foremost national spokesman for the progressive movement. A fine addition to the classic New American Nation Series, this volume includes political, economic, social and intellectual history and offers a well-written analysis of the period.

174 **The great war and the search for a modern order: a history of the American people and their institutions, 1917-1933.**
Ellis W. Hawley. New York: St. Martin's Press, 1979. 264p. bibliog. (St. Martin's Series in Twentieth Century United States History).
Second in a planned four-volume series on 20th century American history, this work's primary focus is on economics. This is an insightful reinterpretation of the period, a fresh look at the 'roaring twenties'. For Hawley the central theme of American history during the period was 'modernization', the search for 'ordering mechanisms' to bring organization to the economy and society. An ample bibliographical essay and a good index supplement the text. This excellent series also includes Chamber's *The tyranny of change: America in the progressive era, 1900-1917* (q.v.) and Nash's *The Great Depression and World War II: organizing America, 1933-1945* (q.v.).

175 **Over here: the First World War and American society.**
David M. Kennedy. New York: Oxford University Press, 1980. 352p. bibliog.
This group of narrative essays analyses the impact of the First World War experience on the development of American society. It explores diverse economic and social issues such as the effect of government efforts to mobilize labour and business in a corporate war economy or the significance of the war for poets and writers.

176 **The perils of prosperity, 1914-1932.**
William E. Leuchtenburg. Chicago: University of Chicago Press, 1958. 313p. bibliog. (Chicago History of American Civilization).
A descriptive work covering the period from the New Freedom of Woodrow Wilson to the policies of the republican years that followed. It examines the trends which led to the stock market crash at the end of the 1920s. This good basic treatment continues to be a useful introduction to the period.

177 **Reform and regulation: American politics, 1900-1916.**
Lewis L. Gould. New York: John Wiley & Sons, 1978. 197p. bibliog. (Critical Episodes in American Politics).
A useful work for the beginner to American politics of the period. Its excellent suggestions for further reading are a special feature of the work. It should be read with Link's *Woodrow Wilson and the progressive era, 1910-1917* (q.v.) and Mowry's *The era of Theodore Roosevelt and the birth of modern America, 1900-1912* (q.v.).

178 **Republican ascendancy, 1921-1933.**
John D. Hicks. New York: Harper & Row, 1960. 318p. bibliog. (New American Nation Series).
This survey emphasizes economic and political history. For Hicks the period was notable for a lack of strong political leadership in either domestic or foreign affairs. Another fine volume in the series.

179 **The tyranny of change: America in the progressive era, 1900-1917.**
John Whiteclay Chambers. New York: St. Martin's Press, 1980. 280p. bibliog. (St. Martin's Series in Twentieth Century United States History).

This study draws on the new social and cultural history, in addition to covering the economic, political and international aspects of the period. It proposes that the dramatic events of the late 19th century - rapid industrialization, massive immigration, the closing of the western frontier, the growth of congested metropolises and the sudden acquisition of an island empire - shook the faith of many Americans in the ideal of a self-regulating society and contributed to a 'new interventionism' which was demonstrated in many forms.

180 **Woodrow Wilson and the progressive era, 1910-1917.**
Arthur Stanley Link. New York: Harper & Row, 1954. 330p. bibliog. (New American Nation Series).

Wilson's biographer and the editor of the Wilson papers, the author is a noted historian. Primarily dealing with Wilson's first term, this concise and detailed overview is obviously the result of extensive scholarship. Essential for every level of study.

1930-1945

181 **The age of Roosevelt.**
Arthur M. Schlesinger, Jr. Boston, Massachusetts: Houghton Mifflin, 1957- . 3 vols.

Three volumes have appeared in this multi-volume comprehensive history by a noted historian. Vol. 1: *The crisis of the old order, 1919-1933*; vol. 2: *The coming of the New Deal*; vol. 3: *The politics of upheaval*. Vol. 3 brings the narrative through to Roosevelt's renomination in 1936. This is a detailed and vivid source for Roosevelt's early years.

182 **Dust bowl: the southern plains in the 1930s.**
Donald E. Worster. New York: Oxford University Press, 1979. 277p. maps. bibliog.

A fine scholarly study of the creation of the dust bowl on the southern plains of Kansas, Oklahoma, Texas, Colorado and New Mexico during the 1930s. It analyses the creation of dust bowl conditions and focuses on two counties and their people in detail. It assesses New Deal policies and the situation and applies its conclusions to current world ecological problems created by the pressures of population and increasing demands for foodstuffs.

183 **The Federal Writers' Project: a study in government patronage of the arts.**
Monty N. Penkower. Urbana, Illinois: University of Illinois Press, 1977. 266p. bibliog.
A well-written, carefully researched account of the aims and programmes of the Federal Writers' Project during the New Deal era of the 1930s. The volume contains an extensive explanation of how the noted *American guide series* (q.v.) was developed. There is an excellent use of interviews with the writers involved in the project, including Arna Bontemps, Sterling Brown and Studs Terkel. This is a superb introduction to an important New Deal phenomenon.

184 **Franklin D. Roosevelt and the New Deal, 1932-1940.**
William E. Leuchtenburg. New York: Harper & Row, 1963. 393p. bibliog. (New American Nation Series).
Another in the classic Harper series, this volume by a noted New Deal scholar surveys the period from Roosevelt's 1932 campaign to his re-election to a third term in 1940. It is a comprehensive treatment which details the development of various agencies of the New Deal and examines leading personalities of the period such as Hopkins, Lilienthal and Tugwell. The study includes a look at developing foreign events in addition to its careful analysis of domestic policy.

185 **The glory and the dream: a narrative history of America, 1932-1972.**
William Raymond Manchester. Boston, Massachusetts: Little, Brown, 1974. 2 vols. bibliog.
A good basic overview of the period and a readable narrative, this work will provide the general reader with a useful framework for further study as well as an extensive bibliography to structure a reading programme.

186 **The Great Depression and World War II: organizing America, 1933-1945.**
Gerald D. Nash. New York: St. Martin's Press, 1979. 184p. bibliog. (St. Martin's Series in Twentieth Century United States History).
An excellent basic treatment of the Depression and the Second World War eras. The lucid text is supplemented by a fine bibliography.

187 **The United States and World War II.**
Albert R. Buchanan. New York: Harper & Row, 1964. 2 vols. bibliog. (New American Nation Series).
A comprehensive narrative history of the Second World War. This work includes details of strategy, battles and domestic mobilization. An excellent overall study.

1945-

188 American dreams: lost and found.
Studs Terkel. New York: Pantheon, 1980. 470p.

Terkel has become something of a legend as an oral historian-biographer. All his important and very popular books - *Division street: America* (1960), *Hard times* (1970) and *Working* (1974) - have been aimed at reassessing heroism and hunting for it among people who ordinarily do not enjoy the limelight. In his latest effort Terkel travelled the country for three years and taped 300 interviews. The hundred he considered to be best are included here. They range from a Miss USA, a celebrated muscleman, a few second-rung politicians to an ex-Ku Klux Klansman, among others. This is a fascinating look at contemporary America.

189 America's longest war: the United States and Vietnam, 1950-1975.
George C. Herring. New York: John Wiley & Sons, 1979. 298p. bibliog.

One of the best syntheses of US involvement in Vietnam to date. There is a good use of secondary sources to trace American policy in Vietnam from 1950-75. Vietnam is presented as part of the failure of Truman's containment policy. This study compares well with other works by Frances Fitzgerald, Bernard Fall and Edgar O'Ballance. The text is supplemented by a good annotated bibliography.

190 The changing world of the American military.
Edited by Franklin D. Margiotta. Boulder, Colorado: Westview Press, 1979. 488p. bibliog.

A collection of essays by experts from a variety of disciplines which surveys the factors that will shape the American military during the 1980s. The primary emphasis is on military manpower problems. Diverse views on the solutions to the problems of increasingly sophisticated technology and the necessity to develop military professionalism are represented here.

191 The culture of narcissism: American life in an age of diminishing expectations.
Christopher Lasch. New York: Norton, 1979. 268p.

This work consists of ten chapters of analysis and comment on the contemporary American scene. It focuses on the ethos of self-indulgence and the hedonism pervading US society today. It is a well-written and provocative book by a prominent historian.

192 Fire in the streets: America in the 1960s.
Milton Viorst. New York: Simon & Schuster, 1979. 591p. bibliog.

A well-written, vivid account of the decade's most tumultuous movements. A professional reporter, Viorst succeeds in discerning coherent patterns and in writing with style, clarity and balance about controversial issues during a period of social upheaval.

193 Kennedy and Roosevelt: the uneasy alliance.
Michael R. Beschloss. New York: Norton, 1980. 318p. bibliog.

An excellent comparative study of John F. Kennedy and Franklin D. Roosevelt - the differences in backgrounds, careers and philosophies. Readable and well researched, this is much more than a biographical treatment of either leader.

194 The military-industrial complex: a historical perspective.
Paul A. Koistinen, foreword by Representative Les Aspin, introduction by Major Robert K. Griffith. New York: Praeger, 1980. 186p. bibliog.

The author demonstrates that the military-industrial complex is not a recent phenomenon and emphasizes the 20th century development of the links between the military establishment and industry. It is remarkably free of the statistical jargon that makes many such studies unreadable at a non-specialist level.

195 The progressive presidents: Roosevelt, Wilson, Roosevelt, Johnson.
John Morton Blum. New York: Norton, 1980. 221p.

A study of four American presidents which considers the men, the office and their different uses of and views of presidential power. A good bibliographical essay adds to the value of the work.

196 Setting national priorities: agenda for the 1980s.
Edited by Joseph A. Pechman. Washington, DC: Brookings Institution, 1980. 563p.

The eleventh in an annual series analysing federal foreign and domestic policy issues. The volume contains fifteen previously unpublished articles and a summary. It includes material on energy, health, education, defence, the Middle East, US-Soviet relations and a variety of other issues. This set of papers published by the liberal Brookings Institution should be considered with the conservative Hoover Institution's counterpart volume, *The U.S. in the 1980's* (q.v.) edited by Duignan.

197 The third century: America as a post-industrial society.
Edited by Seymour Martin Lipset. Stanford, California: Hoover Institution Press, 1979. 471p.

This collection of sixteen original chapters by some of the country's leading sociologists and political scientists analyses basic social trends in areas of their expertise. It represents one of the most comprehensive recent efforts to interpret the direction of American institutions and sub-groups. Although there is no superimposed political orthodoxy, a large number of contributors express what is called the 'neo-conservative' outlook. All are recognized experts in their fields. The work is an outgrowth of a series of lectures at Stanford University.

198 A thousand days: John F. Kennedy in the White House.
Arthur M. Schlesinger, Jr. Boston, Massachusetts:
Houghton Mifflin, 1965. 1,087p.

Not a comprehensive history but a 'personal memoir by one who served in the White House during the Kennedy Years'. Nevertheless, this account by the noted historian is an insightful overview of the principal events and personalities of that administration. It should be supplemented with former Kennedy staff member Theodore C. Sorenson's biography *Kennedy* (New York: Harper & Row, 1965. 783p.). Sorenson's work includes the Kennedy of pre-presidential years and the 1960 election campaign. The two volumes represent both personal history and good scholarship.

199 The Truman Doctrine and the origins of McCarthyism: foreign policy, domestic politics, and internal security, 1946-1948.
Richard M. Freeland. New York: Knopf, 1971. 419p.
bibliog.

This study asserts that anti-communist fervour was promoted throughout the country by the Truman administration in order to ensure support for the Marshall Plan which entailed substantial economic aid for western Europe. Freeland seeks the origins of the McCarthyism of the 1950s in the policies of the Truman administration. A well-written book, this should prove useful at every level.

200 The United States in the 1980s.
Edited by Peter Duignan, Alvin Rabushka. Stanford,
California: Hoover Institution Press, 1980. 868p. map.
(Hoover Institution Publications, 228).

Thirty-two experts address major domestic and foreign policy questions facing the USA in the coming decade. They analyse central issues, describe the policy options open to the country and recommend specific courses of action. Their suggestions are meant to 'restore faith in the U.S. as the leader of the free world'. The contributors include a host of conservative luminaries, among them Milton Friedman and Alan Greenspan. A convenient collection of the best conservative policy analysis of our time. The Brookings Institution, the leading liberal think-tank has produced a counterpart volume, *Setting national priorities: agenda for the 1980s* (q.v.). The two collections should be read for balance.

Nationalities and Minorities

General

201 **Harvard encyclopedia of American ethnic groups.**
Edited by Stephan Thernstrom. Cambridge, Massachusetts: Harvard University Press, 1980. 1,076p. 87 maps.
This important new reference tool surveys the ethnic groups that constitute the American nation. Their histories, culture, distinguishing characteristics and current status in American society are analysed. There are 106 group entries ('Acadians' to 'Zoroastrians') and 29 thematic essays ('American identity' to 'Survey research'). This is a landmark work, essential to every reader interested in American ethnicity.

202 **The ethnic dimension in American history.**
James Stuart Olson. New York: St. Martin's Press, 1979. 440p. bibliog.
A chronological treatment of all the various groups that have appeared in the USA. It is divided into four periods: 1607-1776; 1776-1877; 1877-1945; 1945-present. Of twenty-five chapters, fourteen deal with Indians, Afro-Americans, Hispanic Americans and Asians; the remainder are concerned with 'white ethnic groups'. The underlying assumption is that the melting pot 'has not overtaken us' and that 'ethnicity is the central theme of American history'. A fine synthesis of the ethnic experience in the USA, the text is supplemented by good bibliographies at the end of each chapter.

203 **Ethnic leadership in America.**
Edited by John Higham. Baltimore, Maryland: Johns
Hopkins University Press, 1978. 214p. (Johns Hopkins
Symposia in Comparative History, 9).

These papers result from a series of seven lectures, given at Johns Hopkins in
1976, on the forms and patterns of ethnic leadership in seven different groups in
the USA. The essays include Nathan Glazer writing on the Jews, Nathan Hug-
gins on Afro-Americans, and Roger Daniels on the Japanese.

204 **Natives and strangers: ethnic groups and the building of
America.**
Leonard Dinnerstein, Roger L. Nichols, David M.
Reimers. New York: Oxford University Press, 1979. 333p.
bibliog.

A concise summary of the role of Indians, Afro-Americans and other immigrants
in American history. A readable survey of current scholarship on racial, religious
and other ethnic minorities from the colonial period to the present, this work is
an excellent introduction to the field.

205 **Strangers in the land: patterns of American nativism,
1860-1925.**
John Higham. New York: Atheneum, 1966. rev. ed. 440p.
bibliog.

This basic work by a noted scholar examines American attitudes toward immigrants. The book ends with an analysis of the results of the Immigration Act of
1924, which placed strict limitations on the entrance of certain immigrant groups.

206 **To seek America: a history of ethnic life in the United
States.**
Maxine Seller. Englewood, New Jersey: Jerome S. Ozer,
1977. 328p. bibliog.

A well-written general history of the role of ethnic groups in the American
experience. Chapter one contains an incisive definition of ethnicity and there are
detailed examinations of a variety of racial and ethnic elements in the population.
A useful bibliographical essay supplements the text.

207 **We who built America.**
Carl F. Wittke. Cleveland, Ohio: Case Western Reserve
University Press, 1964. rev. ed. 550p. bibliog.

A survey of American immigration throughout American history. The pattern of
immigration from colonial times is examined and each ethnic group is sketched in
detail, as are American reactions to succeeding waves of newcomers. This remains
a useful overview for the non-specialist.

208 **The Asian in North America.**
Edited by Stanford M. Lyman. Santa Barbara, California:
ABC-Clio, 1977. 299p. bibliog.
A useful collection of essays about the experience of Chinese and Japanese groups in North America. There are twenty-eight selections exploring a variety of subjects including marriage and family relations, generational differences and political dynamics within the ethnic communities. Some of the essays were previously published in Lyman's *The Asian in the West* (1971), but are no longer readily available and contribute to the broad concept of the current work.

209 **The Irish in America.**
Carl F. Wittke. New York: Russell & Russell, 1970. 316p.
bibliog.
A careful examination of the Irish immigrant experience, beginning with the great migrations of the 1830s and 1840s. This reprint of the 1956 edition is a fine basic introduction that remains useful today.

210 **Island of hope, island of tears.**
David M. Brownstone, Irene M. Franck, Douglass L.
Brownstone. New York: Rawson, 1979. 307p. bibliog.
Captures the essence of the experience of the over 10 million immigrants from central and eastern Europe who passed through Ellis Island on their way into the USA between 1892 and 1930. It makes excellent use of a variety of oral history sources and includes material from interviews with Czechs, Greeks, Poles, Italians, eastern European Jews, Christian Armenians and others. It is supplemented by good black-and-white illustrations.

211 **The Mexican-American people: the nation's second largest minority.**
Leo Grebler (and others). New York: Free Press, 1970.
786p. bibliog.
A detailed survey of Mexican-Americans. It includes economic, social and political aspects of their life in the USA, their impact on the West and Southwest and the reaction of the general population to their increasing immigration.

Afro-Americans

212 **The age of segregation: race relations in the South, 1890-1945.**
Edited by Robert Haws. Jackson, Mississippi: University
Press of Mississippi, 1978. 156p.
A series of essays assessing the impact of segregation. Three particularly fine contributions are by Derrick Bell, Dan Carter and George B. Tindall. This series of papers should be read in combination with C. Vann Woodward's *The strange*

career of Jim Crow (q.v.) and Howard Rabinowitz's recent reinterpretation of Woodward's thesis, *Race relations in the urban South* (q.v.).

213 The American slave: a composite autobiography.
Edited by George P. Rawick. Westport, Connecticut: Greenwood Press, 1972. 19 vols.; suppl. series 1, 1978. 12 vols.; suppl. series 2, 1979. 10 vols.

A major publishing event in 1972, the initial set of volumes of slave narratives from fourteen states has twice been supplemented as new material has been discovered and edited. Volume 1 in the 1972 series is Rawick's *From sundown to sunup*, which contains his analysis of the materials in the initial collection. The total series offers a vital reference source for anyone studying slavery in the United States.

214 Been in the storm so long: the aftermath of slavery.
Leon F. Litwack. New York: Knopf, 1979. 651p. bibliog.

This is Litwack's second significant study of American race relations. His first book, *North of slavery* (1961), analysed the difficulties of free negroes in the North before the Civil War. His new study examines the response of bondsmen and their masters to the destruction of slavery. The work is beautifully written and researched. It should be read with Eugene D. Genovese's *Roll Jordan Roll* (q.v.), Herbert Gutman's *The black family in slavery and freedom, 1750-1925* (q.v.), and Lawrence W. Levine's *Black culture and black consciousness* (q.v.).

215 Black culture and black consciousness: Afro American folk thought from slavery to freedom.
Lawrence W. Levine. New York: Oxford University Press, 1977. 522p.

A well-written, incisive book that broadens our understanding of the Afro-American experience in America through the use of folklore sources. Levine writes a history of black American thought.

216 The black family in slavery and freedom, 1750-1925.
Herbert G. Gutman. New York: Pantheon, 1976. 664p.

One of the most important books on race relations of the last decade. New methodology uses records from as far back as the 18th century to document a strong tradition of black family life during slavery and after, independent of white models. This controversial work challenges E. Franklin Frazier and Daniel Patrick Moynihan, whose work contended that slavery destroyed black family life.

217 Black labor and the American legal system.
Herbert Hill. Washington, DC: Bureau of National Affairs, 1977- .

Volume 1 of this projected two-volume work, *Race, work and the law*, places the patterns and systems of employment discrimination in historical perspective. Hill studies a variety of industries and unions. Volume 2, *The developing law of equal opportunity*, will study the effects of Title VII of the Civil Rights Act of 1964, concentrating on the activities of the Equal Employment Opportunity Commission during its first decade.

218 **The black worker: a document history from colonial times to the present.**
Edited by Philip Sheldon Foner, Ronald L. Lewis. Philadelphia: Temple University Press, 1978. 3 vols.
Vol. 1: *Black worker in 1869*; vol. 2: *Black worker during the era of the National Labor Union*; vol. 3: *The black worker during the era of the Knights of Labor*. Foner, a prolific writer on labour, including his standard *History of the labor movement in the U.S.* (q.v.), here edits a projected four-volume work on black workers in the United States. The first three have appeared and are well organized and carefully selected. Each major section of documents is introduced by explanatory material. Many of the documents contain tables of data. This is a useful reference tool.

219 **Black workers in white unions: job discrimination in the United States.**
William B. Gould. Ithaca, New York: Cornell University Press, 1977. 506p. bibliog.
Studies the roles played by strong white unions in persistent patterns of job discrimination. He concentrates on the effects of Title VII of the 1964 Civil Rights Act and considers the legal decisions that have followed that watershed legislation. His conclusions about expanding employment opportunities are pessimistic.

220 **A documentary history of the Negro people in the United States.**
Herbert Aptheker. Secaucus, New Jersey: Citadel Press, 1951-74. 3 vols.
Vol. 1: *From colonial times to 1910*; vol. 2: *From 1910-1932*; vol. 3: *From 1932-1945*. Includes material written by blacks from periodicals, letters, pamphlets, etc. The documents are supplemented by incisive introductory comments.

221 **The Dred Scott case: its significance in American law and politics.**
Don E. Fehrenbacher. New York: Oxford University Press, 1978. 741p. bibliog.
One of the best books written on the famous 1857 case in which the Supreme Court ruled on complex questions of Negro citizenship, congressional power over the territories and the constitutionality of the Missouri Compromise. The middle section of the work is a fine legal and constitutional examination of the case itself and the court's ruling. The author goes further and examines the constitutional and political difficulties involving congressional power over slavery and the divisive issue of the expansion of the slave system.

222 **From slavery to freedom: a history of Negro Americans.**
John Hope Franklin. New York: Knopf, 1980. 5th ed. 624p. bibliog.
The fifth edition of this classic study of the history of blacks in America. It contains a fully updated bibliography and takes into consideration the most recent

writings in the field. It is essential introductory reading and suitable as a source
at every level.

223 **International library of Afro-American life and history.**
Charles H. Wesley, Patricia W. Romero. Cornwall
Heights, Pennsylvania: Publishers Agency under the auspices
of the Association for the Study of Afro-American Life &
History, 1976. 10 vols.
A variety of historical and cultural themes are treated by the experts who have
contributed to this multi-volume reference work. Every reader interested in the
Afro-American experience should utilize this source.

224 **The Negro almanac: a reference work on the Afro-American.**
Compiled and edited by Harry A. Ploski, Warren Marr,
II. New York: Bellwether, 1976. 3rd ed. 1,206p. maps.
bibliog.
A comprehensive reference work on the history and culture of black Americans.
There is a detailed subject index, chronology, selected bibliography, selected docu-
ments and excellent articles on special topics such as 'The black worker in the
labor movement', 'The black woman', and 'Perspectives on black education'.
There is a good biographical section. The work has been cited by the American
Library Association and *Library Journal* for its outstanding quality.

225 **The Negro in the United States: a selected bibliography.**
Compiled by Dorothy B. Porter. Washington, DC: Library
of Congress, 1970. 313p.
This concise yet comprehensive bibliography on the Afro-American experience
was compiled by the noted former librarian of the Negro Collection at Howard
University. It is extremely detailed, carefully organized and well indexed,
although it lacks annotations. A superb guide for the reader seeking bibliographic
guidance.

226 **A new deal for blacks: the emergence of civil rights as a
national issue.**
Harvard Sitkoff. New York: Oxford University Press,
1978. 397p.
The first volume, entitled *The Depression decade*, of a projected three-volume
study of the rise of civil rights as a national issue, this is a good combination of
original research and synthesis. Sitkoff ranges over the broad spectrum of institutional, individual and intellectual forces of change. He discusses the contribution
of a variety of individuals and groups, including Eleanor Roosevelt, the CIO
(Congress of Industrial Organizations), individual blacks, Southern liberalism and
Supreme Court decisions to the changing atmosphere. A balanced overview.

227 **Race relations in the urban South, 1865-1890.**
Howard N. Rabinowitz. New York: Oxford University
Press, 1978. 441p. maps. bibliog. (Urban Life in America
Series).
Concentrating on several Southern cities (New Orleans, Charleston, Birmingham,
Savannah, Baltimore, Louisville and Washington, DC), Rabinowitz revises C.
Vann Woodward's thesis on the origins of segregation as set forth in the classic
The strange career of Jim Crow (q.v.). He argues that the 'forgotten alternative'
in Southern race relations was exclusion, not a choice between segregation and
integration.

228 **Roll Jordan roll.**
Eugene D. Genovese. New York: Pantheon, 1974. 823p.
bibliog.
A detailed inquiry into the everyday lives of American slaves is combined with an
articulate and coherent theory which attempts to explain the meaning of that
experience for both masters and slaves.

229 **The slave community.**
John W. Blassingame. New York: Oxford University Press,
1979. rev. ed. 448p. bibliog.
This extensively revised edition eloquently describes how black culture and social
institutions endured and adapted. A new chapter compares white slaves in North
Africa with black slaves in the American South. The work draws on statistics,
interviews, letters and autobiographies. New tables and illustrations complement
this authoritative study.

230 **Slavery remembered: a record of twentieth-century slave
narratives.**
Paul D. Escott. Chapel Hill, North Carolina: University of
North Carolina Press, 1979. 236p.
Library Journal calls this 'a direct and telling attack' on Eugene Genovese's *Roll
Jordan roll* (q.v.). This work rejects Genovese's central idea of an organic rela-
tionship between masters and slaves. Escott uses modern quantitative methods,
applying them to slave narratives. A fine interpretative study.

231 **The strange career of Jim Crow.**
C. Vann Woodward. New York: Oxford University Press,
1974. 3rd rev. ed. 250p.
This classic work contends that segregation was a product of the late 19th and
early 20th century, demonstrating that 'Jim Crow' laws were not a result of the
reconstruction, but that separation of the races occurred gradually at the end of
the 19th century. His thesis has recently been questioned by Rabinowitz in *Race
relations in the urban South, 1865-1890* (q.v.).

232 They have no rights: Dred Scott's struggle for freedom.
Walter Ehrlich. Westport, Connecticut: Greenwood Press,
1979. 266p. bibliog. (Contributions in Legal Studies, 9).
A well-written and carefully researched study that will probably become the
standard treatment of the Dred Scott case. Ehrlich departs from general practice
and closely analyses the case, examining hitherto unused Circuit Court tran-
scripts. A significant feature of the work is a chronologically arranged bibliographical essay on all aspects of the Dred Scott case.

233 The voice of black America.
Edited by Philip Sheldon Foner. New York: Simon &
Schuster, 1972. 1,215p.
A collection of major speeches by blacks in the USA, 1797-1971. The arrangement is chronological. Many have been produced in their entirety because of their
historical significance, but in general passages have been extracted. Each speech
is preceded by biographical and introductory notes to place it in historical context. A useful ready-reference tool.

American Indians

234 The American Heritage history of the Indian wars.
Robert M. Utley, Wilcomb E. Washburn. New York:
American Heritage, 1977. 352p. map.
A top-quality illustrated history of the Indian wars. Although lacking in footnotes
or bibliography, the volume is nevertheless readable and factually sound. Good
introduction for the non-specialist.

**235 Bury my heart at Wounded Knee: an Indian history of the
American West.**
Dee Alexander Brown. New York: Holt, Rinehart &
Winston, 1971. 487p. bibliog.
An attempt, in novel form, to describe the settlement of the West as the Indians
saw it. An emotional presentation, this thoroughly researched provocative study
will stimulate all readers and cause them to consider events from a new perspec-
tive.

236 The civilization of the American Indian series.
Norman, Oklahoma: University of Oklahoma Press, 1932- .
The more than eighty volumes in this long series have as their purpose 'the
reconstruction of American Indian Civilization by presenting aboriginal, historical
and contemporary Indian life'. The volumes are diverse, including memoirs,
scholarly monographs and general histories such as Debo's *History of the Indians
of the United States* (q.v.). This series is an excellent source for all aspects of
American Indian life.

237 **A concise dictionary of Indian tribes of North America.**
Barbara A. Leitch. Algonae, Michigan: Reference
Publications, 1980. 646p. maps. bibliog.

A useful reference volume for the general reader. It contains concise entries for
about 280 tribes, each statement briefly outlining the culture, history and present
status of the tribe. Entries are free of anthropolgical jargon and summarize the
significant facts. Several maps illustrate language groups, culture areas and
regional distribution of tribes.

238 **Everyday life of the North American Indian.**
Jon Manchip White. New York: Holmes & Meier, 1979.
256p. maps. bibliog.

A narrative history of the North American Indian from the earliest period to the
present. The emphasis is on various cultures at their peak. Detailed chapters on
the role of the hunter, warrior, artist, etc., are extremely useful. A good collection
of pictures and maps supplement the text.

239 **Handbook of North American Indians.**
Edited by William C. Sturtevant. Washington, DC:
Smithsonian Institution, 1978- . bibliog.

To be completed in 20 volumes, this series is intended to supersede *Handbook of
American Indians north of Mexico*, edited by F. W. Hodge (1907-10. 2 vols.),
which has been a standard reference for more than half a century. Two volumes
have so far appeared in the new venture: vol. 15: *Northeast*, edited by Bruce G.
Trigger (1978), and vol. 8: *California*, edited by Robert F. Heizer (1979). The
new handbook fully incorporates the research of the last five decades and is
arranged not alphabetically, but topically. The volumes published so far are well
balanced and show high standards of scholarship. The first four volumes will deal
with general topics. Eleven more, of which *Northeast* is one, will deal with
individual tribes grouped by regions. There will be a separate volume on technology and the visual arts; one on languages; two of biographies and a final general
index volume. They will be published at an expected rate of two a year through
to 1987. This promises to be a major achievement in American Indian studies for
our generation.

240 **A history of the Indians of the United States.**
Angie Debo. Norman, Oklahoma: University of Oklahoma
Press, 1970. 386p. bibliog. (Civilization of the American
Indian Series).

An historical survey of the Indians of the USA, including the Eskimos and Aleuts
of Alaska. It provides one of the best available examinations of the relations
between Europeans and Indians from the days of the early explorers to date.
There are some over-simplifications and a few factual errors, but overall this is a
balanced lucid narrative for the non-specialist.

241 **Indian treaties: two centuries of dishonor.**
Rupert Costo, Jeannette Henry. San Francisco: Indian
Historian Press, 1977. 243p. (American Indian Reader
Series: Current Affairs, 5).
Costo, founder of the American Indian Historical Society, and Henry, editor of
the *Indian Historian*, offer a response to charges that American Indians do not
deserve property held by treaty rights. Appendixes include a chronology of Indian
treaties and a list of major laws that apply to American Indians.

242 **Man's rise to civilization: the cultural ascent of the Indians
of North America.**
Peter Farb. New York: E. P. Dutton, 1978. 2nd ed. 314p.
maps. bibliog.
An updated version of the author's 1968 work, this is a well-written, extensively
illustrated exploration of the cultural history of the American Indian. There is a
useful detailed bibliography.

243 **Peoples of the coast: the Indians of the Pacific Northwest.**
George Woodcock. Bloomington, Indiana: Indiana
University Press, 1977. 223p. bibliog.
Noted for his writings on the Canadian peoples, Woodcock here surveys the
northwest coast Indians, their history and current living conditions. A readable
exploration of the changing Indian life style, the work is filled with detailed
information on the principal tribes in the area: the Nootka, Haida, Tsimshian and
Kwakiutl. It is beautifully illustrated.

244 **Reference encyclopedia of the American Indian.**
Barry Klein. Rye, New York: Todd, 1978. 3rd ed. 2 vols.
bibliog.
A basic reference work. The first volume includes tribal council listings, government agencies relating to Indian affairs, Indian associations, urban centres,
museums, etc. The second volume is a 'who's who' of individuals prominent in
Indian affairs. There is a detailed bibliography in the first volume which includes
government publications and periodical articles on the American Indian.

245 **The urban American Indian.**
Alan L. Sorkin. Lexington, Massachusetts: Lexington and
D. C. Heath, 1978. 158p.
A good concise survey which studies American Indians who have left the reservation for the city. Extensive statistical evidence supports the narrative (data on
unemployment, alcoholism, school dropouts, etc). There is constant comparison
between the urban experience and life on the reservation. This is a clear statement of the problems of native Americans in the urban environment.

246 **The white man's Indian: images of the American Indian from Columbus to the present.**
Robert F. Berkhofer. New York: Knopf, 1978. 261p. bibliog.
A readable and well-researched work whose thesis is that the preconceptions of white Americans, rather than the objective realities they observed, determined in large part the Indian image they shaped and passed on to later generations.

Women

247 **The American woman: her changing social, economic, and political roles, 1920-1970.**
William Henry Chafe. New York: Oxford University Press, 1972. 236p. bibliog.
A good introductory survey on women in 20th century America. The decade of the 1970s is not included, but this work provides an excellent prologue to a study of that period.

248 **At odds: women and the family in America from the revolution to the present.**
Carl N. Degler. New York: Oxford University Press, 1980. 527p. bibliog.
Pulitzer prize winning historian Degler examines the tensions between the social demands of the family and women's struggle for equality. He emphasizes the 19th century, a transitional period during which the women's rights movement came into increasing conflict with the cult of domesticity. Non-white and working class women are included along with white middle class women in this excellent interpretive study.

249 **Beginnings of sisterhood: the American women's rights movement, 1800-1850.**
Keith E. Melder. New York: Schocken, 1977. 287p. bibliog.
A readable introduction to the origins of American feminism.

250 **Beyond her sphere: women and the professions in American history.**
Barbara J. Harris. Westport, Connecticut: Greenwood Press, 1978. 212p. bibliog.
This intelligent review of the secondary literature provides an introduction to the field. The core of the argument is that traditional assumptions about woman's intellectual inferiority and domestic obligations have restricted her career opportunities. Beginning with a brief overview of European developments, Harris moves quickly to concentrate on American women and traces events through the 1960s.

251 **Black women in white America: a documentary history.**
Edited by Gerda Lerner. New York: Pantheon, 1972. 666p.
A useful anthology covering the period from the 1830s to the 1960s. The selections include a variety of sources - letters, speeches, articles, etc. Most of the material is by black women and there are helpful introductory notes.

252 **The bonds of womanhood: 'woman's sphere' in New England, 1780-1835.**
Nancy F. Cott. New Haven, Connecticut: Yale University Press, 1977. 225p. bibliog.
A clear concise introduction to the changing perceptions of women by themselves and others during the early period in US history. Five essays deal with different aspects of female experience: work, domesticity, education, religion and sisterhood. The study explores the development of a female belief in a 'separate nature' rather than an 'inferior' place in the male society.

253 **Century of struggle: the woman's rights movement in the United States.**
Eleanor Flexner. Cambridge, Massachusetts: Belknap Press of Harvard University Press, 1975. rev. ed. 398p. bibliog.
A revised edition of a basic history of the women's rights movement in America. The emphasis is on the suffrage movement, but abolition, labour and other reform efforts are discussed.

254 **Everyone was brave: the rise and fall of feminism in America.**
William L. O'Neill. Chicago: Quadrangle, 1969. 380p. bibliog.
An examination of the struggle for female suffrage in America, emphasizing the final victory in 1920 and the difficulties for feminism immediately following that event. Provides a careful analysis of the disillusionment that came as women realized that votes left many basic inequalities essentially untouchable.

255 **Feminine mystique.**
Betty Friedan. New York: Norton, 1963. 410p.
Now a classic, this examination of the American female experience since the Second World War was a cornerstone of the new feminism of the 1970s. Friedan's analysis of the dissatisfaction of many American women is essential reading for anyone interested in the origins of the contemporary women's liberation movements in the United States.

256 **Feminism and suffrage: the emergence of an independent women's movement in America, 1848-1869.**
Ellen Carol DuBois. Ithaca, New York: Cornell University Press, 1978. 220p. bibliog.
An exploration of the women's rights movement from its birth at Seneca Falls in 1848 to its institutionalization with the formation of the National and the American Woman Suffrage Associations in 1869. The work places women's struggle for rights in perspective with other reform efforts such as the abolition movement.

257 Feminism in American politics.

Clair Knoche Fulenwider. New York: Praeger, 1980. 182p.

Studies the impact of feminism on contemporary American political attitudes and behaviour. The work considers the difference in the feminism of white and minority women. A good analytical study of current trends and behaviour.

258 The feminization of American culture.

Ann Douglas. New York: Knopf, 1977. 403p. bibliog.

An extensively researched study which should become a classic analysis of the close connection between the sentimentalization of 19th century American culture and modern mass culture. Douglas asserts that the disestablishment of the clergy and women between 1820 and 1875 led to the dehumanization of both groups and the sentimentalization of American culture.

259 A history of women in America.

Carol Hymowitz, Michaele Weissman. New York: Bantam, 1978. 400p.

A readable and accurate history of American women. Well illustrated. It gives significant space to the problems of black and working class women and concludes with a good summation of the 'new feminism'.

260 If all we did was to weep at home: a history of white working-class women in America.

Susan Estabrook Kennedy. Bloomington, Indiana: Indiana University Press, 1979. 331p. bibliog.

A narrative interpretation of working class women and paid labour from 1600 to the present. There are three sections, with chronological subdivisions. This is a well-researched analysis of this relatively unexplored field.

261 In transition.

Judith M. Bardwick. New York: Holt, Rinehart & Winston, 1979. 203p. bibliog.

A discussion and analysis of how feminism, sexual liberation and the search for self-fulfilment have altered America. A personal view by an important contributor to women's studies literature. Bardwick considers work, motherhood, sex, marriage, divorce and sexual identity in this fascinating book.

262 Liberty's daughters: the revolutionary experience of American women, 1750-1800.

Mary Beth Norton. Boston, Massachusetts: Little, Brown, 1980. 384p. bibliog.

A study of the changing role of American women during the revolutionary period. Norton develops her view that the experience of self-reliance during the war combined with revolutionary ideology to raise the self-esteem of American women during this period. This book is valuable for every level.

263 **Personal politics: the roots of women's liberation in the civil rights movement and the new left.**
Sara Evans. New York: Knopf, 1979. 274p.
An effective and stimulating analysis of the origins of a social movement. Evans traces the development of the women's liberation movement, the 'second wave' of American feminism, from the experiences of women in earlier social movements. This is an excellent example of the value of oral history sources.

264 **The politics of the Equal Rights Amendment: conflict and the decision process.**
Janet K. Boles. New York: Longman, 1979. 214p. bibliog.
This is the first scholarly study of the ratification process of the ERA, attempted while that process is still going on. It is intelligently written and provides many interesting little-known details of ERA politics. It attempts to present a balanced consideration of arguments, pro and con.

265 **The remembered gate: origins of American feminism: the woman and the city, 1800-1860.**
Barbara J. Berg. New York: Oxford University Press, 1978. 334p. bibliog. (Urban Life in America Series).
An important addition to the literature on the origins of American feminism. Berg finds its roots in female benevolent societies of 1800-60, not in the abolitionist movement. A readable and provocative study.

266 **Seven days a week: women and domestic service in industrializing America.**
David M. Katzman. New York: Oxford University Press, 1978. 374p. bibliog.

267 **Sexual politics.**
Kate Millett. New York: Doubleday, 1970. 393p. bibliog.
This important work of early 1970s women's liberation asserts that the relationship between the sexes has been and remains a political one - a continuing power struggle. A provocative book that illuminates the women's movement of the 1970s and the 1980s in America.

268 **The Southern lady, from pedestal to politics, 1830-1930.**
Anne Firor Scott. Chicago: University of Chicago Press, 1970. 235p. bibliog.
An exploration of the evolution of the female role from the antebellum period to the 20th century in the American South. A well-written interpretative work for student and scholar alike.

269 **Wage-earning women: industrial work and family life in the United States, 1900-1930.**
Leslie Woodcock Tentler. New York: Oxford University Press, 1979. 266p. bibliog.
Focuses on the half-dozen years between the completion of education and entry into marriage, examining the employment experiences of young working class women in major industrially mature cities of the East and Midwest. An excellent analysis.

270 **Woman's proper place: a history of changing ideals and practices, 1870 to the present.**
Sheila M. Rothman. New York: Basic Books, 1978. 322p.
The author examines American definitions of woman's place *vis-à-vis* reform proposals affecting that role. She identifies four definitions since 1870: virtuous womanhood, educated motherhood, wife-companion, and woman as a person. She relates these role models to reform efforts during each era.

271 **Women and the American labor movement: from colonial times to the eve of World War I.**
Philip Sheldon Foner. New York: Free Press, 1979. 621p. bibliog.
The first of a projected two-volume work. Making good use of original sources, Foner focuses on the inter-relationships of male and female workers in the organized labour movement.

272 **Women in modern America: a brief history.**
Lois W. Banner. New York: Harcourt Brace Jovanovich, 1974. 276p. bibliog. (Harbrace History of the United States).
A good introductory overview. The simple narrative provides a clear framework for further reading. For the beginning student.

273 **Women of America: a history.**
Edited by Carol Ruth Berkin, Mary Beth Norton. Boston, Massachusetts: Houghton Mifflin, 1979. 442p. maps. bibliog.
An excellent series of articles on the female experience in America. There are essays on Chinese, Irish immigrant and black women as well as middle class white women. Many original documents are included in the work and the bibliography is excellent.

Language and Dialects

274 American dialects: a manual for actors, directors, and writers.
Lewis Helmar Herman, Marguerite Shalett Herman. New York: Theatre Art Books, 1959. 328p.

Designed to be used by those who must reproduce vernacular speech, this volume provides studies of the representative dialects of every major section of the United States. The authors include musical inflection charts, diagrams for placement of lips, tongue and breath and exercises to help the student reproduce the sounds needed.

275 The American language: an inquiry into the development of English in the United States.
H. L. Mencken. New York: Knopf, 1936. 4th ed. 729p. bibliog. Suppl. 1-2, 1945-48. 2 vols.

A classic work, originally published in 1919, enlarged in 1921, again in 1923, and finally in 1936. The fourth edition was brought out in a single-volume abridged form in 1963. These volumes treat the historical growth of the American language and include a myriad of topics, such as pronunciation, spelling, slang, and an appendix discussing non-English dialects in the United States.

276 American talk: where our words come from.
Joey Lee Dillard. New York: Random House, 1976. 187p. bibliog.

An interesting study of the origins of American jargon, tracing words from the colonial period to the present. There are eight chapters, each devoted to a small collection of terms and phrases belonging to a specialized lingo: pidgin English, black English, Dutch, French and Cajun, gambler-talk, cowboy-talk, booze-and-sin talk and adman-ese.

277 **Americanisms: a dictionary of selected Americanisms on historical principles.**
Mitford M. Mathews. Chicago: University of Chicago Press, 1966. 304p. bibliog.
An abridgment of the author's earlier work, *A dictionary of Americanisms on historical principles* (q.v.).

278 **Current American usage.**
Edited by Margaret M. Bryant. New York: Funk & Wagnalls, 1962. 280p. bibliog.
A survey of how Americans speak and write. This book covers the areas of the United States sharing certain usage variations: namely, the North, the North midland, the South midland, the South, the North Central states, and the upper Midwest. Included is information on how education affects usage as well as cultural experiences.

279 **Dictionary of Afro-American slang.**
Clarence Major. New York: International, 1970. 127p. bibliog.
A glossary of terms used characteristically by blacks. This work contains over 2,500 entries and gives definitions as well as dates of greatest use. Nicknames for real-life and legendary characters are also included.

280 **A dictionary of American-English usage, based on Fowler's** *Modern English usage.*
Margaret Nicholson. New York: Oxford University Press, 1957. 671p.
An American version of Fowler's *A dictionary of modern English usage*, first published in 1926. The author has added American spellings, pronunciations and meanings, and has included notes on words not included in Fowler (some of which were not current in his day).

281 **A dictionary of American idioms.**
Edited by Maxine Tull Boatner, John Edward Gates. Woodbury, New York: Barron's Educational Series, 1975. rev. ed. 392p.
First published in 1966 under the title *A dictionary of idioms for the deaf*, this new edition has over 250 additional modern idiomatic expressions, many originating within recent cultural movements, and others gathered from space technology terms in popular usage. This dictionary is very useful to foreigners who have learned English and would like to understand American idiomatic speech - which makes up much of daily conversation.

282 **Dictionary of American slang.**
Harold Wentworth, Stuart Berg Flexner. New York: Thomas Y. Crowell, 1975. 766p. bibliog.
First published in 1960 and updated in 1967, this new edition contains about fifty additional pages of new usage. A useful reference tool containing a wide variety

Language and Dialects

of American slang - including special terms of vocations and avocations, regionalisms and colloquialisms. Included is an appendix containing a discussion of the processes of slang formation.

283 **A dictionary of Americanisms on historical principles.**
Mitford M. Mathews. Chicago: University of Chicago Press, 1951. 2 vols. bibliog.
A historical dictionary of words and expressions that have originated in the United States. Included also are words and phrases that were already in the English language, but took on new meanings in America. Some of the categories of words are: slang expressions, American nicknames, phrases first used in America, and terms made by combining older terms.

284 **Dictionary of contemporary American usage.**
Bergen Evans, Cornelia Evans. New York: Random House, 1957. 567p.
A lively, practical dictionary of American usage, dealing with grammar, word preferences, style, punctuation, idioms, spelling, etc. The authors provide some comparison with British usage, always emphasizing the American preference.

285 **I hear America talking.**
Stuart Berg Flexner. New York: Van Nostrand Reinhold, 1976. 505p.
An illustrated story of American language, relating it to American history. This lively presentation offers groups of definitions gathered together by subject, such as the Civil War, hot dogs, the Pony Express, etc., and tells the story behind the words or expressions.

286 **Language in America.**
Edited by Neil Postman, Charles Weingartner, Terence P. Moran. New York: Pegasus, 1969. 240p.
A witty collection of essays, most of which have appeared elsewhere, by a variety of authors on contemporary American English. The authors investigate the language of politics, censorship, racism, computers, love, law, etc., and attempt to expose language pollution in all these areas.

287 **Our own words.**
Mary Helen Dohan. New York: Knopf, 1974. 315p. bibliog.
A readable history of American language, tracing its development from early Indian words, through early English, French and German contributions, pioneer-coined expressions, and finally to modern slang and jargon. A fascinating social history reflected in language.

288 **The underground dictionary.**
Eugene E. Landy. New York: Simon & Schuster, 1971. 206p.

A dictionary designed to provide a guide to the language of an American subculture - drug users, 'hippies', 'dropouts', etc. This book was compiled by a clinical psychologist to provide a communication link between the 'establishment' and this underground culture.

289 **What's the difference? A British/American dictionary.**
Norman Moss. New York: Harper & Row, 1973. 138p.

A very useful dictionary, divided into a list of British to American words and a list of American to British words. The book gives definitions of words where common usage differs and gives the corresponding word used, such as British 'flat' for American 'apartment'.

Religion

290 **American Catholic thought on social questions.**
Edited by Aaron Ignatius Abell. Indianapolis, Indiana:
Bobbs-Merrill, 1968. 571p.
An anthology of writings representing Catholic opinion on various social questions from the mid-19th century to the 1960s. A variety of viewpoints by Catholic spokesmen are presented, and the book provides interesting reading for students of American history.

291 **American civil religion.**
Edited by Russell Earle Richey, Donald G. Jones. New York: Harper & Row, 1974. 278p. bibliog. (Harper Forum Books).
A collection of twelve essays by a variety of authors studying the phenomenon of an American creed as a separate form of religious behaviour. This is an interesting source-book on non-church-based religion in America.

292 **American mosaic: social patterns of religion in the United States.**
Edited by Phillip E. Hammond, Benton Johnson. New York: Random House, 1970. 342p. bibliog.
An anthology of works expressing the changing character of American religion as seen by two sociologists. The three parts of the book discuss definitions and expressions of religion; organized religion; and religious influence on individual and national life.

293 **The American religious experiment: piety and practicality.**
Edited by Clyde L. Manschreck, Barbara Brown Zikmund. Chicago: Exploration Press, 1976. 145p. bibliog. (Studies in Ministry and Parish Life).
A collection of essays by various religious leaders and teachers of theology (namely the faculty of the Chicago Theological Seminary, a Jewish rabbi and a

Roman Catholic priest) on various aspects of religion in America. Included are sections on historical perspectives, biblical reflections, Jewish/Catholic views and social inter-relationships.

294 American religious thought: a history.
William A. Clebsch. Chicago: University of Chicago Press, 1973. 212p. bibliog. (Chicago History of American Religion).
Focuses on three essayists who contributed spirituality and a particular perception of the universe to the American Protestant heritage: Jonathan Edwards, Ralph Waldo Emerson and William James.

295 American religious values and the future of America.
Edited by Rodger Van Allen. Philadelphia: Fortress Press, 1978. 211p. map. bibliog.
A bicentennial study, undertaken at Villanova University, yielded this collection of essays by the following authors: Sydney E. Ahlstrom, Martin E. Marty, Benjamin Mays, Michael Novak, David O'Brien, Rosemary R. Reuther and Marc Tanenbaum. They discuss the relation of religion to culture in America and its role in the future.

296 Bible in pocket, gun in hand: the story of frontier religion.
Ross Phares. Garden City, New York: Doubleday, 1964. 182p.
A survey of American frontier religion, documented by excerpts from diaries, church court trial minutes, and anecdotes. The author describes the preacher who had to be able to 'shoot it out' as well as speak the language of the people. This book is an entertaining bit of Americana, as well as one providing religious background.

297 Catholic America.
John Cogley. New York: Dial Press, 1973. 304p. bibliog. (Two Centuries of American Life).
An introductory history on the Catholic church in the United States. The book is divided into two parts: the first deals with the chronological history of the Catholic church in America; the second discusses the role of the Catholic community today.

298 Christian churches of America: origins and beliefs.
Milton Vaughn Backman. Provo, Utah: Brigham Young University Press, 1976. 230p. bibliog.
A description of the history and tenets of the major Christian denominations in America. The religions included are: Roman Catholic, Eastern Orthodox, Lutheran, Presbyterian, United Church of Christ, Episcopal, Methodist, Baptist, Society of Friends, Unitarian Universalist, Disciples of Christ, Church of Christ, the Church of Jesus Christ of Latter-day Saints, Seventh-day Adventist, Watch Tower Bible and Tract Society, Church of Christ, Scientist and Holiness-Pentecostal.

Religion

299 **A critical bibliography of religion in America.**
Nelson Rollin Burr. Princeton, New Jersey: Princeton
University Press, 1961. 2 vols. (Religion in American Life,
vol. 4).

This two-volume bibliography completed the series Religion in American Life,
edited by James Ward Smith and A. Leland Jamison. The faculty teaching the
seminars upon which this series is based drew up a suggested reading list for their
students, using brief critical essays to describe the sources recommended. They
then prevailed upon Dr. Nelson R. Burr of the Library of Congress to compile
the completed bibliography from this material.

300 **The deacon wore spats: profiles from America's changing
religious scene.**
John T. Stewart. New York: Holt, Rinehart & Winston,
1965. 191p.

A history of 20th century American Protestantism as recorded by a former newspaper correspondent and religion editor of the *St. Louis Post-Dispatch*. The
author provides his impressions of major Protestant figures and events during this
period.

301 **A directory of religious bodies in the United States.**
Edited by J. Gordon Melton, James V. Geisendorfer. New
York: Garland, 1977. 305p. bibliog. (Garland Reference
Library of the Humanities, vol. 91).

An alphabetical listing of over 1,200 of America's religious bodies, compiled by
the Institute for the Study of American Religion which was founded in 1969. The
directory provides the address of each group, plus the names and addresses of the
group's major periodicals. Religious 'family groups' are defined and described in
the second chapter.

302 **Dissent in American religion.**
Edwin Scott Gaustad. Chicago: University of Chicago
Press, 1973. 184p. (Chicago History of American Religion).

A lively survey of religious dissent in America from colonial times to the present.
In this short study the author treats the subject from a biographical point of
view, and provides a readable addition to any collection on American religious
history.

303 **The eagle and the rising sun: Americans and the new
religions of Japan.**
Robert S. Ellwood. Philadelphia: Westminster Press, 1974.
224p. bibliog.

An introductory study of five Japanese religions that are practised in the USA:
Tenrikyo, Nichiren Shoshu, the Church of World Messianity, Seicho-no-Ie, and
Perfect Liberty. The book is useful to the student of American religions as well
as of the 1960s in America.

304 **The encyclopedia of American religions.**
J. Gordon Melton. Wilmington, North Carolina: McGrath,
1978. 2 vols.

Vol. 1 provides overviews of religious bodies, including world heritage, ideological surveys and descriptions of general styles of living. Vol. 2 provides similar material for American branches of religious bodies and is especially useful for new and more esoteric religious groups. An excellent reference guide to a difficult field.

305 **Four paths to one God: today's Jew and his religion.**
Gilbert S. Rosenthal. New York: Bloch, 1973. 323p.
bibliog.

Clarifies the differences in ritual patterns both in home and in synagogue observances, and discusses ideological differences between orthodoxy, reform, conservatism and reconstructionism. The author traces the history in America of the various Jewish movements and analyses the ideas of famous personalities in American Jewish religious life.

306 **From sacred to profane America: the role of religion in American history.**
William A. Clebsch. New York: Harper & Row, 1968.
242p. bibliog.

An interesting analysis of the influence of religion on American society. The author discusses the social utility of religion in such areas as the education system, welfare and morality, equality and nationality. He also considers the role of religion in the 'American dream' from colonial to modern times.

307 **From state church to pluralism: a Protestant interpretation of religion in American history.**
Franklin Hamlin Littell. New York: Macmillan, 1971.
225p. bibliog.

A book which, the author writes, 'was conceived as an introduction to American Protestantism, its history and present prospects'. The history of American religion presented here covers the colonial period to modern times, and discusses dialogue between faiths, as well as areas of conflict.

308 **The future of the Jewish community in America: essays prepared for a Task Force on the Future of the Jewish Community in America of the American Jewish Committee.**
Edited by David Sidorsky. New York: Basic Books, 1973.
324p. bibliog.

A collection of essays presented to an American Jewish Committee Task Force which was formed to study the survival of Jewish identity in America. The four major areas covered are: historical and ideological movements; demographic trends and social patterns of American Jews; communal institutions (synagogues and Jewish schools); and issues for the future (youth direction, priorities, etc.).

Religion

309 Handbook of denominations in the United States.
Frank Spencer Mead. Nashville, Tennessee: Abingdon Press, 1975. 6th ed. 320p. bibliog.
A descriptive listing of the many religious denominations in the United States, including information concerning history, beliefs and practices. Also included are addresses of denominational headquarters and a glossary of terms. A very useful addition to any religious collection.

310 Historical atlas of religion in America.
Edwin Scott Gaustad. New York: Harper & Row, 1962. 179p. maps. bibliog.
A useful reference tool for the student of American religious history. This well-researched sourcebook contains maps, graphs and statistical tables which present information on the various religious bodies in the United States, arranged within chronological periods. Included are the histories of fifteen major religious traditions, documented by selections from original papers (diaries, sermons, etc.).

311 A history of the Catholic church in the United States.
Thomas Timothy McAvoy. Notre Dame, Indiana: University of Notre Dame Press, 1969. 504p. bibliog.
A broad general history, designed to interest the general reader, tracing developments in the Catholic church in America since 1634. The wealth of material, conveyed in a narrative style and punctuated by excerpts from primary sources, makes this book useful to the historian as well as to the layman.

312 Immigrants and religion in urban America.
Edited by Randall M. Miller, Thomas D. Marzik. Philadelphia: Temple University Press, 1977. 170p.
A collection of eight essays which discuss late 19th century migration to the United States. Each essay discusses a different immigrant group, focusing on the group's religious life in America. Those groups discussed are Poles, Slovaks, Jews, Czechs, German Catholics, Italians, Armenians and Irish.

313 The Jewish community in America: an annotated and classified bibliographical guide.
William W. Brickman. New York: Burt Franklin, 1977. 396p. (Ethnic Bibliographical Guides).
A useful reference tool containing over 800 writings, in English and other languages, which contribute to the understanding of over 300 years of Jewish life in the United States. Included is an introductory essay on the history of Jews in America.

314 The Jewish experience in America: selected studies from the publications of the American Jewish Historical Society.
Edited by Abraham J. Karp. Waltham, Massachusetts: American Jewish Historical Society, 1969. 5 vols. bibliog.
A comprehensive work covering all aspects of Jewish experience in America - including, of course, religious experience. The volumes are arranged chronologi-

cally: vol. 1: *The colonial period*; vol. 2: *In the early republic*; vol. 3: *The emerging community*; vol. 4: *The era of immigration*; vol. 5: *At home in America*. Included are eighty-three articles by distinguished contributors.

315 **The Jews in America, 1621-1970: a chronology and fact book.**
Edited by Irving J. Sloan.   Dobbs Ferry, New York: Oceana, 1971. 151p. bibliog. (Ethnic Chronology Series, no. 3).
A collection of facts on the history of Jews in America. This volume begins with a chronology, goes on to a section of selected documents, and concludes with a series of appendixes, containing material such as lists of American Jewish civic organizations, newspapers, etc.

316 **The Mormon establishment.**
Wallace Turner.   Boston, Massachusetts: Houghton Mifflin, 1966. 343p.
A study of Mormon society written for the interested layman. This book describes church principles and rites, discusses the church in politics and also examines sociological aspects.

317 **New gods in America: an informal investigation into the new religions of American youth today.**
Peter Rowley.   New York: David McKay, 1971. 208p. bibliog.
An informal introduction to twenty-one contemporary religious movements - especially those joined by many young Americans. The author bases his information on interviews with members of the sects and observations of their rituals.

318 **The new heavens and new earth; political religion in America.**
Cushing Strout.   New York: Harper & Row, 1973. 400p. bibliog.
An examination of the interaction between religion and politics in America. The author first discusses Alexis de Tocqueville's views on the role of religion in American society, as found in *Democracy in America*. He then surveys America's religious history with a view to studying the role of religion in important political and social conflicts throughout the years.

319 **The political pulpit.**
Roderick P. Hart.   West Lafayette, Indiana: Purdue University Press, 1977. 141p. bibliog.
An analysis of civil religion in American political and social history. The author discusses the unspoken agreement between church and state: maintaining separation but having non-official contacts.

Religion

320 The religion business.
Alfred Balk.   Richmond, Virginia: John Knox Press, 1968.
96p.

A short analysis of the practice of allowing churches to engage in tax-exempt business operations, as well as the tax squeeze put on the economy by the tax-exempt status of church property. This readable volume is an expansion of an article written by the author for *Harper's*, October 1967, entitled 'God is rich'.

321 Religion in America.
Winthrop S. Hudson.   New York: Charles Scribner's Sons, 1965. 447p.

A history of religion in America, tracing it from colonial times to the present. The book is organized into chronological periods and discusses the major religious force within each time period. A comprehensive study, suitable for the general reader and the scholar in the field.

322 Religion in America, 1950 to the present.
Jackson W. Carroll, Douglas W. Johnson, Martin E.
Marty.   New York: Harper & Row, 1979. 123p. maps.

A study of religious trends in America from 1950 to 1975, using charts, graphs and maps to document such areas as church membership, attendance and financial contributions. Included is a discussion of future development.

323 Religion in the American experience: the pluralistic style.
Edited by Robert T. Handy.   Columbia, South Carolina: University of South Carolina Press, 1972. 246p.

A series of essays selected to illustrate religious pluralism in American life (e.g. the pluriform religion of the American Indian, the many forms of Christianity transplanted from Europe, plus the newer forms added in America, and the evolution of Judaism in the United States into three main branches).

324 Religions in America.
Edited by Herbert L. Marx, Jr.   New York: H. W. Wilson, 1977. 208p. bibliog. (Reference Shelf, vol. 49, no. 6).

A survey of religions in America, placing emphasis on recent changes and developments. This book is divided into seven sections entitled 'The changing role of religions'; 'Protestant diversity'; 'The Catholic church in America'; 'Varieties of religious experience'; 'Youth and religion'; 'Religious education'; 'A view to the future'.

325 Religions of America: ferment and faith in an age of crisis: a new guide and almanac.
Edited by Leo Calvin Rosten.   New York: Simon & Schuster, 1975. 672p. bibliog.

In 1955 *Look Magazine* published a series on religions in America. This was later issued as a book which has twice been revised and updated. This latest edition has two sections: part one contains a series of articles by authorities from each religious creed, describing the tenets of his faith; part two is an almanac, containing statistics, polls, a glossary and much more. A useful reference tool on American religion.

326 Religious America.
Philip Garvin, Julia Welch. New York: McGraw-Hill, 1974. 189p.

A beautiful collection of photographs taken by the author to provide an intimate view of the many religious groups that make up America. He supplements his photographs with personal interviews and impressions.

327 A religious history of America.
Edwin Scott Gaustad. New York: Harper & Row, 1966. 421p. maps. bibliog.

A well-illustrated survey of American religious history which covers a variety of topics, including the involvement of religion in the lives of the early settlers and the efforts of religious leaders of all faiths to establish equal rights in the latter half of the 20th century. Excerpts from many original documents add dimension to the well-illustrated text.

328 A religious history of the American people.
Sydney E. Ahlstrom. New Haven, Connecticut: Yale University Press, 1972. 1,158p. bibliog.

A comprehensive history of American religion. It relates the origins of the religious life of early American settlers, and traces the roots of each subsequent religious group that settled in America. This detailed work deals with American religious history within the framework of America's social, political and intellectual development.

329 Religious movements in contemporary America.
Edited by Irving I. Zaretsky, Mark P. Leone. Princeton, New Jersey: Princeton University Press, 1974. 837p. bibliog.

A scholarly collection of essays by twenty-eight contributors, describing the various religious movements within contemporary American society. The three categories of movements include: 1. churches that have had a long tradition in the USA or were offshoots of 19th century Protestantism; 2. recently founded religious groups; 3. groups based on important cults. Each of the contributors analyses a single aspect of a specific movement.

330 Religious perspectives in American culture.
James Ward Smith. Princeton, New Jersey: Princeton University Press, 1961. 427p. (Religion in American Life, vol. 2).

Volume two in this series edited by James Ward Smith and A. Leland Jamison. It contains essays dealing with the role of religion in America's social, political and cultural life.

Religion

331 **Righteous empire: the Protestant experience in America.**
Martin E. Marty. New York: Dial Press, 1970. 295p.
bibliog. (Two Centuries of American Life: a Bicentennial
Series).
An interpretive history of American evangelical Protestantism which explores the
influence of Protestantism on American society. An interesting addition to any
collection on American religion.

332 **The rise of Adventism: religion and society in mid-nineteenth
century America.**
Edited by Edwin Scott Gaustad. New York: Harper &
Row, 1974. 329p. bibliog.
A series of essays which focus on the birth and development of Adventism in the
1840s and 1850s. This important contribution to religious history discusses the
religious climate of the mid-19th century in America.

333 **The shaping of American religion.**
James Ward Smith. Princeton, New Jersey: Princeton
University Press, 1961. 514p. (Religion in American Life,
vol. 1).
The first in a four-volume series edited by James Ward Smith and A. Leland
Jamison. The series grew out of a seminar given at Princeton University and
deals with four broad segments of American religion: Protestantism, Roman
Catholicism, Judaism, and 'new religions'. The series is made up of essays by
theologians and other specialists.

334 **The story of religion in America.**
William Warren Sweet. Evanston, Illinois; London: Harper
& Row, 1950. 492p. bibliog.
A standard work on American religious history which relates religious life to the
political, economic and social climate of the time. The author wrote the first
edition of this work in 1930 and revised it to include the period since 1939. The
book is arranged chronologically and traces religion in America from its earliest
colonial days.

335 **They gathered at the river: the story of the great revivalists
and their impact upon religion in America.**
Bernard A. Weisberger. Boston, Massachusetts: Little,
Brown, 1958. 345p.
An interesting and comprehensive history of revivalism in America from the early
1800s to the 1920s. The author writes as a historian, and treats a colourful
subject in a readable, yet scholarly manner. A useful addition to any collection of
American religious history.

336 **Turning east: the promise and peril of the new orientalism.**
Harvey Gallagher Cox. New York: Simon & Schuster,
1977. 192p. bibliog.

The author describes his personal contact with Eastern religious groups, and analyses the movements to see what draws converts from other religions. He participated in groups such as Hare Krishna, practised Zen and Yoga, and here talks of his experiences. An interesting look at a modern phenomenon in American religious life.

Social Conditions

337 Aging in America.
Bert Kruger Smith. Boston, Massachusetts: Beacon Press, 1973. 239p. bibliog.
This survey of the problems of aging - chronologically, physiologically and psychologically - grew out of the White House Conference for the Aging held in 1971. It reviews some of the conference recommendations and includes a list of resources which can be consulted.

338 All our children: the American family under pressure.
Kenneth Keniston. New York: Harcourt Brace Jovanovich, 1977. 255p. bibliog.
A study of the American family and its anxieties in today's society - parents' jobs, the costs of raising children, the status of children in our society, etc. In this study done with the Carnegie Council on Children, the author investigates American attitudes towards children and families, and makes specific recommendations for reforms in terms of available health, educational and legal services.

339 The American family in social-historical perspective.
Edited by Michael Gordon. New York: St. Martin's Press, 1973. 428p. bibliog.
A collection of material on the social history of the American family. Included in this study are statistical data and material on such groups as Italians in Buffalo, New York, blacks in Boston, and whites in Chicago.

340 The American future.
Washington, DC: Congressional Quarterly, 1976. 192p. bibliog.
A collection of nine reports originally published as separate Editorial Research Reports (put out by a reference service for newspapers, broadcasting networks and libraries). The topics covered in this volume include such social issues as under-employment in America, the future of welfare, rural migration and the volunteer army.

72

341 **The anguish of change.**
Louis Harris. New York: Norton, 1973. 306p.
The author, a pollster, presents a study, based on his organization's research, of change in America since 1960. He discusses such topics as feelings about the quality of life, new aspirations of women, the growth of consumerism, and differing tastes of young people.

342 **Behind bars: prisons in America.**
Edited by Richard Kwartler. New York: Vintage, 1977. 178p.
In 1974 the Ford Foundation funded *Corrections Magazine* devoted to reporting on prison systems in America. This book is based on that research, first published between September 1974 and June 1976. Illustrated with photographs, the study provides a look at the state of American criminology today.

343 **Beyond despair: directions for America's third century.**
Robert Theobald. Washington, DC: New Republic, 1976. 169p. bibliog.
A survey of today's problems in the areas of work, education, health and justice. The author presents a variety of possible solutions to the complex problems confronting modern America.

344 **Chemical coping: a report on legal drug use in the United States.**
Carl D. Chambers, James A. Inciardi, Harvey A. Siegel. New York: Spectrum, 1975. 157p. bibliog.
A statistical survey of users of legal psychoactive drugs such as barbiturates, alcohol, tranquilizers, and stimulants. The aim of the authors is to characterize the extent to which the United States population copes with life through the use of chemicals. They break their study down into the use of three general categories of substances: prescription drugs, over-the-counter nonprescription drugs and alcohol.

345 **Child development: day care.**
United States. Department of Health, Education and Welfare. Washington, DC: US Government Printing Office, 1971- . (DHEW Publication).
A series of handbooks covering all aspects of a comprehensive day-care programme. The handbooks available include: 1. *A statement of principles*; 2. *Serving infants*; 3. *Serving preschool children*; 4. *Serving school age children*; 5. *Staff training*; 6. *Health services*; 7. *Administration*; 8. *Serving children with special needs*; 9. *Family day care.*

346 **Community health: its needs and resources.**
Edited by John D. Porterfield. New York: Basic Books, 1966. 250p.
A basic reader for the layman on the subject of community health programmes in the United States. This book is based on a series of lectures prepared for the

Voice of America, explaining public health in the USA (e.g. communicable disease control, maternal and child care, nutrition, etc.).

347 **Conscience and convenience: the asylum and its alternatives in progressive America.**
David J. Rothman. Boston, Massachusetts: Little, Brown, 1980. 464p. bibliog.
Contends that progressive reforms reinforced and extended the institutional faults of the prisons and asylums they were intended to improve. The study contains reviews of probation, parole and prison reform programmes. A similar analysis of the treatment of juvenile delinquents and the mentally ill is attempted. A well-written and important book with excellent documentation.

348 **Dealing with drug abuse: a report to the Ford Foundation.**
Drug Abuse Survey Project. New York: Praeger, 1972. 396p.
The Ford Foundation sponsored a study to investigate the problem of drug abuse in the United States, and to offer recommendations for effective ways to deal with the problem. This book contains a survey report and a group of background papers dealing with such subjects as drug education, effects and economics.

349 **The development of rural America.**
George Loris Brinkman. Lawrence, Kansas: University Press of Kansas, 1974. 140p. bibliog.
A collection of essays which arose from a seminar presented at Kansas State University in 1971 on rural community development. The papers deal with a variety of topics, including social and economic conditions and problems, use of natural resources, and rural poverty and urban growth. This is a useful volume for any collection on rural sociology.

350 **Drugs in American life.**
Edited by Morrow Wilson, Suzanne Wilson. New York: H. W. Wilson, 1975. 212p. bibliog. (Reference Shelf, vol. 47, no. 1).
A series of essays emphasizing youthful involvement with drugs - and aimed for use by high school and college students. The book gives an overview of the problem and deals with the legal aspects of drug use, social and medical aspects of the problem, personal accounts, and possible solutions.

351 **The 8 day week.**
John Ward Pearson. New York: Harper & Row, 1973. 161p. bibliog.
Discusses the interesting concept of changing the country's work week to a four days on, four days off cycle, so that only half the work-force reports to work on a given day. This would change leisure time habits, pressure on transportation, and life-styles in general.

352 **The future of social security.**
Alicia H. Munnell. Washington, DC: Brookings Institution,
1977. 190p. (Studies in Social Economics).
A comprehensive analysis of social security in relation to other sources of retirement income. This study deals with the question of financing the system from
payroll taxes, and the various options for reforms to eliminate inequities within
the system.

353 **The graying of working America: alternative retirement
futures.**
Harold L. Sheppard, Sara E. Rix. New York: Free Press,
1977. 174p. bibliog.
A study dealing with the problems resulting from population changes leading to a
large retirement-age group requiring support (financial, medical and psychological). The authors discuss alternative policies of retaining older workers rather
than forcing them to retire at a mandatory age.

354 **Growing old in America: the Bland-Lee lectures delivered at
Clark University.**
David Hackett Fischer. New York: Oxford University
Press, 1977. 242p.
The author has approached the subject of aging in a novel way - historically -
and has written a fascinating book tracing the shift in American society from
1780 to the present. He notes the changes from a society revering age to one that
idolizes youth. He documents social history and offers suggestions for the future.

355 **Growing old in the country of the young.**
Charles H. Percy. New York: McGraw-Hill, 1974. 214p.
A look at the problems of the aged in relation to poverty, government health
programmes, home health care, housing, etc. The first half of the book is written
in an anecdotal style, but it also includes a resource guide which offers useful
advice and practical information (agency names, phone numbers, etc.).

356 **Health programs in the states: a survey.**
Gary J. Clarke. New Brunswick, New Jersey: Center for
State Legislative Research and Services, Eagleton Institute
of Politics, Rutgers University, 1975. 40p. bibliog.
A study in the Eagleton Institute's series on state legislatures and public policy.
This report provides information on selected state health programmes, focusing
primarily on health care delivery and cost control. Each chapter begins with
historical background and then goes on to summarize more recent developments.
A useful tool for anyone in the public health field.

Social Conditions

357 **A history of social welfare and social work in the United States.**
James Leiby.   New York: Columbia University Press, 1978. 426p. bibliog.
A scholarly work covering American social welfare programmes from 1815 to 1972, and also discussing the social work profession. An important addition to all academic libraries.

358 **The history of violence in America: historical and comparative perspectives.**
Edited by Hugh Davis Graham, Ted Robert Gurr.   New York; Washington, DC; London: Praeger, 1969. 822p. bibliog.
A collection of scholarly articles presented to the National Commission on the Cause and Prevention of Violence. This broad study touches on all aspects of the problem from a historical overview to comparative patterns of violence. Included are articles on crime, racial aggression, rebellion, protest movements, etc.

359 **Innocents at home: America in the 1970s.**
Tad Szulc.   New York: Viking Press, 1974. 342p. bibliog.
A look at American society in the 1970s, by a foreign correspondent recently returned home after an absence of five years. The author touches on the problems that he saw - poverty, urban decay, environmental wreckage, racial conflict, etc. - yet ends with the optimistic observation that change is possible to correct these ills.

360 **Kind and usual punishment: the prison business.**
Jessica Mitford.   New York: Knopf, 1973. 340p. (Distributed by Random House).
A study of the American prison system, which uncovers numerous abuses. The author outlines the defects in the system, makes various reform proposals, and includes an appendix of publications and organizations devoted to various aspects of fighting for prisoners' rights.

361 **Lifeway leap: the dynamics of change in America.**
Luther P. Gerlach, Virginia H. Hine.   Minneapolis, Minnesota: University of Minnesota Press, 1973. 332p.
An important sociological study analysing the process of social change in the United States. The authors describe the influences of counter-culture movements on the established order, and also discuss the differences between evolutionary and revolutionary change.

362 **Lonely in America.**
Suzanne Gordon.   New York: Simon & Schuster, 1975. 318p. bibliog.
An interesting study of loneliness as an experience of white, middle class Americans and of their attempts to cope with this problem through innovations such as

singles' bars, encounter groups, etc. Various aspects of the subject are touched upon, such as the single status, old age, divorce, etc.

363 The marihuana conviction: a history of marihuana prohibition in the United States.
Richard J. Bonnie, Charles H. Whitebread. Charlottesville, Virginia: University Press of Virginia, 1974. 368p. maps. bibliog.

A scholarly history of marihuana use and prohibition in the United States from 1915 to the 1970s. Included are information on legislation and government agencies and a variety of editorial cartoons which reflect official attitudes towards drugs. An important addition to any collection on drug use in the United States.

364 The medical profession and social reform - 1885-1945.
Lloyd C. Taylor. New York: St. Martin's Press, 1974. 168p. bibliog.

A short discussion of the role of physicians as social reformers in areas such as the setting up of social services in hospitals and initiating occupational health and safety measures. The approach is biographical.

365 National health insurance: benefits, costs, and consequences.
Karen Davis. Washington, DC: Brookings Institution, 1975. 182p. bibliog. (Studies in Social Economics).

Studies the objectives of national health insurance and various proposals and options available to meet these objectives. A very useful sourcebook on the topic of health care costs.

366 The new extended family: day care that works.
Ellen Galinsky, William H. Hooks. Boston, Massachusetts: Houghton Mifflin, 1977. 280p. bibliog.

A practical guide for parents seeking a day-care programme for their children. Included are descriptions of fourteen programmes which the authors considered to be outstanding among the many they visited while researching the book. The authors also include a chapter outlining legislation which they feel would help to ensure good child care.

367 On relief: the economics of poverty and public welfare.
Bruno Stein. New York: Basic Books, 1971. 211p. bibliog.

A survey and analysis by an economist on the history of American laws devised to aid the needy. The author discusses a variety of methods, both implemented and suggested, in public assistance: negative income tax, children's allowance programmes, family assistance, etc.

368 Poor people's movements: why they succeed, how they fail.
Frances Fox Piven. New York: Pantheon, 1977. bibliog.

An interesting interpretation of protest movements with an analysis of four particular organizations of the poor: the movement of unemployed during the Great Depression which led to the Workers' Alliance of America; the movement of industrial workers to form the CIO (Congress of Industrial Organizations) at this time; the Southern civil rights movement; and the movement of welfare recipients leading to the formation of the National Welfare Rights Organization.

369 **Prison.**
Leonard J. Berry. New York: Grossman, 1972. 266p. (Subsistence Press Book).
A collection of interviews with inmates, wardens, guards, doctors, chaplains and guidance counsellors in prisons across the United States. The author edited his material to try to present a picture of a typical day in prison life. The book is illustrated with press photographs.

370 **Prisons, protest, and politics.**
Edited by Burton M. Atkins, Henry R. Glick. Englewood Cliffs, New Jersey: Prentice-Hall, 1972. 180p.
A collection of readings dealing with prison unrest and protest in the United States. The book deals with four aspects of this question: living conditions, constitutional rights of prisoners, consequences of these conditions, and the politics of prison reform.

371 **The pursuit of dignity: new living alternatives for the elderly.**
Bert Kruger Smith. Boston, Massachusetts: Beacon Press, 1977. 154p.
A description of the options available for the elderly who need care, as alternatives to nursing homes. Some solutions discussed are day-care centres, home health services, nutrition programmes and cooperative housing.

372 **Raising children in modern America: problems and prospective solutions.**
Edited by Nathan B. Talbot. Boston, Massachusetts: Little, Brown, 590p. bibliog.
A collection of contributions by over twenty experts in a variety of fields treating various aspects of raising children: decisions to have children, the needs and development of children, social institutions devoted to the family, etc.

373 **Regulating the poor: the functions of public welfare.**
Frances Fox Piven, Richard A. Cloward. New York: Pantheon, 1971. 389p. bibliog.
An analysis of the 'Great Society' programmes of the 1960s and a discussion of the evolution of relief programmes from the time of the Great Depression in 1932. The authors correlate relief-giving with the political and social climate, and argue that welfare programmes are designed to control social unrest rather than simply to alleviate suffering.

374 **The seventies: problems and proposals.**
Edited by Irving Howe, Michael Harrington. New York: Harper & Row, 1972. 519p. bibliog.
A series of articles, originally published in *Dissent* magazine, on a variety of current social problems and proposals for solving them. Some of the issues include

poverty, crime, pollution, women's liberation, black politics, etc. An interesting presentation of one point of view.

375 Social history of the United States: a guide to information sources.

Donald F. Tingley. Detroit, Michigan: Gale Research, 1979. 260p. (American Government and History Information Guide Series, vol. 3).

376 Social security: promise and reality.

Rita Ricardo Campbell. Stanford, California: Hoover Institution Press, Stanford University, 1977. 351p. bibliog.

A survey of the social security system, examining how it works in reality, and suggesting how it should ideally work. The author examines the poor future of the system as it now stands and offers proposals for reforms.

377 Social security: the fraud in your future.

Warren Shore. New York: Macmillan, 1975. 238p.

A study, by a consumer advocate, of the present social security system, its short-comings, and recommendations for its improvement. The author explains the benefits available, individual retirement accounts, the Pension Reform Act, and answers many questions frequently asked about social security.

378 State of the nation.

William Watts, Lloyd A. Free. Lexington, Massachusetts: Lexington, 1978. 238p. bibliog.

A portrait of the American national mood as reflected by public opinion surveys conducted by the Gallup Organization. People were asked to express their opinions on national progress in such areas as the economy, crime, housing, health care, educational opportunity, etc. The first edition of this work was published by Universe Books in 1973.

379 Time of transition, the growth of families headed by women.

Heather Ross, Isabel V. Sawhill. Washington, DC: Urban Institute, 1975. 223p.

An analysis of single-parent families headed by women, from economic and psychological points of view. The authors make use of census data and other statistical studies, and make thought-provoking comments on the policies of the present and the needs of the future in this area.

380 Uprooted children: the early life of migrant farm workers.

Robert Coles. Pittsburgh, Pennsylvania: University of Pittsburgh Press, 1970. 142p.

Describes the life of the children of migrant farm workers - the conditions under which they live and how they adjust to the rootless world in which they find themselves. The book is an outgrowth of a Horace Mann Lecture given in 1969 and portrays the despair of poverty in the United States.

Social Conditions

381 **The wagon and the star: a study of American community initiative.**
Margaret Mead, Muriel Brown. New York: Rand McNally, 1966. 223p.
Analyses the involvement of the American community in activities which affect the welfare of the people living within it. Some examples of the variety of activities discussed are volunteer fire companies, nursery schools, the founding of societies such as the National Association for Retarded Children or the Parent-Teacher Association, and activities which illustrate the involvement of the American people in volunteer roles to better their communities.

382 **Welfare: a handbook for friend and foe.**
Timothy J. Sampson. Philadelphia: United Church Press, 1972. 203p. (A Pilgrim Press Book).
A reference source containing jargon, history and statistical data on public welfare. Useful to student and layman alike.

383 **When your parents grow old: information and resources to help the adult son or daughter cope with the problems of aging parents.**
Jane Otten, Florence B. Shelley. New York: Funk & Wagnalls, 1976. 298p. bibliog.
One of a number of useful resource books providing information on how to deal with the problems posed by aging parents and how to help them cope with the daily needs and decisions of life.

384 **Who cares for the baby? Choices in day care.**
Beatrice Glickman, Nesha Springer. New York: Schocken, 1977. 250p. bibliog.
The authors set out to write a book showing that day-care is not good for children. However, after investigating many alternative solutions to caring for children at home, they present many of the day-care systems in a positive, practical light. The study suggests means of choosing care for children based on individual family needs.

385 **Who's minding the children? The history and politics of day care in America.**
Margaret O'Brien Steinfels. New York: Simon & Schuster, 1973. 281p. bibliog.
The author, an advocate of child care, traces the history of day-care in the United States from its origins to its present state. She discusses the workings of day-care and answers the questions that inevitably arise when this subject is analysed: What kind of day-care is helpful? Will day-care support or destroy the family unit? Can day-care be an educational environment or merely a baby-sitting service?

386 **You and your aging parent: the modern family's guide to emotional, physical, and financial problems.**
Barbara Silverstone, Helen Kandel Hyman. New York: Pantheon, 1976. 335p. bibliog.

A practical guide to dealing with the problems of determining and obtaining the care needed by aged parents. This book first discusses family ties, emotions and responsibilities. The second half is devoted to options available and the appendixes list specific resource agencies and directories. Also included is a descriptive list of common diseases of the elderly, and a nursing home checklist.

Politics

General

387 The age of surveillance: the aims and methods of America's political intelligence system.
Frank J. Donner. New York: Knopf, 1980. 554p. bibliog.
A detailed study by a civil liberties lawyer which argues that since the wave of anti-communist sentiment following the Second World War the US government has suppressed all forms of political dissent. J. Edgar Hoover and the FBI are the central villains in Donner's study.

388 The Almanac of American Politics: the Senators, the Representatives, the Governors - Their Records, States and Districts.
Michael Barone (and others). New York: E. P. Dutton, 1972- . annual. maps.
A solid comprehensive reference book providing essential up-to-date information on American politics. For all levels.

389 America votes: a handbook of contemporary American election statistics, 1945-1954-
New York: Macmillan; Washington, DC: Congressional Quarterly, 1956- .
Volume thirteen in this excellent reference series appeared in 1979, bringing the coverage forward to include the 1978 elections. Presidential, senatorial and congressional elections can be studied using the tables in these volumes, which include information on primaries as well as general elections.

390 **American democratic theory: pluralism and its critics.**
William Alton Kelso.   Westport, Connecticut: Greenwood
Press, 1978. 288p. bibliog. (Contributions in Political
Science, 1).
A well-organized defence of pluralism and the pluralist concept of democracy.
Kelso defends the pluralist theory which has been criticized recently and updates
Nelson Polsby's earlier defence *Community power and political theory* (1963). A
useful bibliography supplements the text.

391 **The American political dictionary.**
Jack C. Plano, Milton Greenberg.   New York: Holt,
Rinehart & Winston, 1979. 5th ed. 544p.
Arranged in eighteen topical chapters, this basic reference tool's 1,200 entries
have been thoroughly updated and cross-referenced. Each term is given a paragraph of definition or description and an additional paragraph of analysis indicat-
ing its significance.

392 **The American political tradition and the men who made it.**
Richard Hofstadter.   New York: Knopf, 1973. reprint.
440p.
A series of classic essays on American political leaders from the founding fathers
to Franklin D. Roosevelt. Witty and sharply styled, the twelve portraits are as
essential to the modern reader as they were when first published in 1948.

393 **Bureaucratic government USA.**
David Nachmias, David H. Rosenbloom.   New York: St.
Martin's Press, 1980. 269p. bibliog.
A well-written analysis of American government achieved by an examination of
the bureaucracy. There are fine chapters on the development of bureaucratic
organization within federal legislative and judicial branches. The last chapter
deals with the consequences of bureaucratization and concludes that many Americans feel they can no longer control government and politics through democratic
processes, such as elections.

394 **The cultural pattern in American politics: the first century.**
Robert Kelley.   New York: Knopf, 1979. 368p. bibliog.
The first of a two-volume overview of American political history. It is a synthesis
of recent scholarship resulting in a more comprehensive appreciation of ethno-
cultural forces such as the central role of Scotch-Irish Presbyterians in the coming of the American Revolution. The volume has four sections: the revolutionary
origins; the Jeffersonian and Jacksonian party systems; the Civil War party
system, 1856-94; and a retrospect.

395 **The deadlock of democracy: four-party politics in America.**
James MacGregor Burns.   Englewood Cliffs, New Jersey:
Prentice-Hall, 1963. 376p. bibliog.
An examination of the American political system. Burns concludes that the
system has been paralysed by a Madisonian model in which conflicting interests
check each other and in turn check national power. The system is described as a

four-party system (including two congressional and presidential parties, the former representing local interests, the latter national interests). Burns asserts that a restoration of a Jeffersonian model based on two party competition would improve government functioning in the USA.

396 The divided left: American radicalism, 1900-1975.
Milton Cantor. New York: Hill & Wang, 1978. 248p. bibliog.
An excellent survey incorporating recent research and synthesis, such as that of John P. Diggins' *The American left in the twentieth century* (1973) and James Weinstein's *The ambiguous legacy: the left in American politics* (1975), yet adding its own distinctive analysis. It explores the failure of the left, concluding that 'immediatism', implying a gradual road to socialism, was at the root of radical failure, since by humanizing the existing system, they served only to strengthen it.

397 Domestic intelligence: monitoring dissent in America.
Richard E. Morgan. Austin, Texas: University of Texas Press, 1980. 208p. bibliog.
The ferment of the last decade over the many illegal practices of federal law enforcement agencies in pursuit of domestic intelligence has raised the question of the role of government in these pursuits and the rights of individuals to privacy. Morgan studies the tension between the right to political dissent and the need to protect the community and concludes that a balance can be drawn utilizing responsible guidelines and a system of checks and balances.

398 Electronic democracy.
Anne Rawley Saldich. New York: Praeger, 1979. 142p.
A concise, well-written appraisal of the impact of television on the American political process. It examines television news and its role as a determinant of general perceptions of public affairs, its ability to confer immediate name and face recognition on national leaders and its power to develop credibility for government figures.

399 Emerging coalitions in American politics.
Edited by Seymour Martin Lipset. San Francisco: Institute for Contemporary Studies, 1978. 524p.
Twenty-two academics, political practitioners and journalist David Broder address various aspects of coalition politics, resulting in a useful compilation. The book contains six essays on background and history, two essays on the voting behaviour of the contemporary electorate, four essays on strains in the party system, nine essays on the prospects of new coalitions and a concluding essay by Lipset. Each essay provides a succinct summary of existing scholarship.

400 The end of liberalism: the second republic of the United States.
Theodore J. Lowi. New York: Norton, 1979. 2nd ed. 331p. bibliog.
The first edition of this work (1969) established Lowi as one of the most imaginative and provocative critics of the American political system; in it he indicted

the pluralist politics of the American liberal state. His basic message remains the same: open-ended delegations of authority have led to a condition of policy without law which can be remedied only through legal formalism, which Lowi calls 'juridical democracy'. He carries his study through the Nixon administration into the 1970s. This is a stimulating, discussion-provoking analysis.

401 **Financing politics: money, elections and political reform.**
Herbert E. Alexander. Washington, DC: Congressional Quarterly Press, 1980. 2nd ed. 275p.
Revised to include campaign spending in the 1976 and 1978 elections, this informative work examines the levels, sources and expenditure of campaign funds. It includes a survey of political action committees. A valuable treatment of a subject of great current interest.

402 **Must we bus? Segregated schools and national policy.**
Gary Orfield. Washington, DC: Brookings Institution, 1978. 470p.
This book is a *tour de force* on one of the most divisive political issues in the contemporary USA. An extraordinarily comprehensive work, it reflects an awareness of the historical, legal, sociological and political dimensions of the struggle over school desegregation. The work explores the legal basis for busing, the demography of school enrolment, the economics of busing and the role of the federal government in school desegregation. It is a significant study of a continuing source of political conflict.

403 **The neoconservatives: the men who are changing America's politics.**
Peter Steinfels. New York: Simon & Schuster, 1979. 352p. bibliog.
Designated a 'notable book' by the American Library Association, this is a well-written and vivid portrait of the men and the movement that are bringing about a significant shift in American politics. Well researched.

404 **The new American political system.**
Samuel H. Beer (and others). Washington, DC: American Enterprise Institute for Public Policy Research, 1978. 407p. (AEI Studies, 213).
Nine contributors discuss the major changes in US politics since the inauguration of John F. Kennedy. Each essay is of the highest quality and a final chapter summarizes developments and puts the findings into focus.

405 **The odyssey of the American right.**
Michael W. Miles. New York: Oxford University Press, 1980. 371p.
A comprehensive history of the American right from the Depression to the present day. The work analyses right wing ideology and its position in current American politics. It surveys the movement's supporters from MacArthur to Nixon.

Politics. General

406 The origins of American politics.
Bernard Bailyn. New York: Knopf, 1968. 173p.

Originating as lectures delivered at Brown University, these essays examine the nature of colonial politics. This analysis clearly reveals the modifications to the British heritage that resulted from the influence of the American experience on the colonists.

407 Political profiles.
New York: Facts on File, 1978- .

An exceptional series in which five volumes have so far been published: *The Truman years, The Eisenhower years, The Kennedy years, The Johnson years, The Nixon/Ford years.* The volumes on Kennedy and Johnson were chosen by the American Library Association as being among the outstanding reference books of 1978 and the Truman volume was cited for its quality in 1979. Each volume contains more than 500 biographical sketches and includes a bibliography.

408 The politics of unreason: right wing extremism in America, 1790-1970.
New York: Harper & Row, 1970. 547p. bibliog. (Patterns of American Prejudice Series, 5).

A comprehensive well-documented analysis of right wing political movements throughout American history. It includes examinations of a variety of organizations including the Know-Nothing Party, the Ku Klux Klan and the John Birch Society. Important and well written, this study is recommended for all levels of study.

409 Politics, position and power: the dynamics of federal organization.
Harold Seidman. New York: Oxford University Press, 1970. 311p. bibliog.

Seidman asserts that the essence of government administration is politics. He gives examples from the federal administrative structure which illustrate the political nature of decisions taken on administrative functioning. He identifies informal power élites within agencies as the element determining policy on the basis of specialist rather than broad interests. This is an important scholarly work.

410 Power on the left: American radical movements since 1946.
Lawrence Lader. New York: Norton, 1979. 410p. bibliog.

A readable, anecdotal history of America's left since the 1940s. There is careful coverage of the upsurge of black and student radicalism during the 1960s. A well-researched effort, valuable for its wealth of data, if somewhat lacking in analytical terms. A good introduction for the non-specialist.

411 Public opinion in American politics.
W. Lance Bennett. New York: Harcourt Brace Jovanovich, 1980. 420p. bibliog.

Valuable not only as a text book but for the general reader, this ambitious work analyses the links between politics and public opinion in terms of three closely related dimensions: the individual and society; the formation of public issues and political communication; political institutions and culture. The work shows multiple ways public opinion can vary in origin, evolution, expression and political impact.

412 Top secret: national security and the right to know.
Morton H. Halperin, Daniel N. Hoffman. New York: New Republic, 1977. 158p. bibliog.
A concise attack on what the authors consider excessive secrecy in the executive branch of government. They present new options for classification of information. Appendixes detail the current state of espionage law and court cases on the subject. A stimulating study of an issue of increasing concern.

413 Unions in American national politics.
Graham K. Wilson. New York: St. Martin's Press, 1979. 168p.
A brief, well-written analysis of the role of labour unions in the American political arena. It opens with a historical summary and then considers labour's current political and lobbying activities. Discusses the attitudes of union members, the relation of unions and political parties and labour's role in US foreign policy.

Congress

414 Congress and the budget.
Joel Havemann. Bloomington, Indiana: Indiana University Press, 1978. 247p. bibliog.
A concise account of efforts to reform the congressional budget since the passage of legislation to alter fiscal procedures in 1974. It evaluates the impact of reform on legislative-executive relations in regard to the federal budget. A well-written and researched analysis by a journalist who has covered the issue since 1974.

415 Congress and the nation.
Washington, DC: Congressional Quarterly, 1965- .
Vol. 1: 1945-64; vol. 2: 1965-68; vol. 3: 1969-72; vol. 4: 1973-76. Congressional Quarterly has taken its presidential, legislative and political coverage and condensed it to give researchers an overview and detailed coverage of every major political subject area. The text is supplemented by an extensive index and table of contents, an appendix which includes key congressional votes, biographical data, lists of presidents and cabinets, and state of the union addresses. An indispensable reference on American national politics and policy.

416 Congressional ethics.
Washington, DC: Congressional Quarterly, 1980. 2nd ed. 215p. bibliog.
A revised updated reference volume on ethics and the American Congress. It includes a wealth of factual information and covers the issue through develop-

Politics. Congress

ments in the recent ABSCAM scandal to May 1980. A good bibliography and index contribute to this handy reference introduction to the subject.

417 **Congressional procedures and the policy process.**
Walter J. Oleszek. Washington, DC: Congressional Quarterly, 1978. 256p. bibliog. (Politics and Public Policy Series).

A lively, thorough and clear work on the rules of procedure of Congress. One of the best treatments to date of the congressional environment and the route by which a bill becomes a law. Good illustrative examples, a glossary, end-notes and a bibliography enhance this useful work on the legislative process.

418 **Congressional Quarterly Almanac.**
Washington, DC: Congressional Quarterly News Features, 1945- . annual.

Based on the *Congressional Quarterly Weekly Reports,* this is one of the most valuable sources of information on American politics. Coverage of congressional affairs is detailed and comprehensive. It contains an excellent index and is supplemented by a variety of charts, voting records, etc. Every student of American government should make frequent use of the *CQ Almanac* and *Weekly Reports.*

419 **Congressional Quarterly's guide to Congress.**
Washington, DC: Congressional Quarterly, 1976. 2nd ed. [various]p. bibliog.

Considerably larger than its 900-page predecessor, published in 1972, this comprehensive reference tool contains a wealth of additional information. Especially helpful are the sections on the changes in congressional procedures and the seniority system as well as the section dealing with congressional powers and exploring the War Powers Act of 1973 and the 1974 Budget Act. A useful set of appendixes include the texts of laws affecting congressional reorganization and campaign financing.

420 **Congressional Staff Directory.**
Indianapolis, Indiana: Bobbs-Merrill, 1959- . annual.

Supplements the *Official Congressional Directory* (q.v.) with valuable staff information as well as details of congressional committee assignments, seniority, etc. An invaluable ready-reference tool.

421 **Money in congressional elections.**
Gary C. Jacobson. New Haven, Connecticut: Yale University Press, 1980. 250p. bibliog.

An important contribution to the literature on campaign finance, this candid discussion reveals how money operates in the electoral politics of Congress. Based upon considerable data from the congressional elections of the 1970s Jacobson draws important conclusions about the extent to which campaign spending determines success at the polls. In light of recent and proposed changes to the campaign financing laws, the volume is of considerable significance. A well-written and thoroughly documented study.

422 The new Senate: liberal influence on a conservative institution.

Michael Foley. New Haven, Connecticut: Yale University Press, 1980. 348p.

An extensively researched analysis of the US Senate from the early 1950s to 1972. It studies the ways in which the liberal members altered the structure and institutional norms of the Senate and at the same time assesses the impact of the institution on the liberals themselves.

423 Official Congressional Directory.

Washington, DC: US Government Printing Office, 1809- . semi-annual.

This directory, whose title has varied down through the nation's history, contains biographical information on all members of Congress as well as details regarding the boundaries of the various congressional districts. A useful ready-reference tool.

424 On the hill: a history of the American Congress.

Alvin M. Josephy, Jr. New York: Simon & Schuster, 1979. 414p. bibliog.

A well-written account of congressional history, offering important clarifications of the major political trends of the 19th and 20th centuries.

425 The Senate nobody knows.

Bernard Asbell. Garden City, New York: Doubleday, 1978. 466p.

A well-written study of Edmund Muskie, Democratic Senator from Maine, which goes far beyond the individual legislator. It offers the reader far broader insights into the workings of the Congress as a whole. The book portrays an institution, rather than merely one individual.

426 Unelected representatives: congressional staff and the future of representative government.

Michael J. Malbin. New York: Basic Books, 1980. 279p.

A solid explanation of how congressional staff have assumed and exercised authority. It documents the 'iron triangle', the term used to describe the three-sided entity composed of the executive bureaucracy, a congressional staff and an interest-group lobby, which together undermine representative democracy. The author cites examples of how staff members have made decisions about legislation that two decades ago would have been improper for anyone other than an elected official. Malbin suggests that this situation leads to stalemate, as seen in the difficulty Congress has in a variety of problems of growing current importance, such as energy.

Political parties

427 American political parties.
David Everson. New York: New Viewpoints, 1980. 256p. bibliog.

An insightful evaluation of the traditional two-party system in the USA. The study examines the major changes that have occurred in the presidential nomination process and the nationalization of two-party competition.

428 The creation of a democratic majority, 1928-1936.
Kristi Andersen. Chicago: University of Chicago Press, 1979. 160p. bibliog.

An attempt to rebut the widely held view that the partisan realignment of the 1930s that transformed the Democrats from the minority to the majority party was the result of the conversion of former Republicans who switched their allegiance under the impact of hard times. Andersen explains the new Democratic majority as arising largely from the mobilization of new voters, particularly immigrant-stock residents of the northern cities and young people who first came of age in the 1920s and 1930s. Her thesis is not new, but is well supported by a wealth of data and analysis.

429 National party conventions, 1831-1976.
Washington, DC: Congressional Quarterly, 1979. 2nd ed. 227p. bibliog.

A useful reference work. A major portion gives a chronology of nominating conventions from 1831-1976. A section on the key ballots at the conventions provides a unique compilation of such data. This second edition adds data from the 1976 convention to the material in the earlier edition.

430 National party platforms.
Compiled by Donald Bruce Johnson. Champaign, Illinois: University of Illinois Press, 1978. 6th rev. ed. 2 vols.

Volume 1 covers political party platforms from 1840-1956; volume 2 covers 1960-76. Each volume is indexed by subject and by name. There are concise half-page descriptions of each presidential election.

431 The parties: Republicans and Democrats in this century.
Henry Fairlie. New York: St. Martin's Press, 1978. 236p.

Although undocumented and without an index, this is a stimulating exploration of the recent past of the two major American parties. The parties are not treated kindly, but the reader will delight in and profit from the sharp appraisals.

432 **The Republican Party, 1854-1966.**
George H. Mayer. New York: Oxford University Press, 1967. 2nd ed. 615p. bibliog.

A clear study of the development of the Republican Party, which emphasizes the growth of the national organization rather than politics on the state and local level. A good general introductory work.

433 **The romance of American communism.**
Vivian Gornick. New York: Basic Books, 1978. 265p.

A good descriptive account of day-to-day party activities. Gornick's own recollections of Jewish working class political activities in the 1940s and 1950s are extremely useful. Not an analytical or ideological study, but extremely valuable, nonetheless.

434 **Search for consensus: the story of the Democratic Party.**
Ralph M. Goldman. Philadelphia: Temple University Press, 1979. 417p. bibliog.

The initial chapter is devoted to conceptual theses; seven more carry the reader from the inception of the party to the election of Jimmy Carter. The two final chapters return to conceptual themes for the purpose of speculating about future political developments. A valuable, if highly compressed, party history.

435 **Where have all the voters gone? The fracturing of America's political parties.**
Everett Carll Ladd, Jr. New York: Norton, 1978. 86p.

A brief readable analysis of two principal themes in American politics: the relative strength, social make-up and ideology of the Democratic and Republican coalitions; and the health (or lack of it) of American political parties as the institutions linking citizens to government.

The Presidency

436 **All things to all men: the false promise of the modern American presidency.**
Godfrey Hodgson. New York: Simon & Schuster, 1980. 288p. bibliog.

Contends that the presidency is neither too weak, nor too strong, but rather burdened by unrealistic expectations from citizens of what can be accomplished. The office is also isolated from institutions like the Congress which could facilitate its activities. A well-written synthesis on the current state of the presidency.

437 The American presidency.
Richard M. Pious. New York: Basic Books, 1979. 491p. bibliog.

A readable analysis of the American presidency. The basic discussion of the office is clear and balanced. This is a good modern addition to the work of Clinton Rossiter (see the following item), now somewhat dated.

438 The American presidency.
Clinton Lawrence Rossiter. New York: Harcourt Brace, 1960. 2nd ed. 281p.

A standard historical study, combining in one volume six lectures delivered by Rossiter at the University of Chicago in 1956. Although somewhat out-of-date, this examination of the office and the men who have filled it remains a cornerstone in the literature on the American presidency.

439 History of American presidential elections, 1789-1968.
Edited by Arthur M. Schlesinger, Jr. (and others). New York: Chelsea House and McGraw-Hill, 1971. 4 vols.

Forty-five contributors added to this analysis of presidential elections and accompanying relevant documents. Vol. 1: 1789-1844; vol. 2: 1848-96; vol. 3: 1900-36; vol. 4: 1940-68. Arranged chronologically, election by election, and including selected party platforms, speeches, correspondence, etc., this is an extremely valuable set.

440 The making of the president, 1960.
Theodore H. White. New York: Atheneum, 1961. 400p.

The first in White's series of political narratives on presidential campaigns. He has produced a volume on each succeeding election: *The making of the president, 1964*; *The making of the president, 1968*; *The making of the president, 1972*; and *The making of the president, 1976*, are currently available. They are excellent surveys for readers at every level.

441 The modern presidency.
Grant McConnell. New York: St. Martin's Press, 1976. 2nd ed. 131p. bibliog.

A completely revised edition of the author's fine 1968 examination of the nature of the modern presidency. A useful bibliography and list of presidents and their terms of office supplement the work. This is an excellent concise study. It should be read in conjunction with Rossiter's classic *The American presidency* (q.v.).

442 The past and future of presidential debates.
Edited by Austin Ranney. Washington, DC: American Enterprise Institute for Public Policy Research, 1979. 226p. bibliog. (AEI Studies, 228).

Based on eight papers presented at a 1977 conference. This is a comprehensive, well-written series of essays by a variety of experts. They discuss presidential debates from 1960 to the present day and provide an extensive bibliography for further study.

443 The power of the modern presidency.
Erwin Hargrove. Philadelphia: Temple University Press,
1974. 353p. bibliog.
A good concise analysis of the office of president and its responsibilities in domestic and foreign policy formulation. It defines the crisis of the contemporary presidency, providing a wealth of illustrative detail.

444 Presidential impeachment.
John R. Labovitz. New Haven, Connecticut: Yale
University Press, 1978. 268p.
The author, who served on the Nixon impeachment staff, provides a clear review of the history of the impeachment process in the American political system. The discussion begins with the constructing of the Constitution and ends with an analysis of the Nixon inquiry.

445 Presidential power: the politics of leadership from FDR to Carter.
Richard E. Neustadt. New York: John Wiley & Sons,
1980. 2nd ed. 286p. bibliog.
The second edition of a classic, first published in 1960. Neustadt has added two chapters to the reprint which was issued with an additional chapter in 1968. He attempts to show how presidents gain and use power. He argues that at the beginning of the 1980s the USA has neither an 'imperial president' nor a dominant Congress. In fact, he declares the country is adrift, with no central leadership.

446 Presidential selection: theory and development.
James W. Ceaser. Princeton, New Jersey: Princeton
University Press, 1979. 371p. bibliog.
An ambitious and comprehensive historical analysis of the way US political parties have shaped presidential selection. It treats the central ideas embodied in the present presidential selection process by tracing their history from the founding fathers to the transformations of Jefferson, Van Buren, the Progressives and contemporary times. This is a lucid and informative analysis of a vital American process.

447 The pulse of politics: electing presidents in the media age.
James David Barber. New York: Norton, 1980. 342p.
Deals with twelve elections since 1900 and develops three models for elections: conflict elections, conscience elections and conciliation elections. The first involves a battle for political power, the second is a reaction to exclusively partisan politics and the third offers solace and unity to the electorate. In all of these models the interactions between the candidate and the media are vital. Barber analyses media-candidate relations carefully and concludes with some suggestions to the media for improvement.

448 **Race for the presidency: the media and the nominating process.**
Edited by James David Barber. Englewood Cliffs, New Jersey: Prentice-Hall, 1978. 205p.

This work is the result of three years of study, utilizing interviews, and researching newspaper, magazines and television news in order to provide an understanding of the interaction between news people and the campaigners. A vital source for anyone interested in the key role of the mass media in politics in the electronic age.

449 **The road to the White House: the politics of presidential elections.**
Stephen J. Wayne. New York: St. Martin's Press, 1979. 286p. bibliog.

Examines the strategies and tactics of presidential candidates. A well-researched, lucid volume, it contains numerous examples from recent campaigns. It provides a complete guide to the nomination and election process, the electoral college system, campaign finance, parties and coalitions, delegate organization, the use and influence of the media and the election itself.

450 **The state of the presidency.**
Thomas E. Cronin. Boston, Massachusetts: Little, Brown, 1980. 2nd ed. 417p. bibliog.

This extensively revised and expanded version of the 1975 edition now includes data on the Ford and Carter presidencies. It provides important insights into what Americans look for in a national leader. Useful appendixes.

451 **The unmaking of a president: Lyndon Johnson and Vietnam.**
Herbert Y. Schandler. Princeton, New Jersey: Princeton University Press, 1977. 419p. bibliog.

A readable analysis of a major turning point in American electoral history - the 1968 Tet offensive in Vietnam. This is a consideration of events in terms of their effect on the ability of Lyndon Johnson to function as president. An interesting study of the beginning of the trend toward the one-term president.

Law and Constitution

Legal system

452 **The ages of American law.**
Grant Gilmore. New Haven, Connecticut: Yale University
Press, 1977. 154p. (Storrs Lectures on Jurisprudence, 1974).
A noted American legal scholar surveys the historical and philosophical develop-
ment of American law. The work is divided into three chronological sections: the
age of discovery, extending to the Civil War; the age of faith, between the Civil
War and the First World War; the age of anxiety, beginning after the First
World War. A thoughtful, gracefully written book, projecting an optimistic view
of the ability of American law to grow and change.

453 **American law: the third century: the law bicentennial volume.**
Edited by Bernard Schwartz. New York: F. B. Rothman
for the New York University School of Law, 1977. 456p.
An excellent collection of essays resulting from a conference held at the NYU
School of Law in 1976. A host of leading jurists and legal scholars projected
basic legal trends into the next century and also discussed American law in the
broader context. The volume concludes with essays by Chief Justice Warren
Burger and Lord Widgery, the highest judicial officer in Great Britain.

454 **American legal processes.**
William P. McLauchlan. New York: John Wiley & Sons,
1977. 218p.
A readable survey of the structure and organization of the contemporary American judiciary at all levels. An excellent examination of the local court structure
makes this a particularly useful work.

Law and Constitution. Legal system

455 The American prosecutor: a search for identity.
Joan E. Jacoby. Lexington, Massachusetts: Lexington, 1980. 336p.

An examination of the responsibilities, duties and policies of American prosecuting attorneys.

456 Black's law dictionary; definitions of the terms and phrases of American and English jurisprudence, ancient and modern.
Henry Campbell Black. St. Paul, Minnesota: West, 1979. 5th ed. 1,511p.

The classic legal dictionary. The first revision since 1968, this edition includes over 10,000 new or revised entries. It is thumb-indexed and covers all areas of law, including much more than simple definitions. An essential reference tool for every level.

457 Criminal justice: issues and ironies.
Abraham S. Blumberg. New York: New Viewpoints, 1973. 2nd ed. 432p.

In this thoroughly revised and expanded edition of his landmark 1967 work, Blumberg analyses all aspects of the criminal justice system from arrest to trial and sentencing, probation and parole. Includes considerations of the process of appellate review and plea bargaining.

458 Denial of justice: criminal process in the United States.
Lloyd L. Weinreb. New York: Free Press, 1977. 177p.

A well-written analysis of two sectors of the criminal justice system: criminal investigation and prosecution. Weinreb recommends that a single agency might more effectively handle investigation, case preparation and prosecution. There is a useful appendix on the questioning of defendants.

459 A history of American law.
Lawrence Meir Friedman. New York: Simon & Schuster, 1973. 655p.

A good general overview, examining the evolution of the legal profession and law in the USA from colonial times to the 20th century. The connection between English and American law is explored as well as the changes that occurred in the transfer to the colonies.

460 How to use the Freedom of Information Act (FOIA).
L. G. Sherick. New York: Arco, 1978. 138p.

A practical handbook for every citizen on how to use the FOIA and the Privacy Act. Both acts are included in the appendixes. The legislation is explained in simple language and clear instructions are given on how private citizens may make the bureaucracy respond in this regard.

461 **In the matter of color: race and the American legal process: the colonial period.**
A. Leon Higginbothan, Jr.   New York: Oxford University Press, 1978. 512p. bibliog.
The first volume of a study by a distinguished black jurist. It provides a useful compendium of legal data on oppression and is marvellously infused with a passion for justice. The book focuses on six colonies: Virginia, Massachusetts, New York, South Carolina, Georgia and Pennsylvania. The relationships between law and race from colonial times to the present will be analysed definitively when the work is complete.

462 **The jury: its role in American society.**
Rita J. Simon.   Lexington, Massachusetts: Lexington, 1980. 176p.
Analyses the social-psychological aspects of verdicts and speculates on the jury as an instrument of justice.

463 **Justice in America: courts, lawyers, and the judicial process.**
Herbert Jacob.   Boston, Massachusetts: Little, Brown, 1972. 2nd ed. 237p. bibliog.
A detailed political analysis of the administration of justice in American courts. The roles of lawyers, judges and juries are examined in conjunction with a review of the prospects for judicial reform. A fine overview of the American judicial system.

464 **The law of the land: the evolution of our legal system.**
Charles Rembar.   New York: Simon & Schuster, 1980. 447p. bibliog.
A readable history of the development of the US legal system from 'not quite Anglo-Saxon, more Norman influenced' origins into the complex language and procedures of today. The text contains a number of illustrative examples.

465 **Political crime in the United States: analyzing crime by and against government.**
Julian Roebuck, Stanley C. Weeber.   New York: Praeger, 1978. 244p. bibliog.
Based upon the thesis that class conflict exists in advanced capitalist societies, the volume analyses seven major categories of political crime in the USA from 1960 to 1978. The two principal categories are crimes by government against the people and crimes by people against the government, including domestic and foreign intervention by government, domestic surveillance, and evasion and collusion by and against government. An extensively researched, readable book that should be read by every student of government and every alert citizen.

466 **Popular justice.**
Samuel E. Walker. New York: Oxford University Press, 1980. 288p. bibliog.

This is the first one-volume scholarly analysis of the development of American criminal justice from the colonial period to the present. Examining changing patterns of criminal activity, the institutional growth of the system of criminal justice and the major issues involved in its administration, Walker traces the tension which has always existed in America between popular justice and the rule of law.

Constitution

467 **The American Constitution: its origins and development.**
Alfred H. Kelly, Winifred A. Harbison. New York: Norton, 1970. 4th ed. 1,229p. bibliog.

A comprehensive survey on the American Constitution from colonial to modern times. Appendixes include the text of the Constitution and the Articles of Confederation.

468 **The Bill of Rights: a documentary history.**
Edited by Bernard Schwartz. New York: Chelsea House, 1971. 2 vols.

A well-selected collection of documents on the origins and development of the Bill of Rights. The primary sources are woven together by useful explanations which place the documents in their historical and legal context.

469 **The Constitution: a documentary and narrative history.**
Page Smith. New York: William Morrow, 1978. 546p. bibliog.

Surveys the rise of a secular interpretation of the US Constitution. To illustrate his points, Smith reprints the debates of the 1787 federal convention and the texts of many important cases.

470 **The Constitution and what it means.**
Edward S. Corwin. Princeton, New Jersey: Princeton University Press, 1978. 14th ed. 673p.

A classic clause-by-clause examination of the US Constitution. The work has been revised many times and remains a basic reference source for the beginner.

471 **The Constitution between friends: Congress, the president and the law.**
Louis Fisher. New York: St. Martin's Press, 1978. 274p. bibliog.
A readable study focusing on the constant conflict between short-term political objectives and constitutional principles. Fisher discusses the constitutional framework, the limits of power, treaties, the power to delcare war, the power of removal, and presidential and congressional vetoes. A good table of cases supplements the text.

472 **The Constitution in crisis times, 1918-1969.**
Paul L. Murphy. New York: Harper & Row, 1972. 570p. bibliog. (New American Nation Series).
A good effort to show relationships between the presidential leadership and the Supreme Court and between the court and public opinion. Events are traced from the evolution of the Supreme Court's emphasis on property rights to that of civil rights. The people's growing acceptance of the court as defender of personal freedom is also explored. There is an excellent bibliographical essay to supplement the text.

473 **The Constitution of the United States of America, analysis and interpretation.**
Edited by Norman J. Small, Lester S. Jayson. Washington, DC: US Government Printing Office, 1964. rev. ed. 1,693p. (88th Congress. 1st Session. Senate Document 39).
This document prepared by the Legislative Reference Service provides the full text of the Constitution, supplemented with annotations of cases decided by the Supreme Court through to 22 June 1964. An invaluable reference tool.

474 **Defending my enemy: American Nazis, the Skokie case and the risks of freedom.**
Aryeh Neier. New York: E. P. Dutton, 1979. 182p. bibliog.
A thoughtful study of a sensitive and controversial issue by the former National Executive Director of the American Civil Liberties Union. He considers the role of the ACLU in defending the members of the American Nazi Party and analyses the reasons why he believes such persons must be defended. A well-written compelling treatment of the civil liberties aspects of an issue that is causing increasing concern in America today.

475 **Democracy and the amendments to the Constitution.**
Alan P. Grimes. Lexington, Massachusetts: Lexington, 1978. 190p.
An overview of all twenty-six amendments to the US Constitution, drawing some general conclusions on their passage which the author asserts has led to a democratization of the Constitution. The thesis is arguable, but the concise surveys of the amendments are very valuable.

476 **The development of American citizenship, 1608-1870.**
James H. Kettner. Chapel Hill, North Carolina: University of North Carolina Press for the Institute of Early American History & Culture, Williamsburg, Virginia, 1978. 391p.

An important contribution to US history, this work identifies the period of the American Revolution as central to the development of a sense of nationality. It analyses the legal origins of the concept of citizenship in British history and during the colonial period. Kettner clearly traces the evolution of subjects of the crown into citizens of the state. A good index and useful table of cases and statutes cited supplement the text.

477 **The development of the American Constitution, 1877-1917.**
Loren P. Beth. New York: Harper & Row, 1971. 280p. bibliog. (New American Nation Series).

An important addition to a fine series, this study provides a lucid examination of the relations between the branches of the US federal government, as well as those between the federal, state and local governments. The author, a political scientist, concludes that the shape of the modern Constitution had been determined by 1917, including growing federal regulation, centralization of government functions and a tendency toward executive domination. A useful annotated bibliography adds to the value of the work.

478 **An economic interpretation of the Constitution of the United States.**
Charles A. Beard. New York: Free Press, 1965. reprint. 352p.

This classic study interprets the Constitution's framing in terms of economic interests. It has stimulated controversy and extensive critical literature in the years since it was first published in 1913. It remains an important contribution to constitutional history and and should be read both for its analysis and as an illustration of Beard's economic view of history.

479 **Inventing America: Jefferson's Declaration of Independence.**
Garry Wills. Garden City, New York: Doubleday, 1978. 398p.

Characterized by superb writing, this work concludes that Jefferson's theory did not derive from the natural rights philosophies of John Locke, but rather referred back to the Scottish 'moral sense' school of philosophers that included David Hume and Adam Smith.

480 **World War I and the origin of civil liberties in the U.S.**
Paul L. Murphy. New York: Norton, 1980. 285p. bibliog. (Norton Essays in American History).

By the author of *The Constitution in crisis times, 1918-1969* (q.v.), this new book on the Constitution and civil liberties is concise, well organized and clear in presenting the many complex legal questions and problems. The central argument is that civil liberties as an issue and as a body of law and precedent did not exist before the First World War. Murphy explores the reasons for this change.

US Supreme Court

481 Congressional Quarterly's guide to the U.S. Supreme Court.
Edited by Elder Witt. Washington, DC: Congressional
Quarterly, 1979. 1,022p. bibliog.

Winner of the 1980 American Book Award in general reference, this fine work
includes judicial biographies, landmark cases, a glossary of legal terms and an
appendix on Franklin Roosevelt's 1937 court-packing attempt. Numerous tables
and an opening 650-page history of developing constitutional doctrine add to the
value of the guide. There are exhaustive footnotes and a fine index.

**482 From Brown to Bakke: the Supreme Court and school
integration, 1954-1978.**
J. Harvie Wilkinson. New York: Oxford University Press,
1979. 368p. bibliog.

A readable, general narrative history of the Supreme Court's efforts to deal with
questions of racial discrimination in education. This important book by a constitutional scholar provides a good factual framework for the non-specialist reader in
addition to detailed documentation for the more advanced student.

**483 The justices of the United States Supreme Court: their lives
and major opinions.**
Edited by Leon Friedman, Fred L. Israel. New York:
Chelsea House and R. R. Bowker, 1969-79. 5 vols. bibliog.

This monumental set provides a convenient and comprehensive starting point for
biographical information on justices and a survey of representative opinions by
each one. The fine biographical essays are followed by bibliographical notes and
illustrative opinions. An essential reference tool.

484 The modern Supreme Court.
Robert Green McCloskey. Cambridge, Massachusetts:
Harvard University Press, 1972. 376p. bibliog.

An examination of the development of the court from the Second World War
period to its activist era in the 1960s. Beautifully written, the work provides an
incisive analysis of the influence of public opinion and public policy on Supreme
Court behaviour.

485 Privacy, law and public policy.
David M. O'Brien. New York: Praeger, 1979. 262p.
bibliog.

An extensively researched study on the US Supreme Court and the issue of
privacy. This is a carefully documented survey of the efforts of the court to
define the right of privacy.

486 The Supreme Court and individual rights.
Edited by Elder Witt. Washington, DC: Congressional Quarterly, 1980. 303p. bibliog.

An introduction to the role of the Supreme Court in the protection of individual rights. It includes a historical overview and analyses court decisions, past and present. There is a detailed consideration of individual rights issues such as due process and freedom of ideas. An appendix includes a glossary of legal terms and instructions on how to read a legal citation.

487 The Supreme Court in the federal judicial system.
Stephen L. Wasby. New York: Holt, Rinehart & Winston, 1978. 262p. bibliog.

A clear concise study of the Supreme Court, its role in the US political system, how it functions and its influence on American life. It carefully documents its central thesis that the court is 'a major policy maker in the American political system'. There is a fine analysis of the impact of judicial decisions.

488 Supreme Court policy making: explanation and prediction.
Harold J. Spaeth. San Francisco: W. H. Freeman, 1979. 224p.

A compact descriptive analysis of Supreme Court policy-making. There are eight informative and concisely written chapters. Cases are not cited at great length, but by a good choice of representative samples, Spaeth achieves a lively and accurate commentary based upon illustrative decisions. There is a clear description of the internal procedures and supporting personnel of the court.

489 This honorable court.
Leo Pfeffer. Boston, Massachusetts: Beacon Press, 1965. 470p. bibliog.

A narrative history of the Supreme Court. The author analyses the court's functions and assesses its judicial, political and legislative impact. He also places the court within the context of the US governmental system. An excellent introduction for the non-specialist that remains useful today.

Administration and
Local Government

490 **American local government.**
George S. Blair.   New York: Harper & Row, 1964. 619p.
bibliog.
A survey of the various divisions of local government, including counties, cities,
townships, towns and schools. This standard introduction utilizes a comparative
and functional approach to the various forms of government.

491 **Bosses, machines, and urban voters: an American symbiosis.**
John M. Allswang.   Port Washington, New York: Kennikat
Press, 1977. 157p. bibliog. (Interdisciplinary Urban Series).
Combines an examination of five noted city 'bosses' with an introductory statisti-
cal consideration of election returns. A concise balanced appraisal.

492 **City and suburb: the political fragmentation of metropolitan
America, 1850-1970.**
Jon C. Teaford.   Baltimore, Maryland: Johns Hopkins
Press, 1979. 231p. bibliog. (Johns Hopkins Studies in Urban
Affairs).
Central cities and their surrounding suburbs face increasingly complex problems.
One answer to the metropolitan problem is to create some form of political
integration, whether a federation or some other solution. Yet political fragmenta-
tion and social and economic segregation persist. How and why the trend conti-
nues is Teaford's main theme. An extremely well written book.

Administration and Local Government

493 Crisis and legitimacy: the administrative process and American government.
James O. Freedman. New York: Cambridge University Press, 1978. 324p. bibliog.

A good study of the problems and processes of administrative regulation in the USA. Clearly written with a logical topical development and superb notes, index and bibliography, this work is of enormous help to the layman, illuminating such basic topics as the Administrative Procedures Act of 1964 and the comparative performance of several independent regulatory commissions (Securities and Exchange Commission, Federal Trade Commission, and the Equal Opportunities Commission). It is by no means an elementary work and has breadth and depth as well as readability.

494 Experiments in metropolitan government.
James F. Horan, G. Thomas Taylor, Jr. New York: Praeger, 1978. 238p. bibliog.

A clear analysis of the individual experiences of seven United States and one Canadian city in adjusting their metropolitan government structures to meet current needs. A detailed examination of the alternatives for city government and an emphasis on the possible application of these techniques to other metropolitan areas make this a very valuable study.

495 Goodbye to good-time Charlie: the American governor transformed, 1950-1975.
Larry Sabato. Lexington, Massachusetts: Lexington, 1978. 283p. bibliog.

A readable study of the American governor. Sabato asserts that in the last twenty-five years a 'new breed of governor' has developed. He illustrates the positive changes that have enhanced the integrity of the office since 1950, and includes eight tables and two appendixes to back up his thesis. A useful bibliographical essay supplements the text.

496 Governing at the grassroots: state and local politics.
Nicholas Henry. Englewood Cliffs, New Jersey: Prentice-Hall, 1980. 504p.

A lively survey of the political issues that affect state and local government. Suburban politics, regional politics and local politics are discussed in the context of the conflict between classes.

497 Modern public administration.
Felix A. Nigro. New York: Harper & Row, 1980. 5th ed. 481p. bibliog.

This latest revised edition of a basic text examines the problems of administration at every level of government. It emphasizes the need to adapt to changing societal needs.

498 **The politics of efficiency: municipal administration and reform in America, 1800-1920.**
Martin J. Schiesl. Berkeley, California: University of California Press, 1977. 259p. bibliog.

A favourable examination of the crusade for structural reform in municipal government that occurred during the first twenty years of the 20th century. Schiesl concludes that the efficiency movement and the attack on municipal 'bossism' resulted in 'a concept of public interest' in place of the *laissez-faire* ideology that had supported limited government functioning during the 19th century.

499 **Property tax relief.**
Steven David Gold. Lexington, Massachusetts: Lexington and D. C. Heath, 1979. 331p.

A summary and analysis of recent efforts to reduce property tax burdens in the USA. A discussion of California's controversial Proposition 13 and its effects is included. A sound study of current problems of state and local finance, the work is enhanced by a comprehensive bibliography and a wealth of good recent data.

500 **Proposition 13 and its consequences for public management.**
Edited by Selma J. Mushkin. Cambridge, Massachusetts: Council for Applied Social Research with the assistance of ABT Books, 1979. 171p.

Sixteen essays on public feeling toward tax and expenditure limitation provisions and their effect on public management. The work includes an exchange of views among social scientists and policy analysis. It is based on the proceedings of a September 1978 conference and provides an excellent perspective on the differing viewpoints of federal, state and local planners and administrators.

501 **Taxpayers, taxes, and government spending.**
Robert J. Dworak. New York: Praeger, 1980. 272p.

A simple concise explanation of local government finance from the point of view of the taxpayer. In addition to describing current systems, the author suggests alternative proposals such as a Volunteer Personal Service Program. The narrative is clear and the suggestions are guaranteed to generate spirited discussion at every level of expertise.

502 **Understanding intergovernmental relations: public policy and participants' perspectives in local, state and national governments.**
Deil Spencer Wright. North Scituate, Massachusetts: Duxbury Press, 1978. 410p. (Duxbury Press Series on Public Policy).

A lucid introduction to the workings of American federalism. The focus is on financial inter-relationships between the levels of government in the USA. A set of useful appendixes include a guide to jargon and acronyms currently used in public policy circles.

Administration and Local Government

503 **The ungovernable city: the politics of urban problems and policy making.**
Douglas Yates. Cambridge, Massachusetts: M.I.T. Press, 1977. 219p. bibliog. (M.I.T. Studies in American Politics and Public Policy, 3).
A clear presentation of a prime cause of urban problems in the USA today. Yates identifies the source of difficulty as the inability of the existing urban government structure to formulate policies to deal with the realities of modern urban life. He asserts that the first step toward improvement is the recognition that the urban policy-making process is unworkable.

504 **Urban policy and the exterior city: federal, state and corporate impacts upon major cities.**
H. V. Savitch. Elmsford, New York: Pergamon Press, 1979. 358p.
An attempt to explain why American cities are in such dire straits. Savitch suggests that the city is no longer master of its own fate and outlines external forces that act upon it. What is significant is his assertion that 'public policy is a response to the most dominant corporate needs'. This is a provocative and useful study.

505 **Zero-base budgeting in state and local government.**
Edited by John A. Worthley, William G. Ludwin. New York: Praeger, 1979. 190p. bibliog.
The zero-base budgeting system in public administration has undergone a marked increase in popularity in recent years. This readable account of zero-base budgeting, its successes and failures, is a good introduction to the concept and the controversies surrounding it. The work includes a variety of case-studies of zero-base budgeting in states, localities and individual government agencies.

Foreign Relations

506 Africa and the United States: vital interests.
Edited by Jennifer Seymour Whitaker. New York: New
York University Press, 1978. 255p. map.
A collection of seven essays prepared for a Council on Foreign Relations discussion group. Includes papers on US economic interests in Africa; US strategic interests and military options; US policy toward Africa; Soviet strategic options in the area; and Africa in the context of the international economy.

507 America and the Arab states: an uneasy encounter.
Robert W. Stookey. New York: John Wiley & Sons, 1975.
298p. map. bibliog. (America & the World).
A good survey of American relations with the Arab world. American interests are traced back to dealings with the four Barbary powers in North Africa at the end of the 18th century. About two-thirds of the narrative deals with American-Arab relations since the Second World War. There is a useful concluding bibliographical essay.

**508 American dream, global nightmare: the dilemma of U.S.
human rights policy.**
Sandy Vogelgesang. New York: Norton, 1980. 303p.
bibliog.
The author, a foreign service officer and policy planner, attempts to discern the basis of US foreign policy on human rights. The three sections of the work deal with the diplomacy, politics and economics of human rights. An extensive case-study is part of each section.

509 The American foreign policy library.
Cambridge, Massachusetts: Harvard University Press,
1947- .
More than twenty volumes have been published in this superb series; many have been revised and all are of the highest quality. Those in print include E. O.

Foreign Relations

Reischauer's *Japan* (2nd ed. 1965) and J. K. Fairbank's *China* (4th ed. 1979) as well as the latest addition, H. W. Gatzke's *Germany and the U.S.* (q.v.).

510 American foreign policy since World War II.

John W. Spanier. New York: Holt, Rinehart & Winston, 1980. 8th ed. 320p. bibliog.

This new edition, updated to include the first of the Carter years, is a classic work organized around the interplay of two themes - the international balance of power and America's national style (the nation's perceptions, roles, and behaviour with respect to the world). The work begins with the US effort to rebuild Europe through the Marshall Plan and includes discussions of American intervention in Lebanon and the Dominican Republic, as well as considerations of the cold war and NATO and other world alliance systems.

511 American Foreign Relations: a Documentary Record, 1971-[date].

New York: New York University Press for the Council on Foreign Relations, 1976- . annual.

Originally published as *Documents on American Foreign Relations* (New York: Harper & Row for the Council on Foreign Relations, 1939-70), this annual is an excellent carefully selected reference tool providing primary source material for the student of American foreign relations. The 1977 volume is the most recently published and appeared in 1979. It should be used in conjunction with the US Department of State *Foreign relations series*, which is an essential source for American diplomatic history. The *Foreign relations series* is now being published for the period of the 1950s and remains nearly thirty years behind the times due to legal restrictions and publishing problems.

512 America's ascent: the United States becomes a great power, 1880-1914.

John M. Dobson. De Kalb, Illinois: Northern Illinois University Press, 1978. 251p. bibliog.

A description and analysis of US foreign policy development between 1880 and 1944. Asserts that American expansion during the period resulted from conscious decisions by a small number of leaders. Those decisions were based on the desire for improved markets, yearnings for Great Power status and a belief in the superiority of the American way of life.

513 America's rise to world power, 1898-1954.

Foster Rhea Dulles. New York: Harper & Brothers, 1955. 314p. bibliog. (New American Nation Series).

A narrative history of US foreign relations in the first half of the 20th century. It examines the development of the USA into a major world power. This is a broad survey volume, suitable for the non-specialist.

514 The best and the brightest.
David Halberstam. New York: Random House, 1972. 688p. bibliog.

A partisan, but vivid and illuminating analysis of American involvement in Vietnam under the Kennedy and Johnson administrations. Halberstam argues that officials in Saigon and Washington, including the two presidents, concealed doubts about US policies to maintain their anti-communist credibility and that they suppressed negative intelligence reports.

515 The brink: Cuban missile crisis, 1962.
David Detzer. New York: Thomas Y. Crowell, 1979. 299p. bibliog.

A readable narrative account. A dramatic look at crisis policy-making which makes good use of recently released documents, oral histories and Kennedy library rescurces.

516 China-watch: toward Sino-American reconciliation.
Robert G. Sutter. Baltimore, Maryland: Johns Hopkins Press, 1978. 155p. bibliog.

A concise, carefully researched examination of US-Chinese relations since the beginning of the Second World War. Sutter, Asian affairs analyst for the Library of Congress, has made extensive use of recently declassified US government reports analysing press and radio in the People's Republic of China.

517 The cloud of danger: current realities of American foreign policy.
George Frost Kennan. Boston, Massachusetts: Little, Brown, 1977. 234p.

Noted historian, policy analyst and angry lecturer, are all representative roles for the scholar-diplomat who authored this work which he calls 'something resembling a grand design of American foreign policy' written 'as my duty'. He begins by criticizing the US system of divided powers and concludes with chapters on eastern Europe and the Soviet Union. A provocative book which should be in every foreign policy collection; suitable for all readers.

518 The counterinsurgency era: U.S. doctrine and performance, 1950 to the present.
Douglas S. Blaufarb. New York: Free Press, 1977. 356p. bibliog.

Examines the reasons for the success or failure of 'people's wars'. The author spent twenty years in the CIA. He discusses counter-insurgency efforts in Greece, the Philippines, Latin America and Southeast Asia, assessing US policies toward 'client regimes' and revolutionary efforts. This is a well-written, careful interpretative study.

519 **The crises of power: an interpretation of United States foreign policy during the Kissinger years.**
Seyom Brown. New York: Columbia University Press, 1980. 176p.

An essay on foreign policy during the Nixon and Ford administrations as well as an interpretation of the policies and diplomacy of Henry Kissinger. It closely examines US policies in specific situations, such as the opening of relations with China and the Arab-Israeli conflict of 1973. This is a highly objective, insightful and consistent work, utilizing reliable sources of information.

520 **Dictionary of American diplomatic history.**
John E. Findling. Westport, Connecticut: Greenwood Press, 1980. 622p. bibliog.

Includes entries on diplomatic events, treaties, slogans, and definitions of terms and data on diplomatic figures. Five appendixes, including a chronology of diplomatic events, a listing of key diplomatic personnel by presidential administration, and a guide to manuscript sources on diplomatic history contribute to the usefulness of this volume.

521 **The diplomacy of detente: the Kissinger era.**
Coral Bell. New York: St. Martin's Press, 1977. 278p. bibliog.

Bell contends that *détente* should not be viewed as a US-USSR relationship, but as a triangular balance of power in which America operates *vis-à-vis* both China and the Soviet Union. A positive appraisal of the Kissinger era and *détente*, Bell credits Kissinger's policies with primacy in lessening world tensions. A readable, provocative book with a useful bibliography.

522 **A diplomatic history of the United States.**
Samuel Flagg Bemis. New York: Holt, Rinehart & Winston, 1965. 5th ed. 1,062p. bibliog.

A basic introduction to diplomatic history by a noted authority who has been writing in the field since 1908. This comprehensive survey examines American diplomacy from the nation's beginnings until the 20th century. Bemis' premise in all his work has been that today's problems must be understood in the context of their origin and development.

523 **Eagle entangled: U.S. foreign policy in a complex world.**
Edited by Kenneth A. Oge, Donald Rothchild, Robert J. Leiber. New York: Longman, 1979. 365p. bibliog.

A well-written book resulting from a conference held at the University of California (Berkeley). Noted analysts, the contributors have attempted to identify major new trends in international affairs and then to weigh the Carter administration's foreign policy performance in response to these trends.

524 Egypt and the United States: the formative years.
Gail E. Meyer. Madison, New Jersey: Fairleigh Dickinson, 1980. 230p. bibliog.

A detailed narrative of US-Egyptian relations during the 1950s. This extensively documented survey examines the Egyptian revolution, Nasser's consolidation of power and events through the first Suez conflict and the Eisenhower doctrine.

525 Empire as a way of life.
William Appleman Williams. New York: Oxford University Press, 1980. 226p.

Revisionist historian and current President of the Organization of American Historians, Williams warns that the current binge of consumption and expansion combined with a militaristic mood could spell disaster for the USA. He shows that from colonial times to the present a foreign policy based on a way of life devoted to over-consumption has characterized the USA. This is a strong denunciation of 'imperialist foreign policy', a provocative book with suggestions for alternatives for the 1980s.

526 Encyclopedia of American foreign policy: studies of the principal movements and ideas.
Edited by Alexander DeConde. New York: Charles Scribner's Sons, 1978. 3 vols. bibliog.

An important collection of ninety-five original essays on US foreign policy. It includes material on the balance of power, manifest destiny, revisionism and a host of other foreign policy topics. It contains 150 pages of biographical sketches. There is a good index and bibliographies which contribute to its quality as a first-rate reference work.

527 The fall and rise of the Pentagon: American defense policies in the 1970s.
Lawrence J. Korb. Westport, Connecticut: Greenwood Press, 1979. 192p. bibliog. (Contributions in Political Science, 27).

A concise, readable and informative volume on national defence and the military sector. This brief but well-balanced analysis covers the contemporary history of the military establishment and evaluates the performances of civilian secretaries, military chiefs and a variety of programmes in weaponry and strategy. Good statistical charts and bibliographical information supplement the text.

528 Foreign policies of the founding fathers.
Paul A. Varg. East Lansing, Michigan: Michigan State University Press, 1964. 316p. bibliog.

This narrative history examines the course of American foreign policy from 1773 to 1812. The interpretation illustrates the interplay between domestic and foreign issues.

Foreign Relations

529 **Foreign policy by Congress.**
Thomas M. Franck, Edward Weisband. New York: Oxford
University Press, 1979. 357p. bibliog.
A detailed analysis of the development of the foreign policy role of the US
Congress in the years following the Vietnam War. The authors assert that a
major revolution in the role of Congress occurred in the mid-1970s, a change
made permanent by procedural changes, the politicization of foreign policy issues
and several other factors. A well-researched contribution to foreign policy studies.

530 **Franklin D. Roosevelt and American foreign policy,
1932-1945.**
Robert Dallek. New York: Oxford University Press, 1979.
657p. map. bibliog.
The first comprehensive analysis of Franklin Roosevelt's foreign policy, based on
the enormous amount of primary and secondary material now available. Dallek
focuses on the domestic constraints that shaped Roosevelt's decisions. Unlike
James MacGregor Burns in *Roosevelt: soldier of freedom* (1971), Dallek argues
that factors beyond Roosevelt's control, principally Soviet hostility to the West
and the desire to expand, caused the collapse of the wartime alliance. A balanced
interpretation.

531 **Germany and the United States: a 'special relationship?'**
Hans W. Gatzke. Cambridge, Massachusetts: Harvard
University Press, 1980. 314p. maps. bibliog. (American
Foreign Policy Library).
Designed to acquaint the general public with the course of German-American
relations through more than 200 years, this is the most recent addition to a
long-established valuable foreign policy series.

532 **The giants: Russia and America.**
Richard J. Barnet. New York: Simon & Schuster, 1977.
190p. bibliog.
A former Kennedy administration State Department advisor and currently director of the Institute of Policy Studies in Washington, Barnet presents a concise
and generally pessimistic assessment of US-Soviet relations. He examines the
evolution of *détente* and the US-Soviet economic interchange. His conclusions are
provocative, his examination detailed and vivid.

533 **Japan and the United States: challenges and opportunities.**
Edited by William J. Barnds. New York: New York
University Press, 1979. 286p.
An excellent collection of papers discussing developments in US-Japanese relations during the 1970s. The work pinpoints areas of strain in the relationship
caused by a variety of factors, including the relative decline of American military
power, the increasing productivity and competitiveness of the Japanese economy
and the domestic unrest in both countries. Barnds summarizes the essays and
offers suggestions on likely trends in Japanese-American relations in the 1980s.

534 **The lost peace: America's search for a negotiated settlement of the Vietnam War.**
Allan E. Goodman. Stanford, California: Hoover Institution Press, 1978. 298p.
Traces the escalation of the Vietnam War, the attempts to begin negotiations, the fall of South Vietnam and the ultimate failure of the negotiated settlement. A concise analysis of negotiations from the American perspective. An appendix containing the text of the Paris agreement and statements on its implementation supplement the text.

535 **The national interest and the human interest.**
Robert Johansen. Princeton, New Jersey: Princeton University Press, 1980. 517p. bibliog.
In an attempt to determine the extent to which the USA contributes to creating a preferred system of world order, Johansen considers US foreign policy against the framework of four major global values: peace, economic well-being, social justice and the ecological balance. Each is considered in the context of a different case-study, for instance human rights in US relations with Chile.

536 **The nuclear question: the United States and nuclear weapons, 1946-1976.**
Michael Mandelbaum. New York: Cambridge University Press, 1979. 277p.
Surveys the development of the American nuclear weapons policy. Asserts that the history of the nuclear age, far from giving cause for concern, illustrates the continuing success of international politics and the power of deterrence. This is a controversial assertion, but the book is thoughtfully constructed, free of jargon and a clear introduction to the issue.

537 **On every front: the making of the cold war.**
Thomas G. Paterson. New York: Norton, 1979. 210p. bibliog. (Norton Essays in American History).
Paterson, one of the foremost analysts of the cold war era, gives another example of his trademark: dedicated research and meticulous scholarship. Brief but extremely well documented, the work combines numerous interpretations of the origins of the cold war with the author's own insights. The American and Soviet roles are each examined. One chapter is devoted to Soviet policy. There is a detailed historiographical essay at the end of the volume.

538 **Paved with good intentions: the American experience and Iran.**
Barry Rubin. New York: Oxford University Press, 1980. 320p. bibliog.
Explores the issue of how American foreign policy in Iran became dependent upon the survival of the Shah's régime, and analyses the US role in the fall of the Shah and the revolution that followed. A useful overview of fifty years of US-Iranian relations.

539 **The power peddlers: how lobbyists mold American foreign policy.**
Russell Warren Howe, Sarah Hayes Trott. New York: Doubleday, 1977. 569p. bibliog.
Focuses on lobbying in Washington on behalf of foreign interests. The authors, political journalists, provide a lively look at an informal power structure that contributes to the formulation of American foreign policy.

540 **Roots of involvement: the U.S. in Asia, 1784-1971.**
Marvin Kalb, Elie Abel. New York: Norton, 1971. 336p.
Kalb, a well-known television journalist, and Abel, former Dean of the Columbia School of Journalism, focus on American policy in Vietnam from Roosevelt to Nixon. The book was finished after the Cambodian incursion, but before Laos. This is an excellent overview for the non-specialist.

541 **The SALT experience.**
Thomas W. Wolfe. Cambridge, Massachusetts: Ballinger, 1979. 405p. bibliog.
The author, a Rand analyst who is an expert on Soviet military strategy and behaviour, offers a lucid summary of Soviet and American military policy over the last decade. He focuses on each side's SALT policies, but examines broader foreign policy issues as well.

542 **Shattered peace: the origins of the cold war and the national security state.**
Daniel Yergin. Boston, Massachusetts: Houghton Mifflin, 1977. 526p. bibliog.
A detailed exploration of the people, events and schools of thought that contributed to the US position in the cold war.

543 **Sideshow: Kissinger, Nixon and the destruction of Cambodia.**
William Shawcross. New York: Simon & Schuster, 1979. 467p. maps. bibliog.
A British journalist's vivid historical reconstruction and denunciation of the intervention in Cambodia during the Nixon and Ford administrations. He makes use of several new documents available under the Freedom of Information Act. There are harsh portrayals of the major political figures involved. An intriguing, polemical book.

544 **The transformation of American foreign relations, 1865-1900.**
Charles S. Campbell. New York: Harper & Row, 1976. 393p. bibliog. (New American Nation Series).
Another fine addition to the classic New American Nation Series, this is a detailed diplomatic history of the last half of the 19th century. The bibliography is particularly useful.

545 **Uncertain greatness: Henry Kissinger and American foreign policy.**
Roger Morris. New York: Harper & Row, 1977. 312p.

A foreign service officer, Morris served the National Security Council staff during the the Johnson administration and later under Kissinger. He resigned in 1970 over the Cambodia issue. He has written a fine book on Kissinger, his impact on American foreign policy and his relationship with Richard Nixon. Despite a lack of notes or bibliography, this is an incisive, balanced work suitable for every level.

546 **The United States and China in the twentieth century.**
Michael Schaller. New York: Oxford University Press, 1979. 199p. map. bibliog.

A readable volume, analysing events from the 19th century opium trade and missionary movement to the recent establishment of diplomatic relations. A perceptive overview of the complex modern Sino-American relationship, the work synthesizes the vast literature on US-China relations.

547 **The United States and the Caribbean, 1900-1970.**
Lester D. Langley. Athens, Georgia: University of Georgia Press, 1980. 324p. maps. bibliog.

A survey of 20th century US-Caribbean relations. The work is arranged chronologically in terms of US policy and deals with Central America, Cuba, Haiti, the Dominican Republic and Puerto Rico.

548 **United States foreign relations, 1820-1860.**
Paul A. Varg. East Lansing, Michigan: Michigan State University Press, 1979. 315p. bibliog.

Varg is the author of numerous valuable monographs on aspects of Sino-American relations. He also wrote *Foreign policies of the founding fathers* (q.v.), a stimulating interpretive study organized around a theme of tension between idealism and realism in foreign policy. This current volume has no such central thesis, although it is an extension of that volume on colonial diplomatic history. After two introductory chapters establishing the diplomatic and international setting, Varg presents brisk accounts, organized both geographically and chronologically, of the major problems faced by Washington during the forty years before the Civil War. A balanced and lucid overview.

549 **Velvet on iron: the diplomacy of Theodore Roosevelt.**
Frederick W. Marks. Lincoln, Nebraska: University of Nebraska Press, 1979. 247p. bibliog.

A fine group of essays evaluating Roosevelt's diplomacy, based on multi-archival research and significant secondary work. Roosevelt is placed in the proper context of turn-of-the-century attitudes. A clear, well-designed book which includes a good selection of quotes and useful notes, bibliography and index.

Foreign Relations

550 **White House years.**
Henry Kissinger. Boston, Massachusetts: Little, Brown, 1979. 1,521p. maps.

Winner of the 1980 American Book Award in history. Writing with the combined insights of an accomplished historian and statesman, Kissinger exposes the reader to the foreign policy process in the USA as well as to the form and content of specific policies developed primarily by him under Nixon and Ford. A fascinating series of personality assessments of President Nixon and his staff.

Economics

551 The affluent society.
John Kenneth Galbraith. Boston, Massachusetts: Houghton
Mifflin, 1969. 2nd rev. ed. 333p. bibliog.
In 1958 the noted economist published the first edition of this attack on what he
called the 'conventional wisdom' in American economics. It has become a classic
in the years since and has had a profound effect on economic thinking, introducing such terms as 'affluence', 'dependence effect', and 'public squalor', to economic language. A provocative and witty book that questions the basic social
value of ever-increasing affluence.

552 The American economy in transition.
Edited by Martin Feldstein. Chicago: University of
Chicago Press, 1980. 696p. (National Bureau of Economic
Research Conference Volume).
Contains background papers in nine areas by noted scholars, while two prominent
figures in government or the private sector add commentary on each. This
exploration of the extended economic malaise of the USA includes an essay on
financial markets by Benjamin M. Friedman, with commentary by Milton Friedman and A. W. Clausen, and one on labour by Richard B. Freeman, with
commentary by John T. Dunlop and R. F. Schubert.

553 Decade of decision: the crisis of the American system.
Michael Harrington. New York: Simon & Schuster, 1980.
354p. bibliog.
In eight previous books, including his noted *The other America: poverty in the
United States* (1962), the author has argued for socialism and against what he
calls 'the corporate ideology'. He urges the US government to adopt a programme
including higher taxes, take-over of failing banks, operation of the entire railroad
system and price controls without wage controls.

Economics

554 The economic crisis and American society.
Manuel Castells. Princeton, New Jersey: Princeton
University Press, 1980. 285p.

Analyses the origin and development of the 'structural crisis in the historical
expansion of the capitalist mode of production' in America during the 1970s.
Sexual and racial inequality, unemployment and under-employment are considered
as are the impact of the economic crisis on the American class structure, the US
political process and the nation's foreign policy.

555 The economic mind in American civilization.
Joseph Dorfman. New York: Viking Press, 1946-59. 5 vols.
bibliog.

These five volumes examine economic development in America through 1933 as
influenced by sociology, philosophy, industrial management, psychology and public
policy. Vol. 1-2: 1606-1865; vol. 3: 1865-1918; vol. 4-5: 1918-33.

556 The economics of the tax revolt: a reader.
Arthur B. Laffer, Jan P. Seymour. New York: Harcourt
Brace Jovanovich, 1979. 138p.

Requiring neither economic nor mathematical sophistication, this collection of
papers, primarily in support of the tax revolt philosophy, includes selections on
federal tax reduction and state-local tax revision (California's Proposition 13).
The authors represented in the papers, which have appeared in other earlier
publications, include noted authorities such as Walter Heller, Irving Kristol and
Herbert Stein.

557 The economy of colonial America.
Edwin J. Perkins. New York: Columbia University Press,
1980. 244p. bibliog.

Lively and comprehensive, this study is an excellent introduction to the economy
of the American colonies for both students and scholars.

558 Encyclopedia of American economic history: studies of the principal movements and ideas.
Edited by Glenn Porter. New York: Charles Scribner's
Sons, 1980. 3 vols. maps. bibliog.

A distinguished group of economic historians have contributed some seventy-two
articles. Vol. 1 contains a chronological overview; vol. 2 covers the specific institutional framework; and vol. 3 concerns itself with the social framework. A significant effort, this set is particularly valuable for the non-specialist.

559 The evolution of the American economy.
Sidney Ratner, James H. Soltow, Richard Sylla. New
York: Basic Books, 1980. 548p.

Combines a great deal of recent 'new economic history' into a useful summary.
After tracing the growth of the world economy, the authors try to reconstruct the
options that were available in the USA - in terms of the resources and their

possible alternative uses and to explain how choices were made. A good introduction for the non-specialist.

560 A history of American economic life.
Edward C. Kirkland.   New York: Appleton-Century-Crofts, 1969. 4th ed. 623p. bibliog.

A standard general survey of American economic history from colonial to modern times. This is a detailed overview.

561 In pursuit of happiness: American conceptions of property from the seventeenth to the twentieth century.
William B. Scott.   Bloomington, Indiana: Indiana University Press, 1977. 244p. bibliog.

An excellent survey exploring the meaning of property in American history. The work shows the expansion of the concept of property rights to include the right to adequate wages, a variety of non-landed tangible assets and eventually the right to acquire skills necessary for economic progress.

562 Inflation and national survival.
Edited by Clarence C. Walton.   New York: Academy of Political Science, 1979. 230p. (Proceedings of the Academy of Political Science, vol. 33, no. 3).

Commissioned for a conference held by the American Council of Life Insurance and published in conjunction with the Academy of Political Science, this book of essays cannot be too highly recommended. The authors are distinguished scholars from universities, research institutions and government service, and the papers are devoted to developing a public understanding of the root causes of inflation and the effectiveness of alternative remedies. 'This volume should be required reading as a start to a national dialogue' was one reviewer's appraisal and the comment is apt.

563 Poverty amid plenty: a political and economic analysis.
Harrell R. Rodgers.   Reading, Massachusetts: Addison-Wesley, 1979. 222p.

A concise survey of the nature and extent of poverty in the USA today, this study presents a good discussion of the public programmes that have attempted to deal with the problem. The work examines the causes of poverty in America, exploring the nature of the US economy, its class structure and the economic consequences of American politics. An excellent definition of the problem.

564 Social security and pensions in transition: understanding the American retirement system.
Bruno Stein.   New York: Free Press, 1980. 320p.

A comprehensive survey of the entire American retirement system, which traces the history of income maintenance programmes, examines the ramifications of social security for the American economy and takes positions on alternatives to the social security system. A readable, thought-provoking overview.

Economics

565 **Welfare: the elusive consensus: where we are, how we got there, and what's ahead.**
Lester M. Salamon. New York: Praeger, 1978. 257p.

Readable synthesis of current research on the American welfare system. The studies were sponsored by the Ford Foundation and conducted by Duke University's Institute of Policy Services and Public Affairs. A useful historical overview and analysis of current programmes for all reading levels.

566 **The zero-sum society: distribution and the possibilities for economic change.**
Lester C. Thurow. New York: Basic Books, 1980. 230p.

A ruthlessly honest, tough-minded book on what it will take to restore the US economy to full health. It has been called an 'elegantly reasoned' interpretation of American economic troubles.

Banking and Finance

567 The anatomy of the floor: the trillion-dollar market at the New York Stock Exchange.
Leonard Sloane. New York: Doubleday, 1980. 228p. bibliog.

A vivid portrait of the stock exchange, with emphasis on the men who served as its head, from Richard Whitney in 1930 to William Batten who was elected in 1976. A good introduction that should be supplemented by Robert Sobel's *The big board* (q.v.).

568 The banker's handbook.
Edited by William H. Baughn, Charles E. Walker. Homewood, Illinois: Dow Jones-Irwin, 1978. rev. ed. 1,200p.

A basic reference source on American banking practice, recently revised. There are eighty-seven chapters written by 105 contributors.

569 The banking crisis of 1933.
Susan Estabrook Kennedy. Lexington, Kentucky: University Press of Kentucky, 1973. 270p. bibliog.

This account, based on the author's Columbia University dissertation, makes full use of newly available source material. It provides a readable account of what happened when the banks failed and of the immediate effects of the measures taken during the period of crisis.

570 The big board: a history of the New York stock market.
Robert Sobel. New York: Free Press, 1965. 408p.

A well-written history of the stock market. The work includes an analysis of the influence of political and social conditions on the development of the institution and considers the role of prominent figures such as Vanderbilt and Gould in its history.

Banking and Finance

571 **The day America crashed.**
Tom Schachtman. New York: G. P. Putnam's Sons, 1979.
336p.
A very dramatic account of the 1929 stock market crash. Schachtman interviewed
hundreds of people for the work. It explains the structure of the market in lively
and simple terms with clear examples. A useful annotated bibliography supplements the text.

572 **The economics of money and banking.**
Lester V. Chandler. New York: Harper & Row, 1977. 7th
ed. 629p. bibliog.
A standard textbook, periodically revised, which provides a detailed overview of
the American banking and finance system. A good introductory work.

573 **The Federal Reserve system.**
Edited by Herbert V. Prochnow. New York: Harper &
Row, 1960. 393p. bibliog.
This carefully edited collection of essays comprise a history of the Federal
Reserve system. They examine its operations, assess its role in the financial and
business structure of the country and analyse its general relationship to the
American economy.

574 **Financial invasion of the U.S.A.: a threat to American
society?**
Earl H. Fry. New York: McGraw-Hill, 1980. 202p.
Considers the extent, origins and possible consequences of the increasing flow of
foreign investment into the American market-place. Concludes that this trend
represents no present danger, but suggests consideration of further restriction and
channelling of foreign investment.

575 **The financiers.**
Michael C. Jensen. New York: Weybright & Talley, 1976.
340p.
Jensen has used his years of experience as a journalist investigating the business
and financial community to write a book on investment bankers - the financial
movers and shakers on Wall Street. He describes a variety of money deals and
explains the role of the investment banker in terms understandable by the non-
specialist.

576 **Financing American enterprise: the story of commercial
banking.**
Paul B. Trescott. New York: Harper & Row, 1963. 304p.
bibliog.
A study of the development of American commercial banking and an assessment
of its contributions to American economic progress. A good general survey for
student and scholar alike.

577 **The go-go years.**
John Nixon Brooks. New York: Weybright & Talley,
1973. 375p. bibliog.
A lively and readable description and evaluation of the 1960s on Wall Street,
when feverish trading was followed by a devastating market decline that ushered
in the 1970s. Brooks examines the leading figures of the period and discusses the
significance of the market fluctuations.

578 **A history of accounting in America: an historical**
interpretation of the cultural significance of accounting.
Gary John Previts, Barbara Dubis Merino. New York:
John Wiley & Sons and Ronald Press, 1979. 378p. bibliog.
A chronological history of the economic, political and social aspects of accounting
in the USA from colonial times to the modern period. The central theme is that
accounting in the USA is a unique discipline evolving from a mingling of influences. The work asserts that 'the accounting establishment' has been a major
factor in American public life.

579 **Inside Wall Street: continuity and change in the financial**
district.
Robert Sobel. New York: Norton, 1977. 288p. bibliog.
Author of *The big board* (q.v.), Sobel here writes in clear concise terms of the
rapid changes occurring in the structure and operation of the nation's securities
markets. There is excellent historical perspective and the text is supplemented by
a useful bibliography.

580 **Moody's Industrial Manual.**
New York: Moody's Investors Service, 1954- . annual.
This is only one of a series of Moody's manuals which are of essential importance
to those interested in business investment, banking, finance or other economic
issues. Well-indexed, the Moody manuals provide historical and current data on
industry and other topics. In addition to the *Moody's Industrial Manual* there
are annual manuals for banking and finance, municipalities and government,
public utilities, transport, bond records as well as a complete index of corporations.

581 **The New York Times guide to business and finance: the**
American economy and how it works.
Albert L. Kraus. New York: Harper & Row, 1972. 280p.
bibliog.
Provides the general reader with a picture of American business and finance with
emphasis on investing and the stock exchange. The variety of topics covered
include property, the national budget, mutual funds, tariffs, and a variety of
others which comprise an excellent introduction to a complex subject.

Banking and Finance

582 **The origins of central banking in the United States.**
Richard Henry Timberlake. Cambridge, Massachusetts:
Harvard University Press, 1978. 272p. bibliog.

The first available work on the development of central banking up to the establishment of the Federal Reserve system, except for the periods covering the First
and Second Banks of the U.S. or the Independent Treasury system. The work
includes discussions of paper monetary standards and the usage of gold and silver
standards. It is likely to become a standard reference on the subject.

583 **Poor's Stock Market Encyclopedia.**
New York: Standard & Poor's, 1961- . annual.

This reference tool contains an alphabetical listing of stocks with information on
each, such as balance sheet statistics, recent developments and prospects.

584 **Standard and Poor's Stock Reports.**
New York: Standard & Poor's. weekly.

This looseleaf service containing up-to-date investment information is only one of
a number of services published by the Standard & Poor's corporation which are
essential reference tools for the investor, whether an individual stock-holder or a
professional analyst. These include Standard & Poor's *Register of Corporations,
Directors & Executives* (annual), *Bond Guide* (monthly), *Corporation Records*
(bimonthly), and *Industry Surveys* (quarterly). Each of these services is well-
indexed, highly accurate and absolutely up-to-date.

Commerce

585 **America in the market place.**
Paul H. Douglas. New York: Holt, Rinehart & Winston, 1966. 381p. bibliog.
A useful study of trade, tariffs and the balance of payments, the factors affecting American economic policy.

586 **America's impact on the world: a study of the role of the United States in the world economy, 1750-1970.**
William Woodruff. New York: John Wiley & Sons, 1975. 296p. bibliog.
A survey of the changing position of the United States in world commerce over more than two centuries. This is a good introduction to the study of current developments in US trade.

587 **Distribution's place in the American economy since 1869.**
Harold Barger. Princeton, New Jersey: Princeton University Press, 1955. 222p. bibliog. (National Bureau of Economic Research. General Series no. 58).
This study by the National Bureau of Economic Research remains a good basic overview of the history of American commerce. It is a careful examination of the development of the internal goods distribution system from the mid-19th century.

588 **The Kennedy Round in American trade policy.**
John W. Evans. Cambridge, Massachusetts: Harvard University Press, 1971. 383p. bibliog.
A discussion of the 'twilight' of the General Agreement on Tariffs and Trade (GATT) including an examination of the 'Kennedy Round' negotiations in Geneva, 1964-67. An important period in American commercial policy is carefully explored.

Commerce

589 **The last entrepreneurs: America's regional wars for jobs and dollars.**
Robert Goodman.   New York: Simon & Schuster, 1979. 292p. bibliog.
A clear account of the methods used by state and local governments today to attract business development.

590 **The making of United States international economic policy.**
Stephen D. Cohen.   New York: Praeger, 1977. 236p. bibliog.
A careful examination of the process which results in American international economic policy. Includes such issues as trade, investment, energy and resource transfers to developing nations. This well written and researched study illuminates a complicated government policy-making apparatus.

591 **The United States and the Common Market.**
D. D. Humphrey.   New York: Praeger, 1962. 176p. bibliog.
This background study explores the US tariff and trade programme from the passage of the Trade Agreements Act of 1934 to the trade expansion bill proposed by President Kennedy in 1962 and enacted into law. The author's basic premise is that reduced tariffs and trade expansion increase national economic growth.

592 **The United States and the industrial world: American foreign economic policy in the 1970s.**
William Diebold, Jr.   New York: Praeger for the Council on Foreign Relations, 1972. 463p.
A good general survey of the factors affecting US international policies in the 1970s. A perceptive appraisal of the American economic role among the industrialized nations.

593 **The United States and world trade: changing patterns and dimensions.**
Robert T. Green, James M. Lutz.   New York: Praeger, 1978. 319p. bibliog.
Analyses foreign trade trends since the Second World War, emphasizing US activities. There is a valuable statistical presentation of export patterns, comparing major world powers such as the USA, Britain, Germany, France, Japan and the USSR. The book is statistically detailed and analytical, but still of interest to a wide readership because of current concern about the US balance of payments.

Business and Industry

594 **The American Heritage history of American business and industry.**
Alex Grover.   New York: American Heritage, 1972. 384p. bibliog.
A beautifully illustrated historical survey of American business, aimed at the general reader. It contains a chronological examination of business from 1607 to 1972, and fifty-three capsule articles on business figures and topics, including cost-benefit ratios, depression, economics, etc.

595 **American made: men who shaped the American economy.**
Harold C. Livesay.   Boston, Massachusetts: Little, Brown, 1979. 310p. bibliog.
A well-written exploration of the lives of nine men who, the author believes, were key contributors to the growth and development of American business. They include Eli Whitney and his interchangeable parts, Andrew Carnegie and his steel manufacturing, Henry Ford and his development of a car for all people and Pierre S. du Pont and the development of the giant chemical corporation.

596 **Business in American life: a history.**
Thomas Childs Cochran.   New York: McGraw-Hill, 1972. 401p. bibliog.
Traces the major developments in American business and relates them to the social and physical environment surrounding them. The book is divided into four time periods: 1607-1775; 1775-1850; 1850-1915; and 1915-70. There are discussions in each part of business roles and institutional forms. This is a well-documented work for the non-specialist.

597 **The business of America.**
Edited by Ivan E. Berg.   New York: Harcourt, Brace & World, 1968. 437p.
A collection of articles by a group of experts who consider the impact of corporate action on political, economic and sociological aspects of American life.

Business and Industry

598 Business organizations & agencies directory: a guide to trade, business & commercial organizations, government agencies, stock exchanges, labor unions, chambers of commerce, diplomatic representation, trade & convention centers, trade fairs, publishers, data banks & computerized services, educational institutions, business libraries & information centers & research centers.
Edited by Anthony T. Kruzas, Robert C. Thomas. Detroit, Michigan: Gale Research, 1980. 894p.

An important information source, arranged by twenty-six organizational categories and including a telephone number, contact person and description of the organization's activities within each entry.

599 Consumerism in the United States.
Edited by Joel R. Evans. New York: Praeger, 1980. 470p. bibliog.

Analyses the consumer movement's impact on a variety of industries including banking, chemicals, mail order houses, pharmaceuticals and retail establishments. It includes a retrospective look at consumerism and a survey of current court actions and government consumer protection agencies.

600 The gamesman: the new corporate leaders.
Michael Maccoby. New York: Simon & Schuster, 1977. 285p.

A readable work providing a definition and analysis of corporate leadership during the 1970s in the USA. The study is based on interviews with more than 250 senior executives. A clear provocative look at the corporate structure and its leadership. For all levels of study.

601 Keeping the corporate image: public relations and business, 1900-1950.
Richard S. Tedlow. Greenwich, Connecticut: JAI Press, 1979. 233p. bibliog. (Industrial Development and the Social Fabric, no. 3).

An excellent history of public relations and American corporate policy. A useful contribution to the field by an author who is neither a defender of corporate policy nor a public relations specialist.

602 Lobbying the corporation: citizen challenges to business authority.
David Vogel. New York: Basic Books, 1979. 279. bibliog.

Challenges the legitimacy of strictly profit-oriented operations as evidenced in the modern American corporation. Asserts that private pressure on corporations through the use of tactics like boycotts, stockholder suits and proxy fights can affect corporate behaviour and minimize the need for government regulation. A well-written presentation of one viewpoint in the controversial area of American corporate social responsibility.

603 The managers: corporate life in America.

Diane Rothbard Margolis. New York: William Morrow, 1979. 313p. bibliog.

Based on interviews with forty-seven managers and thirty-four wives of managers. Themes such as absorption by the corporation, rootlessness and weak friendship ties are dealt with. Clearly written and free of jargon, this work is useful for every level of reader.

604 Million Dollar Directory.

New York: Dun & Bradstreet. 2 vols. annual.

Vol. 1 of this directory lists businesses in the USA which have a net worth in excess of $1 million, plus utilities, transport companies, banks and trust companies, stockbrokers and insurance companies. Types of organizations not generally included are foreign corporations, professional and consulting organizations, credit agencies and certain financial and insurance institutions. Vol. 2 is entitled 'The middle market', and lists the same type of institutions with an estimated net worth of $500,000 to $999,000. Each volume contains three listings for businesses: alphabetically, geographically, and by product classification. An essential reference tool.

605 Morals and markets: the development of life insurance in the United States.

Viviana A. Rotman Zelizer. New York: Columbia University Press, 1979. 208p. bibliog.

An examination of the way social, religious and moral attitudes influenced the growth of the life insurance industry. Economic and business explanations are minimized. A well-researched, readable new treatment, this provides an excellent supplement to J. O. Stalson's standard history of the life insurance industry, *Marketing life insurance* (Homewood, Illinois: Richard D. Irwin, 1969).

606 The regulated industries and the economy.

Paul W. MacAvoy. New York: Norton, 1979. 160p.

An excellent brief history of regulation from the 1950s to 1978 by an expert who has written several works on this subject. MacAvoy discusses the impetus toward increased regulation in the late 1960s and the reform and deregulation trend of the late 1970s. He discusses public utilities and the transport industry. He also examines the question of health and safety, including surveys of industries like mining, chemicals and construction.

607 Small business in American life.

Edited by Stuart W. Bruchey. New York: Columbia University Press, 1980. 424p.

An extensive and searching analysis of the nature and benefits of the small business in America from the revolution to the present. Seventeen essays on the role of small businesses in manufacturing, the retail trade and banking from the American Revolution through the 1970s are carefully selected and of consistently high quality.

Business and Industry

608 **The structure of American industry.**
Walter Adams. New York: Macmillan, 1977. 5th ed. 523p. bibliog.

A well-known book of readings describing the economics of twelve American industries, including food distribution, steel, petroleum, computers, banking and pharmaceuticals. Two chapters examine the conglomerate firm and public policy questions. A useful introduction for the non-specialist.

609 **Survey of Current Business.**
US Office of Business Economics. Washington, DC: US Government Printing Office, 1921- . monthly, with weekly statistical suppl.

This publication, along with *Business Statistics*, the annual statistical supplement published since 1951, provides descriptive and statistical material on business in the USA, including commodity prices, foreign trade, transport and communication, etc.

610 **Thomas' Register of American Manufacturers.**
New York: Thomas. annual.

Although the number of volumes varies each year, the first several volumes of the set list products and services alphabetically. There follows an alphabetical list of company names, which includes addresses, telephone numbers, travel offices, capital ratings and company officials. There is a volume of brand name listings, and a catalogue of companies concludes the set, listing all of the firms that appear in any of the first portions of the work.

611 **200 years of American business.**
Thomas Childs Cochran. New York: Basic Books, 1977. 288p. bibliog.

A well-known business historian surveys American business. The work includes comparisons with developments in Britain, Germany, Japan and France and detailed descriptions, arranged chronologically, of methods and trends in business organization, finance, production and marketing.

Agriculture

612 Agricultural Statistics.
US Department of Agriculture. Washington, DC: US
Government Printing Office, 1936- . annual.
Prior to 1936 the information contained here was given in the *Yearbook of
Agriculture* (q.v.), and includes statistical data on acreage, yield, production of
crops, farm resources, livestock production, etc.

613 The American farm: a photographic history.
Maisie Conrat, Richard Conrat. San Francisco: Historical
Society, 1977. 256p. bibliog.
The Conrats have collected a group of about 160 photographs to illustrate their
history of the American farmer from 1860 to 1973. The book traces the changing
nature of American agriculture from the simple self-sustaining way of life to the
modern highly technical and mechanized industry.

614 Another revolution in U.S. farming?
Lyle P. Schertz (and others). Washington, DC: US
Department of Agriculture, 1979. 445p. (US Department of
Agriculture. Economic Statistics and Cooperatives Service.
Agricultural Economics Report no. 441).
Thirteen papers on the transformation of livestock and crop production in the
USA have been carefully selected. Part one gives an overview; part two describes
changes in livestock production; and part three emphasizes regional contracts in
US farming, describing six regions of the country.

615 The farmer's frontier, 1865-1900.
Gilbert Courtland Fite. New York: Holt, Rinehart &
Winston, 1966. 272p. bibliog. (Histories of the American
Frontier).
Gilbert Fite uses contemporary letters, diaries, reports, etc., to explore the agri-
cultural settlement of the West in the post-Civil War period. He emphasizes farm

131

settlement and the adjustments that had to be made in frontier agriculture. This is a scholarly work containing a wealth of detail.

616 **Feast or famine: food farming and farm politics in America.**
Ed Edwin. New York: Charterhouse, 1974. 365p.

A good survey of the state of American agriculture, examining every aspect of food production from the farm to the table. This is a useful introduction for the non-specialist, particularly the interested consumer.

617 **The food lobbyists: behind the scenes of food and agri-politics.**
Harold D. Guither. Lexington, Massachusetts: Lexington, 1980. 352p.

An analysis of the groups influencing agribusiness legislation, their effectiveness and the current issues. It includes a directory of over 400 organizations and names of lobbyists.

618 **Hired hands: seasonal farm workers in the United States.**
Stephen H. Sosnick. Santa Barbara, California: McNally & Loftin, 1978. 453p.

A detailed, extensively researched study of seasonal farm labour in the USA. The book considers working conditions, culture, earnings and examines attempts at unionization. It assesses the influence of undocumented alien labour on domestic migrant farm workers. A good historical perspective adds to the concise survey of current conditions.

619 **Introduction to agribusiness.**
Nolan Omri Rawlins. Englewood Cliffs, New Jersey: Prentice-Hall, 1980. 248p. bibliog.

A concise description of American agribusiness. Tables and figures are well presented and provide excellent data to back up the broad concepts outlined. The text is supplemented by useful bibliographies at the end of each chapter.

620 **Whereby we thrive: a history of American farming, 1607-1972.**
John T. Schlebecker. Ames, Iowa: Iowa State University Press, 1975. 342p. bibliog.

A clear survey of American farming, including the social, economic and technological aspects of the subject. The book is chronologically divided: 1607-1783; 1783-1861; 1861-1914; 1914-45; and 1945-72. In each segment land markets and technology are examined. A fine overview.

621 **Yearbook of Agriculture.**
US Department of Agriculture. Washington, DC: US Government Printing Office, 1894- . annual.

This monograph series provides a volume each year devoted to one broad subject which is of interest to the general public. Some recent titles include *Outdoors*

USA (1967), *Food for us all* (1969), *Landscape for living* (1972), *Handbook for the home* (1973) and *That we may eat* (1975).

Transport

622 American railroads.
John F. Stover.   Chicago: University of Chicago Press, 1961. 302p. bibliog. (Chicago History of American Civilization).

The author, a specialist in railway history, examines the growth and development of the industry, its impact on events in American history and its decline after the First World War. He concludes with the assertion that a healthy railway system is still important despite changes in the American national transport system.

623 Americans on the road: from autocamp to motel, 1910-1945.
Warren James Belasco.   Cambridge, Massachusetts: M.I.T. Press, 1979. 212p. bibliog.

Belasco chronicles Americans' obsession for travel by focusing upon touring as 'a major element in the American infatuation with cars'. This is an interesting study of the evolution of the modern motel with fine photographs.

624 Conestoga wagon, 1750-1850: freight carrier for 100 years of America's westward expansion.
George Shumway, Edward Durrell, Howard C. Frey.   Williamsburg, Virginia: Early American Industries Association, 1964. 206p. bibliog.

A beautifully illustrated, detailed study of the conestoga wagon which was one of the most important in American history: an all-purpose vehicle used as the chief means of overland freight transport.

625 Conquest of the skies: a history of commercial aviation in America.
Carl Solberg.   Boston, Massachusetts: Little, Brown, 1979. 441p. bibliog.

A good history of this 20th century phenomenon. The days of glory for the American railway ended in 1920 and the passenger car and aeroplane captured

134

the popular imagination. Solberg writes the story of the development of commercial air travel, carefully outlining the haphazard developments of the inter-war period and the big business boom that expanded the industry after the Second World War. There is a good use of personal interviews and these are included in an excellent bibliography, along with a variety of government documents and secondary sources.

626 Government promotion of American canals and railroads, 1800-1890.
Carter Goodrich. New York: Columbia University Press, 1960. 382p. bibliog.

A careful analysis of the public campaign for internal improvements during the 19th century in the USA, this study explores the competition and cooperation of government and business in the development of canals and railways.

627 The great American motion sickness, or why you can't get there from here.
John Burby. Boston, Massachusetts: Little, Brown, 1971. 408p.

An entertaining and informative survey of the shortcomings of the American transport system. Pollution, warring lobbies, lack of overall transport policy, delays, accidents are all considered. This book was written as an attempt to stir public interest and force legislative action.

628 Highways to nowhere: the politics of city transportation.
Richard Hebert. Indianapolis, Indiana: Bobbs-Merrill, 1972. 214p.

The focus here is on five representative American cities - Flint, Michigan; Dayton, Ohio; Indianapolis, Indiana; Atlanta, Georgia; Washington, DC - with an attempt to diagnose the condition of transport in each. The chaos of each urban transport system is explored and suggestions are made for reform that might be replicated elsewhere. This remains a useful analysis and the reform attempts are in process today. This is a good introduction to the problems that continue to plague major cities in 1981.

629 Iron road to the West: American railroads in the 1850s.
John F. Stover. New York: Columbia University Press, 1978. 266p. maps. bibliog.

Stover explores the growth and development of the American railway system in the ten years before 1860. He asserts that the decade was the most important in the history of railways in the USA. Provides a detailed discussion, state-by-state and line-by-line, of the American railway system during that early period.

Transport

630 Moving the masses: urban public transport in New York, Boston, and Philadelphia, 1880-1912.
Charles W. Cheape. Cambridge, Massachusetts: Harvard University Press, 1980. 285p. maps. bibliog. (Harvard Studies in Business History, 31).

Urban transit enterprise is viewed in the last half of the 19th century, when expanding industries adopted new strategies administered by a new class of professional manager. Cheape compares the development of mass transit in New York, Boston and Philadelphia.

631 Our maritime heritage: maritime developments and their impact on American life.
Washington, DC: University Press of America, 1979. 322p. bibliog.

A good introduction to American maritime history, covering colonial ship-building, fishing and maritime trade, as well as the later expansion of American ocean use and inland waterways. The concluding chapter considers today's merchant fleet, ship-building and the general maritime future of the nation.

632 The transportation frontier: trans-Mississippi west, 1865-1890.
Oscar Osburn Winther. New York: Holt, Rinehart & Winston, 1964. 224p. bibliog. (Histories of the American Frontier).

Amid tales of the westward expansion of the USA in the post-Civil War era, the reader is given a study of the progress in transport from the covered wagon to the railway. Included in this survey are accounts of travel by stagecoach and steamboat.

633 Transportation in America: users, carriers, government.
Donald V. Harper. Englewood Cliffs, New Jersey: Prentice-Hall, 1978. 599p.

A good general introduction to the transport system in the USA. Individual means of transport are discussed in separate chapters, accompanied by an overview of the inter-urban national system and a discussion of regulatory systems.

634 The urban transportation system: politics and policy innovation.
Alan A. Altshuler, James P. Womack, John R. Pucher. Cambridge, Massachusetts: M.I.T. Press, 1979. 558p. bibliog.

A good non-technical survey which considers energy, air quality, safety, and congestion in relation to urban transport systems. It suggests possible policy alternatives and considers the practical consequences of highway expansion or increased investment in public transit systems.

635 **Wheels across America: a pictorial cavalcade illustrating the early development of vehicular transportation.**
Clarence Pearson Hornung.   New York: A. S. Barnes,
1959. 341p.
A fine illustrated history of transport vehicles in the USA, from early carts to the modern automobile. The author describes and illustrates the use of vehicles such as stagecoaches, steam locomotives, trams, bicycles and self-propelled buggies.

636 **Wheels for a nation.**
Frank R. Donovan.   New York: Thomas Y. Crowell, 1965.
303p.
This lively volume explores the American enthusiasm for automobiles and analyses their impact on everyday life. An enjoyable survey for the non-specialist.

Employment and Manpower

637 **Blue-collar workers: a symposium on middle America.**
Edited by Sar A. Levitan. New York: McGraw-Hill, 1971.
393p. bibliog.
A well-selected collection of essays by a group of economists, political scientists
and sociologists, which attempts to analyse the problems faced by the lower-
middle income American population, especially 'blue-collar' workers.

638 **Coming of age in the ghetto: a dilemma of youth**
unemployment: a report to the Ford Foundation.
Garth L. Mangum, Stephen F. Sininger. Baltimore,
Maryland: Johns Hopkins Press, 1978. 114p. bibliog. (Policy
Studies in Employment and Welfare, 33).
A readable summary of factors affecting teenage unemployment and its causes in
urban ghettos. The work makes good use of current data and analyses of population trends and economic patterns in central cities. Fine sociological and psychological handling of chapters on ghetto life-styles.

639 **Death on the job: occupational health and safety struggles in**
the United States.
Daniel M. Berman. New York: Monthly Review, 1979.
260p.
Asserts that continual struggle by workers is the only means by which progress
will be made against industrial hazards and disease. The national safety system,
Berman contends, is created and controlled by industry and can only be improved
by worker activism. An important book on a controversial issue.

138

640 **Employing the unemployed.**
Edited by Eli Ginzberg. New York: Basic Books, 1980.
209p.
Eleven previously unpublished essays on various aspects of America's manpower
policies and programmes from their inception in 1962 to 1979. Ginzberg provides
a perceptive summary analysis to link the papers.

641 **Good jobs, bad jobs, no jobs.**
Eli Ginzberg. Cambridge, Massachusetts: Harvard
University Press, 1979. 219p. bibliog.
An analysis of recent changes in the number and type of jobs available in the
USA and the corresponding changes in the characteristics of those seeking jobs.
Part one is an overview of the structure of the US economy. Part two studies the
connections between education and employment and considers the prospects for
skilled workers. Part three considers manpower planning in large organizations
and discusses policy planning to cope with the employment problems of the 1980s.
Part four examines the links between American politics and economics.

642 **Injury to insult: unemployment, class and political response.**
Kay Lehman Schlozman, Sidney Verba. Cambridge,
Massachusetts: Harvard University Press, 1979. 393p.
bibliog.
A definitive study of the unemployed and the way in which they take part in
American politics. It closely examines the unemployed as a class: who they are,
how they interpret their joblessness, what they do about it, how they view the
American social order and how they vote or otherwise take part in the American
political process. Well written, with good tables. The book results from large-scale
telephone surveying supplemented by personal interviews.

643 **More than subsistence: minimum wages for the working poor.**
Sar A. Levitan, Richard S. Belows. Baltimore, Maryland:
Johns Hopkins Press, 1979. 179p.
What has been the effect of the minimum wage law on the US economy? Has it
driven up unemployment and inflation rates? Has it improved the lot of
America's working poor as intended? This study addresses these questions and
analyses the theory behind the minimum wage and assesses its effect on the
economy.

644 **Pink collar workers.**
Louise Kapp Howe. New York: G. P. Putnam's Sons,
1977. 301p. bibliog.
A series of portraits of the working life of women in jobs traditionally held by
women (office worker, beautician, waitress, homemaker, etc.). There is an appendix which provides statistical breakdowns of the female labour force in America.
The study is a skilful blend of statistical information and anecdotal experiences, a
readable interpretative analysis.

645 **Understanding the service economy: employment, productivity, location.**

Thomas M. Stanback, Jr.   Baltimore, Maryland: Johns Hopkins Press, 1979. 122p.

Explores the question of whether the demand for services has outstripped the demand for goods in the US economy. Stanback attempts to clarify recent employment trends and assess what we really know about service sector employment.

646 **The work ethic in industrial America, 1850-1920.**

Daniel T. Rodgers.   Chicago: University of Chicago Press, 1978. 300p.

One of the 'outstanding books of 1978', as chosen by *Choice* magazine, this is a study of how men and women reacted to the abundance that the 19th century industrial revolution produced in the USA. Examines how technology affects ideas and explores the tensions created as working people struggled to adjust their old values and work ethic to their new economic situation.

647 **The world of the blue-collar worker.**

Compiled by Irving Howe.   New York: Quadrangle, 1972. 316p. bibliog.

A special issue of *Dissent* magazine, of which Howe was editor, was published in 1972 and was devoted to the topic covered in this book. Most of the essays which appeared in that issue are collected in this work and deal with American industrial workers and the realities of their lives in modern America.

648 **Youth employment and public policy.**

Bernard E. Anderson, Isobel V. Sawhill.   Englewood Cliffs, New Jersey: Prentice-Hall and Spectrum, 1980. 161p. (American Assembly, Columbia University Series).

Six papers on the causes, effects and depth of youth unemployment. Although primarily focused on the USA, one paper considers youth in other industrialized countries. This is an overall assessment of primary problems that emphasizes low-income minority youth and makes recommendations for targeting more specifically in the 1980s to create jobs for this sector of the population.

Labour Movement and Trade Unions

649 American labor in a changing world economy.
Edited by Ward Morehouse. New York: Praeger, 1978.
362p.
Thirty-one essays, published in cooperation with the Carnegie Endowment for International Peace, examining the issues affecting American labour and employment patterns amidst the increasing complexity of world economics. The difficulties of collective bargaining with multinational corporations and the problems of defining effective international fair labour standards are among the problems discussed.

650 History of the labor movement in the United States.
Philip Sheldon Foner. New York: International, 1947-80. 5
vols.
Vol. 1: *From colonial times to the founding of the American Federation of Labor*; vol. 2: *Founding of AFL to the emergence of American imperialism*; vol. 3: *Policies and practices of AFL, 1900-1909*; vol. 4: *Industrial Workers of the World, 1905-1917*; vol. 5: *The AFL in the progressive era, 1910-1915*. The set contains a mass of information on early labour struggles, not readily available so compactly elsewhere.

651 The imperfect union: a history of corruption in American trade unions.
John Hutchinson. New York: E. P. Dutton, 1970. 447p.
bibliog.
No collection of labour history would be complete without a study of the abuses and corrupt practices which have been uncovered over the years within the labour movement. This book covers the period from 1890 to the early 1960s and comments on the causes of corrupt practices, as well as suggesting remedies.

Labour Movement and Trade Unions

652 Labor and communism: the conflict that shaped American unions.
Bert Cochran.   Princeton, New Jersey: Princeton University Press for the Research Institute on International Change, Columbia University, 1977. 394p. bibliog.

The author, once an auto worker and United Automobile Workers official and now associated with the Research Institute on International Change, has written a detailed and sophisticated book. This is the most emotionally detached book on the subject yet to appear. The overwhelming emphasis is on the period from about 1929 to the early 1950s. A good description of party shifts and their effects on the relations of the party with the unions.

653 Labor in America.
Foster Rhea Dulles.   New York: Thomas Y. Crowell, 1960. 2nd rev. ed. 435p. bibliog.

A concise authoritative work on the American labour movement, providing a history of events and personalities. A wealth of information has been well condensed into this study, which provides a fine introduction to the subject for the non-specialist.

654 The lean years: a history of the American worker, 1920-1933.
Irving Bernstein.   Boston, Massachusetts: Houghton Mifflin, 1960. 557p. bibliog.

The first volume in Bernstein's two-volume study of the American worker, this describes the labour movement during the 1920s, with emphasis on the workers, both organized and unorganized, rather than on the unions. The reader will find this a readable well-documented study, which can be supplemented by Bernstein's work on the later period *The turbulent years* (q.v.).

655 A long time coming: the struggle to unionize America's farm workers.
Dick Meister, Anne Loftis.   New York: Macmillan, 1977. 241p. bibliog.

A well-written narrative of the long fight by farm workers to establish their right to collective bargaining. The work covers the period between 1850 and 1976.

656 Organized labor in American history.
Philip Taft.   New York: Harper & Row, 1964. 818p.

A definitive history of the American labour movement from colonial times to the 1960s. The book examines developing unionism, including the organization of the American Federation of Labor and the Congress of Industrial Organizations. It discusses many labour personalities such as Samuel Gompers and John L. Lewis. An excellent comprehensive source for the serious student.

657 A pictorial history of American labor.
William Cahn. New York: Crown, 1972. 341p. bibliog.

The author has enhanced a text of fifteen chronological chapters with over 750 illustrations designed to show the history of the labour movement from early Jamestown days to the present.

658 Technology and woman's work.
Elizabeth F. Baker. New York: Columbia University Press, 1964. 460p. bibliog.

Extensively researched, this study examines the employment of American women outside the home. The author traces the historical and economic factors that have brought women into offices, factories and shops. The professions are considered only briefly, but there is an excellent discussion of the relationship between women and labour unions. The author discusses the impact of protective labour legislation on the female work-force.

659 Toil and trouble: a history of American labor.
Thomas R. Brooks. New York: Delacorte Press, 1971. 2nd rev. ed. 402p. bibliog.

A well-written comprehensive history of the American labour movement. There is a good treatment of the unionization of the public sector, the upsurge of blacks within unions and the changing nature of the new generation of blue-collar youth.

660 The turbulent years: a history of the American worker, 1933-1941.
Irving Bernstein. Boston, Massachusetts: Houghton Mifflin, 1970. 873p. bibliog.

This study continues Bernstein's *The lean years* (q.v.). This volume covers labour's struggles during the the period of the New Deal under Franklin Roosevelt, 1933-41. The emphasis of the book is on the unions and the power those structures achieved during this time.

661 Workers in industrial America: essays on the twentieth century struggle.
David Brody. New York: Oxford University Press, 1980. 257p.

A collection of papers by a noted labour historian who wrote *Steelworkers in America* (New York: Russell & Russell, 1960). The essays cover the period from the labour struggles of the progressive era. They are well-written and perceptive historical studies, which will prove useful to student and scholar alike.

Environment

662 **America's changing environment.**
Edited by Roger Revelle, Hans H. Landsberg. Boston,
Massachusetts: Houghton Mifflin, 1970. 314p. bibliog.
(Daedalus Library, vol. 15).

A collection of papers by economists, political scientists, city planners and conser-
vationists, who discuss environmental problems and suggest the types of planning
that must be utilized in order to remedy them.

663 **The closing circle: nature, man, and technology.**
Barry Commoner. New York: Knopf, 1971. 362p.

An important book on ecology, stating clearly what our environmental problems
are, how they have developed, and suggesting solutions for the future, including a
re-ordering of priorities and changes in social and industrial policies.

664 **Design with nature.**
Ian L. McHarg. Garden City, New York: Natural History
Press, 1969. 197p. maps. bibliog.

A well-illustrated book on planning cities and suburban areas with the ecology in
mind, taking into account geology, watersheds, wildlife, forests, shores, etc.

665 **The ecological conscience: values for survival.**
Edited by Robert Disch. Englewood Cliffs, New Jersey:
Prentice-Hall, 1970. 206p. bibliog.

An anthology of essays by ecologists on the need to add a concern for ecology
and the conservation of our resources to our system of values. The contributors
address themselves to the issues of legislation, politics and financial support, as
well as the ethics involved in the social responsibility.

666 Ecotactics: the Sierra Club handbook for environment activists.
Edited by John G. Mitchell, Constance L. Stallings. New York: Simon & Schuster, 1970. 288p. bibliog.

A practical guide for groups who would like to take action to improve the environment. The information included shows how to: organize actions against factories, stores, etc.; arouse awareness in local communities; get maximum media coverage; make use of the law, etc.

667 Energy and environment.
Edited by Stuart W. Bruchey, Gene Brown. New York: New York Times and Arno Press, 1978. 373p. bibliog. (Great Contemporary Issues).

A collection of articles on energy and the environment which appeared in the *New York Times* between 1907 and 1977. Most of the articles are printed in their entirety and cover conservation, pollution, and the energy crisis.

668 Energy, ecology, economy.
Gerald Garvey. New York: Norton, 1972. 235p. bibliog.

The author studies the subject of energy from the points of view of cost, environmental impact and the needs of the future. He suggests using technological skills and economic solutions (such as charges to polluters set high enough to encourage clean-up) to protect conservation interests.

669 Highways and our environment.
John Robinson. New York: McGraw-Hill, 1971. 340p. maps. bibliog.

A beautifully illustrated volume dealing with the subject of the effect of the automobile and highway industries upon city decay and environmental pollution. The author suggests citizen action that can be taken and changes that can be made to improve the situation.

670 Land use controls in the United States: a handbook on the legal rights of citizens.
Natural Resources Defense Council, edited by Elaine Moss. New York: Dial Press, 1977. 362p. bibliog.

A useful handbook for citizens, discussing state, regional and local land use controls as well as federal law on land utilization in the United States. It provides much information for the environmentalist as well as for the student in the field.

671 Losing ground.
John G. Mitchell. San Francisco: Sierra Club, 1975. 227p.

A series of observations on places visited by the author, a reporter investigating the changes in places he has lived and worked and then revisited. He is deeply disturbed by the despoiling of the land and shows the conflicts between such groups as farmers near a hydroelectric plant needing water, and city dwellers needing the energy provided.

Environment

672 **Managing the environment: an economic primer.**
William Ramsay, Claude Anderson. New York: Basic
Books, 1972. 302p. bibliog.

A study applying modern economic techniques to a variety of environmental
problems, from air pollution to vanishing species. The authors show how government can place economic sanctions on polluters and provide planning for future
needs.

673 **The new American dream machine: toward a simpler lifestyle
in an environmental age.**
Robert L. Sansom. Garden City, New York: Anchor Press,
1976. 251p.

The author, an administrator with the EPA (Environmental Protection Administration), describes the early environmental movement in the United States. He
then discusses those changes in the American lifestyle which must take place in
order to live within necessary energy and environmental limits.

674 **Politics and environment: a reader in ecological crisis.**
Edited by Walt Anderson. Pacific Palisades, California:
Goodyear, 1970. 362p. bibliog.

A collection of articles, previously published, providing an introduction to the
subject of ecological crises in America. Some of the topics touched on include
population, varieties of pollution (air, waste, nuclear, etc.), urban environment,
environmental policy, etc.

675 **The politics of environmental concern.**
Walter A. Rosenbaum. New York: Praeger, 1973. 298p.
bibliog.

A study of the political system and its relationship to environmental issues. The
author discusses the process of regulating air and water pollution, the problems of
strip mining and solid waste disposal, the actions of such agencies as the Department of Health, Education and Welfare and the EPA, and much more. A
scholarly addition to environmental collections.

676 **The politics of pollution.**
J. Clarence Davies. New York: Pegasus, 1970. 231p.
bibliog. (Studies in Contemporary American Politics).

A picture of the relationship between pollution laws, economic pressures and
political personalities. The author describes the processes of pollution control
policy research, setting standards, obtaining compliance - and offers suggestions
for improvements within the system.

677 **Pollution.**
Gaithersburg, Maryland: Social Issues Resources Series,
1975. 2 vols.

A loose-leaf collection of articles reprinted from various magazines on all aspects
of pollution in America (air, water, strip mining, pesticides, etc.). The Social

Issues Resources Series publishes annual supplements to keep it up-to-date. Another title in this series is *Energy*, 1975.

678 **Pollution, prices, and public policy: a study sponsored jointly by Resources for the Future, Inc., and the Brookings Institution.**
Allen V. Kneese, Charles L. Schultze. Washington, DC: Brookings Institution, 1975. 125p.
A summary of the economic and technical aspects of regulations to reduce pollution. The authors discuss past federal control efforts and suggest alternative policies designed to make pollution control financially attractive to individuals, businesses and municipalities.

679 **Priorities for survival.**
Edited by William P. Lineberry. New York: H. W. Wilson, 1973. 223p. bibliog. (Reference Shelf, vol. 44, no. 6).
A series of articles dealing with the problems of survival in modern times. Some of the topics covered include man's prospects for survival, costs and priorities, the need for international cooperation, state and local trends, and what the individual can do.

680 **Property power - how to keep the bull-dozer, the power line, and the highwayman away from your door.**
Mary Anne Guitar. Garden City, New York: Doubleday, 1972. 322p. bibliog.
The author speaks to the American home-owner whose property is threatened by developers, highway builders, and other entrepreneurs. She describes grass-roots campaigns to enlist public opinion, pressure law-makers and promote careful planning to avoid despoiling the land.

681 **The quality of the environment.**
James L. McCamy. New York: Free Press, 1972. 276p. bibliog.
The results of a seminar held at the University of Wisconsin in 1967 by a variety of specialists (in physics, engineering, landscape architecture, etc.) to investigate the environment (air, land and water). Its purpose is to acquaint the layman with the state of the environment and with the private and public agencies which can affect change.

682 **State environmental management: case studies in nine states.**
Elizabeth H. Haskell, Victoria S. Price. New York: Praeger, 1973. 282p. bibliog.
Discusses the environmental departments created in five states (Illinois, Minnesota, Washington, Wisconsin, and New York) as a result of the environmental concern of the late 1960s. Other states' approaches to environmental management (Vermont, Maine, Maryland, and Michigan) are shown in later chapters. A useful guide in the field of environmental management.

Environment

683 **The unfinished agenda: the citizen's policy guide to
environmental issues; a task force report sponsored by the
Rockefeller Brothers Fund.**
Edited by Gerald O. Barney.   New York: Thomas Y.
Crowell, 1977. 184p. bibliog.
The report of a study undertaken by a group of sixty-three environmentalists who
were asked to describe our most critical environmental problems and to make
recommendations on how to solve them. The various problems studied include
population size, energy, pollution, etc., and the recommendations deal with legislation, research and education.

684 **The un-politics of air pollution; a study of
non-decision-making in the cities.**
Matthew A. Crenson.   Baltimore, Maryland: Johns Hopkins
Press, 1971. 227p. bibliog.
A study of air pollution, focusing upon the experience of the cities of East
Chicago and Gary, and surveying fifty American cities with populations from
50,000 to 750,000. The author analyses why many cities and towns failed to
make an issue of their pollution problems, and contends that political and industrial interests were responsible.

685 **What we save now: an Audobon primer of defense.**
Edited by Les Line.   Boston, Massachusetts: Houghton
Mifflin, 1973. 438p. (Audobon Library).
A series of articles which appeared in *Audobon*, the official organ of the National
Audobon Society, showing present threats to the environment. The essays provide
a literate plea for public awareness and concern for preservation of the ecosystem.

686 **Your environment and what you can do about it.**
Richard Saltonstall, Jr.   New York: Walker, 1970. 299p.
bibliog.
A guide for the average citizen to steps that can be taken to solve environmental
problems: air, water, noise and chemical pollution, crowded highways, litter, etc.
Included are lists of useful tables such as pesticides to avoid, agencies to consult,
etc.

City Planning

687 **American city planning since 1890: a history commemorating the fiftieth anniversary of the American Institute of Planners.**
Mel Scott. Berkeley, California: University of California Press, 1969. 745p. maps. bibliog. (California Studies in Urbanization and Environmental Design).
An account of the city planning profession in the United States, emphasizing its place in the contemporary scene. This book provides an important supplement to Reps' history, *The making of urban America* (q.v.).

688 **Civilizing American cities: a selection of Frederick Law Olmsted's writings on city landscapes.**
Frederick Law Olmsted, edited by S. B. Sutton. Cambridge, Massachusetts: M.I.T. Press, 1971. 310p.
A selection of writings by a noted planner on designing urban parks and planned communities. Mr. Olmsted is most famous for planning New York's Central Park, and his ideas make interesting reading.

689 **The contemporary new communities movement in the United States.**
Gideon Golany, Daniel Walden. Urbana, Illinois: University of Illinois Press, 1975. 154p. bibliog.
A collection of nine monographs on various aspects of the 'new communities' movement: history, urban design, social planning, etc., plus descriptive accounts of three new towns. The contributors are all involved in the field as planners, developers, government officials, etc.

City Planning

690 **Downtown USA; urban design in nine American cities.**
Kenneth Halpern. New York: Whitney Library of Design,
1978. 256p. bibliog. (Distributed by Watson-Guptil).
A study of the state of urban design in nine cities including New York, San
Francisco, Philadelphia, Chicago and Houston. The book is illustrated by 350
black-and-white photographs, and contains information on history, demography,
historic preservation, zoning, urban renewal, and many other related topics. Very
useful for students in the field of city planning.

691 **Guerrillas in the bureaucracy; the community planning
experiment in the United States.**
Martin L. Needleman, Carolyn Emerson Needleman. New
York: John Wiley & Sons, 1974. 368p. bibliog. (Wiley
Series in Urban Research).
An analysis of six community planning experiments, pointing out the conflicts
among the conservative elements of the planning profession, citizens groups, and
new planners playing an undercover role to accomplish their goals. An interesting
work on urban planning.

692 **The making of urban America; a history of city planning in
the United States.**
John William Reps. Princeton, New Jersey: Princeton
University Press, 1965. 574p. maps. bibliog.
A comprehensive history of city planning in the United States, beginning with
European influence in the 18th century and continuing to the early 20th century.
This book is well illustrated and chronologically arranged, and is a must for all
collections on American history and architecture.

693 **The New Deal in the suburbs; a history of the greenbelt town
program, 1935-1954.**
Joseph L. Arnold. Columbus, Ohio: Ohio State University
Press, 1971. 272p. bibliog.
A study of a major government-sponsored city planning programme which originated in the days of the New Deal in the 1930s. The study documents the
inception of the programme and the later experiments in community life which
were undertaken in the towns after 1938. An important work on the subject.

694 **Suburban land conversion in the United States: an economic
and governmental process.**
Marion Clawson. Baltimore, Maryland: Johns Hopkins
Press, 1971. 406p. (Resources for the Future Series).
A view of urban expansion, suburban land conversion and the problems in general
of 'suburban sprawl'.

695 **Urban land use planning.**
Francis Stuart Chapin.   Urbana, Illinois: University of
Illinois Press, 1965. 2nd ed. 498p. bibliog.
A useful text for city planning agencies, schools and architectural firms. It covers
urban land use planning and the techniques and skills needed to accomplish
planning goals. The book deals with theory, tools, and the planning process itself.

696 **Zoned American.**
Seymour I. Toll.   New York: Grossman, 1969. 370p.
bibliog.
An interesting history of the development of zoning in the United States, tracing
its role in urban development for controlling the use of buildings, land, etc. An
important addition to all planning collections.

Education

697 American boarding schools: a historical study.
James McLachlan. New York: Charles Scribner's Sons, 1970. 381p.

A comprehensive history of such famous American boarding schools for boys as Lawrenceville, Choate, Groton, etc., tracing their creation and development from the 19th and early 20th centuries. The author shows that these early schools were not modelled on English schools such as Eton, but were influenced by experimental schools in Switzerland and Germany. McLachlan attempts to relate the creation of these schools to the social history of the times.

698 American education in the twentieth century.
Isaac Leon Kandel. Cambridge, Massachusetts: Harvard University Press, 1957. 247p. (Library of Congress Series in American Civilization).

A discussion of the state of American education at the mid-20th century from the point of view of what had emerged as a result of the attempt to provide equal opportunity for all. The author explores the strengths and weaknesses of the US education system, and includes chapters on the education of children and adolescents, and on the teaching profession. An interesting survey of the subject.

699 American education: the colonial experience, 1607-1783.
Lawrence Arthur Cremin. New York: Harper & Row, 1970. 688p.

A history of American education which treats the subject in the broad sense - not limiting its discussion to formal schooling alone. The book thereby becomes a history of American culture in the 18th and 19th centuries.

700 The American experience in education.
Edited by John M. Barnard, David Burner. New York: New Viewpoints, 1975. 268p.

An interesting anthology containing writings by various authors on the history of American education. The editors followed four guidelines in selecting the essays:

1. to reflect the educational experiences of more than white, middle class boys, e.g. American Indians, blacks and women; 2. to show the educational impact of institutions outside of the classroom; 3. to show the impact of education on the young; 4. to select articles that expressed more than one interpretive viewpoint.

701 American universities and colleges.
Washington, DC: American Council on Education, 1928- .
A quadrennial sourcebook on higher education, this comprehensive directory describes American colleges and universities and includes information on enrolment, fees, student aid, admission requirements, faculty, student life, etc.

702 America's other children.
Edited by George Henderson. Norman, Oklahoma: University of Oklahoma Press, 1971. 430p.
A collection of fifty articles, reprinted from other sources, which focus attention on the education of children who do not fit into the pattern of middle class children in suburban schools. The 'other' children of this book include those who go to small schools in isolated areas, migrant farm workers' children who seldom get to school, poor white and Indian children in sparsely populated areas, and black children in inner-city schools.

703 Barron's profiles of American colleges.
Woodbury, New York: Barron's Educational Series, 1964- . 2 vols.
This useful college guide is updated every year or two, and includes profiles of each college listed, and an index which lists all the colleges according to the degree of admissions competition: most competitive, highly competitive, very competitive, competitive, less competitive, non-competitive, and special schools (religious, music and art).

704 The college handbook.
New York: College Entrance Examination Board, 1941- . 2 vols.
A handbook prepared by the colleges in conjunction with the College Entrance Examination Board. It gives information to help students choose colleges on the basis of their own interests and needs.

705 The commonwealth of learning.
Henry Steele Commager. New York: Harper & Row, 1968. 277p.
Contains some twenty essays which have appeared previously in such magazines as *Saturday Review* and *The New York Times Magazine*. The author discusses a variety of topics relating to education - from elementary school readers to academic freedom in the university. A thought-provoking book by an eminent historian and teacher.

Education

706 **The comprehensive high school: a second report to interested citizens.**
James Bryant Conant. New York: McGraw-Hill, 1967. 95p.

This book follows an earlier volume written by Dr. Conant in 1959, *The American high school today*, in which he made twenty-one recommendations for improving American schools. This second report shows which of the recommendations have been acted upon, and discusses the need for a national effort to solve educational problems.

707 **The control of urban schools: perspectives on the power of educational reformers.**
Joseph M. Cronin. New York: Free Press, 1973. 262p. bibliog.

An important study, useful for educators and others concerned with the subject of urban education. The author traces the histories of school boards in fourteen American cities from the 1890s to the present and summarizes the major criticisms of urban schools and the proposals for reform.

708 **Crisis in the classroom: the remaking of American education.**
Charles E. Silberman. New York: Random House, 1970. 552p.

An indictment of American schools, with suggestions for changes in schools as well as in teacher education. The author states that he has aimed his book at laymen and professionals alike.

709 **Does anybody give a damn?**
Nat Hentoff. New York: Knopf, 1977. 245p. (Distributed by Random House).

A follow-up of the 1966 work *Our children are dying*, in which Hentoff wrote about conditions in inner-city schools. In this book, he describes the teachers and administrators who have been effective in spite of the odds against them, and provides a readable account of how they have succeeded. Hentoff also tackles such subjects as corporal punishment in schools, parental involvement, and the politics of education.

710 **Editorial Research Reports on issues in education: timely reports to keep journalists, scholars, and the public abreast of issues, events, and trends.**
Washington, DC: Congressional Quarterly, 1976. 184p. bibliog.

Editorial Research Reports is a reference service for newspapers, broadcasting networks and libraries. The reports are issued on topics attracting wide public attention, and this particular volume includes nine reports on vital issues in contemporary education that were previously mailed individually to subscribers.

Education

711 Education in the United States: a documentary history.
Edited by Sol Cohen. New York: Random House, 1974. 5 vols.

A comprehensive source-book on the history of American education. The editor has attempted to collect the most significant documents in this field, from the early European backgrounds and colonial education, up to the present time. The arrangement is chronological within topical chapters, and each volume is prefaced by a brief historical chapter on the period covered. This reference work is invaluable to any scholar working with original source material.

712 Education in the United States: an interpretive history.
Robert L. Church, Michael W. Sedlak. New York: Free Press, 1976. 489p. bibliog.

A study of the role of schools in American society, this book chronologically traces American education from the common school movement of the early 19th century to the changing standard of educational equality in the 1970s. The author analyses the relationships between educational developments and American social history. This book provides an interesting interpretation of the nature of mass education in American life.

713 The education of American teachers.
James Bryant Conant. New York: McGraw-Hill, 1963. 270p.

Discusses the complex issue of how teachers should be educated. The author proposes that teacher education be made the responsibility of each individual college or university having a teacher training programme, rather than resting with state departments of education. He outlines what he thinks should be covered in academic and professional courses and provides a thought-provoking study on this subject.

714 Education of the disadvantaged: a book of readings.
Edited by Aaron Harry Passow. New York: Holt, Rinehart & Winston, 1967. 503p.

A collection of scholarly articles written by educators, sociologists, and psychologists on the education of people living in economically depressed areas. Includes articles on such topics as teaching techniques, language problems, styles of learning, etc.

715 The enrollment explosion: a half-century of attendance in the U.S. colleges and universities.
Garland G. Parker. New York: School & Society, 1971. 163p.

An analytical review of enrolment in American universities and colleges from 1920-70. The information is examined in relation to economic, political and social conditions of the decade in which it was gathered. Reports on this subject have appeared annually in *School and Society* for over fifty years.

Education

716 Every kid a winner: accountability in education.
Leon M. Lessinger.   New York: Simon & Schuster, 1970.
239p.

The author proposes a new concept which he calls 'educational engineering': specifically designed programmes to meet measurable requirements. He contends that education must work as an efficient industry, with accountability for results and with emphasis placed on each child's mastery of the essentials. The book contains some examples of the method actually in operation in specific school systems, and outlines what schools can do to improve education results.

717 Free to learn: unlocking and ungrading American education.
John Henry Martin, Charles H. Harrison.   Englewood
Cliffs, New Jersey: Prentice-Hall, 1972. 185p.

An interesting series of suggestions for improving the US educational system by restructuring its institutions. The authors advocate such bold moves as removing courses like guidance, the arts, and physical education from schools and providing them instead in family-oriented community centres. A provocative addition to any education collection.

718 Growing up in America.
Fred M. Hechinger.   New York: McGraw-Hill, 1975. 451p.
bibliog.

A thought-provoking book on educational experiences in American life as they have been affected by politics and social conditions. The topics covered are traced through American history and up to contemporary times.

719 Handbook on contemporary education.
Edited by Steven E. Goodman.   New York, London: R. R.
Bowker, 1976. 622p.

A useful reference for both students and practitioners in education. This handbook contains information on contemporary topics in education, an index by subject field, and articles summarizing the current status of specific issues in education.

720 History of education in American culture.
R. Freeman Butts, Lawrence A. Cremin.   New York:
Henry Holt, 1953. 628p.

A basic history of American education, tracing its beginnings in colonial times to its development until 1865, through its expansion during industrial times to 1918, and finally contemporary education to mid-century. The book, of course, does not cover the last twenty-five years, but it is a very useful tool for anyone wanting a historical survey of the subject.

721 Lovejoy's college guide.
Clarence Earle Lovejoy.   New York: Simon & Schuster,
1940- .

Periodically updated, this popular college guide contains concise information for students selecting colleges. There is information on expenses, financial aid, admissions, a very useful list of career curricula and which schools offer them, and descriptions of the individual colleges.

722 **The modern family guide to education.**
Benjamin Fine. New York: Doubleday, 1962. 648p.

A useful guide to education, intended as a reference for the family library. This volume provides a historical summary as well as a picture of current education, including trends, techniques, and problems, from elementary school to college and university level.

723 **New careers and roles in the American school.**
Edited by Gerda Bowman, Gordon J. Klopf. Washington, DC: Office of Economic Opportunity, 1968. 256p.

This book is the result of a study of auxiliary personnel in education, conducted by the Bank Street College of Education for the Office of Economic Opportunity. The study attempts to define the roles of people with various skills and training in the educational process, especially as seen in disadvantaged communities.

724 **New trends in the schools.**
William P. Lineberry. New York: H. W. Wilson, 1967. 211p. bibliog. (Reference Shelf, vol. 39, no. 2).

A collection of articles discussing innovations in American education in the 1960s. A few of the topics included are: schools without grades, 'new math', civil rights enforcement in education, and vocational education. The book is divided into five sections: the first contains background articles, the second discusses the effects of reform, the third describes the role of the federal government in education, the fourth and fifth assess the new trends themselves.

725 **Nongraded schools in action: bold new venture.**
Edited by David W. Beggs, III, Edward G. Buffie. Bloomington, Indiana: Indiana University Press, 1967. 270p. bibliog.

A selection of articles by educators discussing the concept of the non-graded school, as well as describing a number of operating programmes. Much essential information is included, and this volume would be a useful tool in any education collection.

726 **The real world of the public schools.**
Harry S. Broudy. New York: Harcourt Brace Jovanovich, 1972. 271p. bibliog.

A highly readable and informed discussion of the American public school system, pointing out its strengths, weaknesses and hopes for the future.

Education

727 **Reforming American education: the innovative approach to improving our schools and colleges.**
Alvin C. Eurich. New York: Harper & Row, 1969. 269p. bibliog.

Discusses the future of education, and the need to utilize such devices as teaching machines, language laboratories, and educational television. There is an interesting chapter entitled 'A 21st century view of American higher education', in which the author talks about the role of computers, the internationalization of higher education, and changes in the traditional concept of set courses of study in a prescribed time period, such as four years in a college.

728 **The school book: for people who want to know what all the hollering is about.**
Neil Postman, Charles Weingartner. New York: Delacorte Press, 1973. 308p. bibliog.

A book addressed to parents, aiming to bring them up to date on school changes over the past fifteen years. The second half of the book is devoted to a glossary of terms used in educational circles, such as 'Montessori method' or 'team teaching', plus a description of some seventy people who have been influential in educational circles.

729 **Sex education and the schools.**
Edited by Virginia Hilu. New York: Harper & Row, 1967. 153p. bibliog.

A discussion of the controversial issue of sex education in the schools, this book is the result of a meeting of headmasters arranged by the Committee on Educational Practices of the National Association of Independent Schools. The meeting took place in 1966, and many schools have since initiated sex education programmes of one sort or another. Much of the material presented is quite useful to educators, parents, clergymen, etc., who might be involved with the subject.

730 **Slums and suburbs: a commentary on schools in metropolitan areas.**
James Bryant Conant. New York: McGraw-Hill, 1961. 147p.

An important study contrasting conditions and aims of suburban schools with those of slum schools in big cities. Although written in 1961, the points made in this book are quite pertinent today.

731 **Standard Education Almanac.**
Chicago: Marquis Academic Media, 1968- . annual.

Designed to provide current, comprehensive coverage of all fields of education (elementary, secondary, higher, and adult). This volume reviews the current status of education, historical developments since 1919, and offers projections for the future. Included are statistics dealing with trends in education and gathered from a variety of government and private sources.

732 Traditions of American education.
Lawrence Arthur Cremin. New York: Basic Books, 1977. 172p.

A novel approach to the subject of education, showing the major ways that Americans have educated themselves - both through formal schooling and through informal means. The volume is made up of three lectures which span American education from 1607 to the present.

733 The transformation of the school: progressivism in American education, 1876-1957.
Lawrence Arthur Cremin. New York: Knopf, 1961. 387p. bibliog.

A definitive history of the progressive education movement from its onset to its collapse after the Second World War. This scholarly work is written in an interesting style and is well documented. An important addition to any collection on American education.

734 The twelve-year sentence.
Edited by William F. Rickenbacker. La Salle, Illinois: Open Court, 1974. 236p. bibliog.

A collection of six papers, prepared for a 1972 symposium co-sponsored by the Institute for Humane Studies and the Center for Independent Education, on the subject of compulsory schooling. The issue is examined from historical, legal, sociological, biological, political and economic points of view.

735 What schools can do.
Joseph Featherstone. New York: Liveright, 1976. 212p.

An interesting collection of essays which originally appeared in journals such as the *New Republic* and the *Harvard Educational Review*. The author evaluates various reform movements in education and discusses classroom innovations, the philosophy of John Dewey, racial imbalance and school busing, parent participation, and many other topics.

Science and Technology

736 **American men and women of science: a biographical directory.**
Lancaster, Pennsylvania: Science Press, 1906- .

Previously named *American men of science*, the title was changed to *American men and women of science* with the 12th edition published in 1971. The directory covers the physical and biological sciences in six volumes. Also available are volumes covering the social and behavioural sciences. Biographies are arranged alphabetically, and material is gathered from questionnaires filled out by the scientists.

737 **Astronautics and Aeronautics, a Chronology.**
United States National Aeronautics and Space Administration. Scientific and Technical Information Office. Washington, DC: Superintendent of Documents, US Government Printing Office, 1961- . annual. (NASA SP).

A series of day-by-day records of aeronautical and space events, including appendixes which list such information as major NASA launches, space probes, etc. A useful reference for anyone working in the field of space technology and research. The previous edition was published in 1961 under the title *Aeronautics and astronautics: American chronology of science and technology in the exploration of space, 1915-1960* (240p.) by Eugene M. Emme.

738 **Dividends from space.**
Frederick Ira Ordway, Carsbie C. Adams, Mitchell R.
Sharp. New York: Thomas Y. Crowell, 1972. 309p.
bibliog.
A discussion of the beneficial achievements which have been by-products of the
space programme, in the fields of medicine, communications, flood control, etc.
The possibilities for future improvements are also considered.

739 **For all mankind: America's space programs of the 1970s and
beyond.**
L. B. Taylor, Jr. New York: E. P. Dutton, 1974. 307p.
An interesting book discussing the aerospace developments originating in the
Apollo and Skylab programmes of the 1960s and 1970s and their possible
applications to society's problems (pollution control, fuel research, food source
development, etc.). Includes much material on space operations and future predic-
tions, plus many illustrations.

740 **The formation of the American scientific community: the
American Association for the Advancement of Science,
1848-1860.**
Sally Gregory Kohlstedt. Urbana, Illinois: University of
Illinois Press, 1976. 264p. bibliog.
An important contribution to the literature on the history of American science,
this scholarly work describes the formation of the American professional scientific
community. Included is material on such diverse topics as the Smithsonian
Institution, the United States Geological Survey and charts showing biographical
data on members of the American Association for the Advancement of Science.

741 **From spinning wheel to spacecraft: the story of the industrial
revolution.**
Harry Edward Neal. New York: Julian Messner, 1964.
191p. bibliog.
A readable history of the American industrial revolution, illustrated with photographs, discussing inventions in connection with social and political changes of
their times.

742 **The healers: the rise of American medicine.**
John Duffy. New York: McGraw-Hill, 1976. 385p. bibliog.
A fascinating history of medicine in America from pre-colonial practices to
modern medical technology. The author, a historian, relates medical practice to
the times, and discusses such modern problems as national health insurance,
malpractice suits, euthanasia, abortion, bio-engineering, etc.

743 **History of American technology.**
John William Oliver. New York: Ronald Press, 1956.
676p.
A survey of America's technology from colonial times to the mid-20th century,
including profiles of famous inventors and chapters on various industries such as
steel, petroleum, clothing, communication, etc.

744 **The ingenious Yankees.**
Joseph Gies, Frances Gies. New York: Thomas Y. Crowell,
1976. 376p. bibliog.
An interesting illustrated look at 100 years of America's technological history,
1776 to 1876. Included are biographical sketches and descriptions of the work of
many inventors - both famous and relatively obscure.

745 **The physicists: the history of a scientific community in
modern America.**
Daniel J. Kevles. New York: Knopf, 1977. 489p. bibliog.
A history of American physicists starting from the end of the Civil War and
tying their work to the trends and historical events of their times. The author
describes the personalities of the scientists as well as their work. An important
contribution to scientific history.

746 **The pursuit of knowledge in the early American republic:
American scientific and learned societies from colonial times
to the Civil War.**
Edited by Alexandra Oleson, Sanborn C.
Brown. Baltimore, Maryland: Johns Hopkins Press, 1976.
372p.
The first volume of a projected three-volume work, this collection presents papers
from a five-day workshop held by the American Academy of Arts and Sciences in
Cape Newagen, Maine, in June 1973. The papers view the contributions of early
learned societies and the objectives of the scientists prior to the Civil War. A
valuable addition to history of science collections.

747 **Science in American society: a social history.**
George H. Daniels. New York: Knopf, 1971. 390p. bibliog.
A history of American science from colonial times to the present, relating science
to social, economic and political influences. The emphasis of the book is on the
period before the Civil War, with a short epilogue describing events since that
time.

748 **Scientific elite: Nobel laureates in the United States.**
Harriet Zuckerman. New York: Free Press, 1977. 335p.
bibliog.
An interesting study of ninety-two Nobel prize winners between 1901 and 1972
who did their research in the United States. The author touches on such aspects
as the educational process, the age at which most Nobel research is done,

experiences after receiving the prize, etc. A worthwhile addition to scientific biography collections.

749 The story of medicine in America.

Geoffrey Marks, William K. Beatty. New York: Charles Scribner's Sons, 1973. 416p. bibliog.

A good general history of medicine in America from colonial times to modern aerospace and nuclear medicine. It touches on such topics as medical research, public health, the fight against communicable diseases, etc.

750 Thinkers and tinkers: early American men of science.

Silvio A. Bedini. New York: Charles Scribner's Sons, 1975. 520p.

A historical survey of 'mathematical practicioners' up to the early 19th century who contributed to such fields as navigation, surveying, and map-making. Included are photographs of scientific instruments and the men who made them.

751 Those inventive Americans.

Washington, DC: National Geographic Society, 1971. 231p. (National Geographic Special Publications).

A beautifully illustrated, highly readable work on inventors in American society which discusses both their inspiration and their contributions. Included are such men as Benjamin Franklin, Robert Fulton, Samuel F. B. Morse, the Wright brothers and many others.

752 Two centuries of American medicine, 1776-1976.

James Bordley, A. Harvey McGehee. Philadelphia: W. B. Saunders, 1976. 844p. bibliog.

A history of American medicine, particularly useful for its coverage of the 20th century. Included is an appendix providing a chronological survey of major events in medical history.

753 Two centuries of federal information.

Burton W. Adkinson. New York: Academic Press, 1978. 235p. bibliog. (Publications in the Information Sciences).

An invaluable history of the dissemination of scientific and technical information by the United States government from 1790 to 1972. Federal policies and programmes are discussed, and the author includes his own view of trends and future directions from his vantage point as former head of the Office of Science Information Service at the National Science Foundation.

754 The visible scientists.

Rae Goodell. Boston, Massachusetts: Little, Brown, 1977. 242p. bibliog.

A study of scientists (Paul Ehrlich, Linus Pauling, Margaret Mead, B. F. Skinner, Carl Sagan, Barry Commoner, and William Shockley) who influence the public on science-related issues because of their celebrity status and direct approach in communicating with the public.

Science and Technology

755 **AIChE Journal.**
New York: American Institute of Chemical Engineers, 1955- .
bi-monthly.

756 **Chemical and Engineering News.**
Washington, DC: American Chemical Society, 1923- .
weekly.

757 **Civil Engineering.**
New York: American Society of Civil Engineers, 1930- .
monthly.

758 **IEEE Spectrum.**
New York: Institute of Electrical and Electronics Engineers,
1964- . monthly.

759 **Physics Today.**
New York: American Institute of Physics, 1948- . monthly.

Each of the many disciplines of science and technology has a representative professional society or organization, many of which publish journals. These provide information on current developments in the field, book reviews, reports of technical meetings, calendars of activities, and statistical information. This journal and the previously cited four publications are representative of such periodicals.

Literature

760 All the happy endings: a study of the domestic novel in America, the women who wrote it, the women who read it, in the nineteenth century.
Helen Papashvily.   New York: Harper & Row, 1956. 231p. bibliog.

A witty and entertaining study of the 'domestic novel' of the 19th century, viewing the sentiments it expressed, the feminine role it established, and the women who read it. The author provides a sociological look at the time, and shows how the status of women was quietly recorded in the domestic novel.

761 America begins: early American writing.
Edited by Richard Mercer Dorson.   New York: Pantheon, 1950. 438p. bibliog.

An anthology of American authors who wrote during the 17th and 18th centuries. Their work reflects America's early years and includes mythology, folklore and superstition.

762 American authors and books; 1640 to the present day.
W. Burke, Will D. Howe, augmented and revised by Irving R. Weiss.   New York: Crown, 1962. 834p.

A comprehensive directory of American authors and works, providing a wealth of information on obscure as well as prominent authors (biographies, lists of works, poems, digests of novels, etc.). This volume is an indispensable reference for any library.

763 The American 1890s: life and times of a lost generation.
Larzer Ziff.   New York: Viking Press, 1966. 376p.

The author portrays the 1890s as a decade filled with writers of a 'lost generation', and traces their literary careers and analyses their work in light of the time. He discusses such authors as Hamlin Garland, Ambrose Bierce and Stephen Crane, and provides us with a lively account of the period.

Literature

764 **The American Heritage history of the writers' America.**
Marshall B. Davidson. New York: American Heritage,
1973. 403p. (Distributed by McGraw-Hill).
A beautifully illustrated survey of American literature which makes good general reading on the subject.

765 **American Indian prose and poetry: we wait in the darkness.**
Edited by Gloria B. Levitas, Frank Robert Vivelo,
Jacqueline J. Vivelo. New York: G. P. Putnam's Sons,
1974. 325p. bibliog.
An anthology of American Indian writings divided into works dating from before the white man's arrival, after it, and contemporary times. Included is a collection of oral material and folklore.

766 **American literary naturalism: a reassessment.**
Edited by Yoshinobu Hakutani, Lewis Fried. Heidleberg,
GFR: Carl Winter, 1975. 207p. bibliog. (Anglistische
Forschungen: Heft 109).
A series of essays written by a number of scholars, each discussing a naturalist in American literature. Some authors analysed are Stephen Crane, Henry Adams, John Steinbeck and Theodore Dreiser.

767 **American Literature: a Journal of Literary History, Criticism
and Bibliography.**
Durham, North Carolina: Duke University Press, 1928- .
quarterly.
Each issue contains about a half-dozen articles on various aspects of American literary history, criticism and bibliography, as well as a bibliography of articles appearing in current periodicals. This publication is sponsored by the Modern Language Association's American literature section.

768 **The American novel: from James Fenimore Cooper to
William Faulkner.**
Edited by Wallace Earle Stegner. New York: Basic Books,
1965. 236p.
A collection of essays written by sixteen authorities on the American novel, originally designed for oral presentation over the Voice of America. The essays lack a unified theme and instead present a variety of viewpoints on the nineteen American novelists who are discussed.

769 **American poetry.**
Edited by Gay Wilson Allen, Walter B. Rideout, James K.
Robinson. New York: Harper & Row, 1965. 1,274p.
This anthology of American poetry is intended for both the student and the general reader, and it contains representative selections from colonial times to the present day. The book is arranged chronologically, and provides a biographical sketch of each poet whose works are represented as well as notes on the works.

770 **The American Puritan imagination: essays in revaluation.**
Edited by Sacvan Bercovitch. New York: Cambridge
University Press, 1974. 265p. bibliog.
A collection of essays by a number of authors on the literary achievements of the
Puritan colonists. The book contains both general articles and those discussing
individual literary figures such as William Bradford or Anne Bradstreet.

771 **American transcendentalism: an anthology of criticism.**
Edited by Brian M. Barbour. Notre Dame, Indiana:
University of Notre Dame Press, 1973. 302p. bibliog.
Contains a collection of seventeen critical essays on the transcendentalist movement in America in the 19th century. The essays cover a broad range of subjects,
including the vocabulary of the movement, its attitude towards nature, its place in
the history of ideas, and its theological aspects. This is a useful addition to any
literary collection.

772 **American treasury, 1455-1955.**
Edited by Clifton Fadiman, assisted by Charles Van
Doren. New York: Harper & Row, 1955. 1,108p.
An anthology of poetry and prose which is enjoyable reading as well as a reference book of American quotations. Included are selections from 1,300 authors,
arranged in three sections: 'We look at ourselves and our country'; 'Poets and
versifiers'; and 'Various Americans on things in general'. Includes useful indexes
of subjects, familiar words and phrases, authors and titles.

773 **American writers: a collection of literary biographies.**
Edited by Leonard Unger. New York: Charles Scribner's
Sons, 1974. 4 vols.
The essays in this work were originally published as a series called the University
of Minnesota Pamphlets on American Writers, and appeared from 1959 to 1972.
Each essay provides an account of the author's career, giving biographical
information and analyses and interpretations of individual works.

774 **American writing in the twentieth century.**
Willard Thorp. Cambridge, Massachusetts: Harvard
University Press, 1960. 353p. bibliog. (Library of Congress
Series in American Civilization).
A comprehensive survey of American literature during the first half of the century. The book is arranged chronologically as well as topically, and its greatest
value is in the large number of authors and works which are included. The author
has devoted one chapter to the 'Southern Renaissance' because of the prolific
work produced in the region during this period.

775 **And I worked at the writer's trade: chapters of literary
history, 1918-1978.**
Malcolm Cowley. New York: Viking Press, 1978. 276p.
An interesting history by a leading critic who writes from the experience of sixty
years on the American literary scene. The author recreates the literary world

Literature

from the First World War and carries his narrative to the 1970s. A fascinating look at literary figures by a critic who was their contemporary.

776 The art of Southern fiction: a study of some modern novelists.
Frederick John Hoffman. Carbondale, Illinois: Southern Illinois University Press; London, Amsterdam: Feffer & Simons, 1967. 198p. (Crosscurrents: Modern Critiques).

A study of the younger, more contemporary writers of Southern fiction; it puts aside discussion of William Faulkner's work in favour of that of his contemporaries. The author examines such authors as Eudora Welty, Carson McCullers, James Agee, Flannery O'Connor and William Styron.

777 The beat generation.
Bruce Cook. New York: Charles Scribner's Sons, 1971. 248p.

An informative and readable literary history of the writers of the 1950s known as the 'Beats', the forerunners of the hippies and protest generation of the 1960s. The author interviewed such figures as Jack Kerouac, Gregory Corso and Allen Ginsberg, and his portraits of these men and their work make interesting reading.

778 Bibliographical guide to the study of the literature of the U.S.A.
Clarence Louis Frank Gohdes. Durham, North Carolina: Duke University Press, 1976. 4th ed. rev. and enl. 173p.

An invaluable guide for research in American literature, this book includes works in history, art, religion, etc. The fourth edition has over 400 new titles, and has updated the earlier entries. A useful reference for students of American literature.

779 Bibliography of American literature.
Jacob Nathaniel Blanck. New Haven, Connecticut: Yale University Press, 1955-73. 6 vols.

A selective bibliography of American authors from the federal period to 1930. The work is arranged alphabetically by author, and the information on each author entered chronologically. Such information includes first editions of books and pamphlets and any other books which contained the first appearance of a work; reprints containing changes; and a selected list of biographical, bibliographical, and critical works.

780 Black American writers past and present: a biographical and bibliographical dictionary.
Theressa Gunnels Rush, Carol Fairbanks Myers, Esther Spring Arata. Metuchen, New Jersey: Scarecrow Press, 1975. 2 vols. bibliog.

A useful reference providing biographical and bibliographical information about more than 2,000 black American writers from the early 1700s to the present. Included are photographs and quotations from the writers on their ideas and philosophies.

781 **Black fiction.**
Roger Rosenblatt. Cambridge, Massachusetts: Harvard
University Press, 1974. 211p. bibliog.
This work differs from many studies of black fiction in that it is primarily a work
of literary criticism rather than a sociological study. The author analyses the
work of such authors as Richard Wright, James Baldwin, Ralph Ellison and
Langston Hughes, and includes many textual references to illustrate his points.

782 **Black writers of the thirties.**
James O. Young. Baton Rouge, Louisiana: Louisiana State
University Press, 1973. 257p. bibliog.
A scholarly study of the work of black writers who published during the Depres-
sion years. This work examines poetry and novels, and provides a useful history of
the time as reflected in these works.

783 **Bright book of life: American novelists and storytellers from
Hemingway to Mailer.**
Alfred Kazin. Boston, Massachusetts: Little, Brown, 1973.
334p.
Examines American fiction since 1940, selectively discussing one or two books by
each author and bringing out the essence of the novelists' work. This book is a
welcome addition to any American literature collection, as it sorts out current
trends and clarifies critical generalizations.

784 **The Cambridge history of American literature.**
Edited by William Peterfield Trent, John Erskine, Stuart P.
Sherman, Charles Van Doren. New York: Macmillan;
Cambridge, England: Cambridge University Press, 1917. 3
vols. in 1; New York: G. P. Putnam's Sons, 1917-21. 4 vols.
bibliog.
A comprehensive and authoritative reference work on American writers from the
colonial period to the 20th century. It contains sixty-four contributions by distinguished American scholars. The one-volume edition is a reprint which is complete
except for the extensive bibliographies available in the original four-volume set.
One of these editions is a must for every reference collection.

785 **Cavalcade of the American novel: from the birth of the nation
to the middle of the twentieth century.**
Edward Charles Wagenknecht. New York: Holt, Rinehart
& Winston, 1952. 575p. bibliog.
A highly readable, informative study of the American novel from colonial times
to mid-20th century. The author provides an interpretive survey and includes an
appendix which contains notes on some novelists not discussed in the main body
of the book. This book will be useful to both the student and the general reader.

Literature

786 **A certain morbidness: a view of American literature.**
Edward Stone. Carbondale, Illinois: Southern Illinois
University Press; London: Feffer & Simons, 1968. 183p.
bibliog. (Crosscurrents: Modern Critiques).

A series of studies of the works of a number of authors: Herman Melville, Henry
James, Stephen Crane, Robert Frost, William Faulkner and J. D. Salinger. The
studies explore the psychology of the morbid or irrational characters included in
their writings.

787 **The chief glory of every people: essays on classic American
writers.**
Edited by Matthew Joseph Bruccoli. Carbondale, Illinois:
Southern Illinois University Press, 1973. 295p. bibliog.

A series of critical essays on the work of the following classic American writers:
James Fenimore Cooper, Stephen Crane, John Dewey, Ralph Waldo Emerson,
Nathaniel Hawthorne, William Dean Howells, Washington Irving, Herman Mel-
ville, William Gilmore Simms, Henry Thoreau, Mark Twain and Walt Whitman.
The essays are written by scholars in the field, and give a modern perspective to
the works discussed.

788 **Comic relief: humor in contemporary American literature.**
Edited by Sarah Blacker Cohen. Urbana, Illinois:
University of Illinois Press, 1978. 339p. bibliog.

An interesting collection of essays discussing American humour of the 1950s and
1960s. The work includes analyses of the comedy of such authors as Vladimir
Nabokov, Philip Roth, Kurt Vonnegut and Saul Bellow, as well as material on
such comic forms as black comedy, ethnic humour, etc.

789 **Contemporary American literature, 1945-1972.**
Ihab Habib Hassan. New York: Frederick Ungar, 1973.
194p.

A compact, critical survey of American literature since 1945. The author deals
with short stories; science fiction; trends in fiction such as the war novel, the
Southern novel, the Jewish novel and the black novel; and poetry and drama. This
is a very useful introduction to the subject.

790 **Crowell's handbook of contemporary American poetry.**
Karl Malkoff. New York: Thomas Y. Crowell, 1973. 338p.
bibliog.

This handbook is a comprehensive guide to modern American poetry, covering
many poets, discussing movements and schools of poetry and containing a bibliography of works by the poets included. A recommended addition to all collections
on the subject.

791 **Cycle of American literature: an essay in historical criticism.**
Robert Ernest Spiller. New York: Macmillan, 1955. 318p.
A study of American literary history, tracing cycles of interpretation, and relating the writings to the growth of the nation. This work is a scholarly discussion which will be useful to any student of the subject.

792 **Cyclopedia of American literature embracing personal and critical notices of authors, and selections from their writings, from the earliest period to the present, with portraits, autographs, and other illustrations.**
Evert Augustus Duyckinck, George L. Duyckinck. Detroit, Michigan: Gale Research, 1965. 2 vols.
A reprint of a work originally published in 1875 by William Rutter. It is arranged chronologically and covers the period 1626-1875. This reference tool is still useful for its coverage of minor earlier writers in American literature.

793 **Desperate faith: a study of Bellow, Salinger, Mailer, Baldwin and Updike.**
Howard M. Harper. Chapel Hill, North Carolina: University of North Carolina Press, 1967. 200p.
The work of five contemporary writers is studied in order to show how each responds to the universal problems which he shares with those of his time. The book contains analyses of many individual works and finally places these authors in terms of traditional American fiction.

794 **Early Puritan writers: a reference guide: William Bradford, John Cotton, Thomas Hooker, Edward Johnson, Richard Mather, Thomas Shepard.**
Edward Joseph Gallagher, Thomas Werge. Boston, Massachusetts: G. K. Hall, 1976. 207p. (Reference Guides in Literature, no. 10).
A bibliography of the works of the writers named in the title.

795 **Fact and fiction: the new journalism and the nonfiction novel.**
John Hollowell. Chapel Hill, North Carolina: University of North Carolina Press, 1977. 190p. bibliog.
An interesting study of a new literary form that has developed since the Second World War: the non-fiction novel. This is a narrative style which fuses fictional and journalistic techniques in writing about events and personalities. One example is Truman Capote's *In cold blood* and Hollowell analyses this and other such works which emerged in the 1960s.

796 **Family reader of American masterpieces.**
Ralph Louis Woods. New York: Thomas Y. Crowell, 1959. 487p.
A collection of excerpts from every form of writing (novels, short stories, poetry, journalism, history, etc.) which contains representative pieces from a great many

important American writers. The book is arranged by geographical sections of the country, and within these sections the selections are placed in chronological order.

797 **The ferment of realism: American literature 1884-1919.**
Warner Berthoff. New York: Free Press, 1965. 330p. bibliog.

Deals with the literary history of the period, tracing the currents of realism, regionalism and other aspects of the literature of 1884-1919. The author discusses the novel as the chief form of the realists, and evaluates such writers as William Dean Howells, Mark Twain and Henry James. This book is the first volume of a series planned to treat the entire history of American literature; each volume is to be undertaken by an author specializing in the period covered.

798 **Fifteen modern American authors: a survey of research and criticism.**
Edited by Jackson R. Bryer. Durham, North Carolina: Duke University Press, 1969. 493p.

A useful reference which surveys the research and criticism on fifteen of the most important modern American writers, as selected by a poll of about 150 college and university teachers of American literature. The contributors to the volume are scholarly authorities on the figures they are discussing. The authors included are Sherwood Anderson, Willa Cather, Stephen Crane, Theodore Dreiser, T. S. Eliot, William Faulkner, F. Scott Fitzgerald, Robert Frost, Ernest Hemingway, Eugene O'Neill, Ezra Pound, E. A. Robinson, John Steinbeck, Wallace Stevens and Thomas Wolfe.

799 **Five novelists of the progressive era.**
Robert W. Schneider. New York: Columbia University Press, 1965. 290p.

An analysis of the work of William Dean Howells, Stephen Crane, Frank Norris, Theodore Dreiser, and Winston Churchill - all authors who wrote during the period between 1890 and the end of First World War. The author discusses the novelists' underlying commitment to the ideals of the 19th century, in contrast to their belief that they had thrown off the shackles of the past in their writing.

800 **The forties: fiction, poetry, drama.**
Edited by Warren French. Deland, Florida: Everett/Edwards, 1969. 330p. bibliog.

A collection of essays on the literature of the 1940s, arranged into two sections. The first section contains three long essays dealing with the fiction, drama and poetry engendered by the Second World War. The second part is arranged chronologically around the dates of events of literary importance. The book includes an appendix listing Pulitzer prizes for the 1940s, and there is also a biographical list of contributors.

801 **Frontier: American literature and the American West.**
Edwin S. Fussell. Princeton, New Jersey: Princeton University Press, 1965. 450p.

Studies the impact of the American West on six Eastern writers of the early 19th century: James Fenimore Cooper, Nathaniel Hawthorne, Herman Melville, Edgar

Allen Poe, Henry David Thoreau, and Walt Whitman. The author shows how these writers used the frontier as a symbol in their writings, and provides an interesting addition to the literary criticisms of the period.

802 **Gentlemen, scholars, and scoundrels: a treasury of the best of Harper's Magazine from 1850 to the present.**
Edited by Horace Knowles. New York: Harper's Magazine, 1959. 696p.
An anthology of writings that have appeared in *Harper's Magazine* over the years, including short stories, poems, and articles. Much good reading for the browser.

803 **The growth of American literature: a critical and historical survey.**
Edited by Edwin Harrison Cady, Frederick J. Hoffman, Roy Harvey Pearce. New York: American Book Company, 1956. 2 vols. bibliog. (American Literature Series).
An anthology of American literature, arranged chronologically, which relates the literature of each era to the culture of the time. Included are introductory essays discussing the period and some biographical details of the authors presented.

804 **Guide to American literature and its backgrounds since 1890.**
Howard Mumford Jones, Richard M. Ludwig. Cambridge, Massachusetts: Harvard University Press, 1972. 4th ed. rev. and enl. 264p.
A selective bibliography in two parts, covering American literature since 1890. The first half provides a list of books on the backgrounds of American literature, an annotated list of magazines of concern to the student of American literature, and a chronological list of the chief historical events from 1890-1971. The second half lists important titles in modern American literature, arranged by period, and divided into fifty-two reading lists.

805 **The Harlem renaissance remembered: essays, edited with a memoir.**
Arna Wendell Bontemps. New York: Dodd, Mead, 1972. 310p. bibliog.
Arna Bontemps was one of a number of black writers who contributed to what was known as the 'Harlem renaissance' in the 1920s. In this book, the author provides a picture of the era, some informative appraisals and profiles of writers of the time (Langston Hughes, Wallace Thurman, Theophilus Lewis) and a collection of essays which were the result of a study at Yale University on the Harlem renaissance.

806 **Harvest of change: American literature, 1865-1914.**
Jay Martin. Englewood Cliffs, New Jersey: Prentice-Hall, 1967. 382p.
Studies the years between the Civil War and the First World War, and discusses the influence of ideological and social changes on the writers of the time. Martin

shows how authors such as Henry James, Mark Twain, Edward Bellamy, Theodore Dreiser, etc. created new literary forms and used literary themes to reflect the new forces of the time.

807 A homemade world: the American modernist writers.
Hugh Kenner. New York: Knopf, 1975. 221p.

A witty, perceptive, critical book on the work of six American writers: William Faulkner, Wallace Stevens, William Carlos Williams, Marianne Moore, Ernest Hemingway and F. Scott Fitzgerald.

808 The image of the Jew in American literature: from early republic to mass immigration.
Louis Harap. Philadelphia: Jewish Publication Society of America, 1974. 586p. bibliog.

An exhaustive study of the image of the Jew as portrayed in American poetry and fiction from colonial days to the end of the 1800s.

809 Images of the Negro in American literature.
Edited by Seymour Lee Gross, John Edward Hardy. Chicago: University of Chicago Press, 1966. 321p. bibliog. (Patterns of Literary Criticism).

A collection of sixteen critical articles on the work of both black and white authors who have dealt with the blacks in fiction and poetry from colonial times to the present. The first part of the book contains a historical introduction and essays on broad historical periods; the second deals with the black as portrayed by individual authors: e.g. Mark Twain, Langston Hughes, Eudora Welty and James Baldwin.

810 Imaginary gardens: a study of five American poets.
Rosemary Sprague. Philadelphia: Chilton, 1969. 237p.

Examines the poetry of Emily Dickinson, Amy Lowell, Sara Teasdale, Edna St. Vincent Millay and Marianne Moore, and shows how each poet expressed her attitudes toward life and poetry.

811 The inclusive flame: studies in American poetry.
Glauco Cambon. Bloomington, Indiana: Indiana University Press, 1963. 258p. bibliog.

The author, an Italian, originally published this book in Italy in 1956, and he later translated it for an American audience. It brings a fresh approach to the study of American literature and includes studies of the work of Edwin Arlington Robinson, Wallace Stevens, Hart Crane, William Carlos Williams and Robert Lowell.

812 An introduction to American literature.

Jorge Luis Borges, translated and edited by L. Clark Keating, Robert O. Evans. Lexington, Kentucky: University Press of Kentucky, 1971. 94p.

An interesting short work by an Argentine essayist and author. This book is meant to be read as a long essay, for it has no index which limits its use as a reference work. It provides a brief guide to the literature of the United States, and includes such areas as science fiction, detective stories and Westerns, as well as the more traditional forms.

813 A library of literary criticism: modern American literature.

Edited by Dorothy Nyren. New York: Frederick Ungar, 1960. 552p.

An invaluable reference which surveys literary criticism of the works of 170 American authors who became famous after 1900. The critical excerpts are chronologically arranged, and the full bibliographical information leads the reader to the source should more detail be required. The list is selective and attempts to reflect the variety of critical standards of the period.

814 The literary decade.

Allen Churchill. Englewood Cliffs, New Jersey: Prentice-Hall, 1971. 329p. bibliog.

A breezy popular account of the American literary scene during the 1920s. It contains profiles of personalities and the plots of the major novels of the time. The author states that his aim is to present a picture of commercial publishing in the 1920s and to portray it in a popular style.

815 Literary history of the United States.

Edited by Robert E. Spiller, Willard Thorp, Thomas H. Johnson, Henry Seidel Canby, Richard M. Ludwig. New York: Macmillan; London: Collier-Macmillan, 1963. 3rd rev. ed. 2 vols. bibliog.

A comprehensive literary history, originally published in three volumes in 1948; it was later updated with two additional chapters, one on the period between the two world wars, and the other on the era since 1945. Fifty-seven scholars contributed to the work, and they examine all forms of American literature. Volume two provides a bibliographical supplement divided into four main sections: guide to resources; literature and culture; movements and influences; individual authors. An essential item for every reference collection.

816 Literary transcendentalism; style and vision in the American renaissance.

Lawrence Buell. Ithaca, New York: Cornell University Press, 1973. 336p. bibliog.

A fresh look at the subject of transcendentalism, giving attention to principles and theories of the movement and to particular works and individuals. This study is worthwhile reading for the scholar in the field.

Literature

817 Main currents in American thought.
Vernon Louis Parrington. New York: Harcourt Brace Jovanovich, 1958. 3 vols.

The first two volumes of this work brought the author the Pulitzer prize for history in 1928. Volume one covers 1620-1800, volume two 1800-60; volume three deals with 1860-1920 and was incomplete at the time of the author's death in 1929, but it was posthumously published as a fragment in 1930. This is a reprint of an important scholarly work which examines the history of men and ideas throughout American literature.

818 Major writers of America.
Edited by Perry Miller. New York: Harcourt, Brace & World, 1962. 2 vols.

An anthology for the student of American literature, as well as for the general reader. Each contributor presents the works of a particular author and provides introductory information.

819 Major writers of early American literature.
Edited by Everett H. Emerson. Madison, Wisconsin: University of Wisconsin Press, 1972. 301p.

A collection of essays by specialists in the field, providing a chronological survey of almost 200 years of American literature. Included are studies of such early writers as Anne Bradstreet, Cotton Mather and Benjamin Franklin. An important addition to collections on American literature.

820 Makers and finders: a history of the writer in America, 1800-1915.
Van Wyck Brooks. New York: E. P. Dutton, 1940-53. 5 vols.

Vol. 1: *World of Washington Irving*, 1944. 495p.; vol. 2: *Flowering of New England, 1815-1865*, 1940. 550p.; vol. 3: *Times of Melville and Whitman*, 1953. 499p.; vol. 4: *New England: Indian summer*, 1940. 557p.; vol. 5: *Confident years, 1885-1915*, 1952. 627p. These volumes comprise a scholarly and impressive study which provides a cultural history as well as literary criticism. The authors discussed are depicted in terms of the environment in which they wrote. An invaluable addition to any collection of American literature.

821 A many-windowed house: collected essays on American writers and American writing.
Malcolm Cowley. Carbondale, Illinois: Southern Illinois University Press, 1970. 261p.

A collection of Malcolm Cowley's critical essays on 19th and early 20th century American writers. The author's style and theories on literary criticism make this book appealing to the general reader as well as to the scholar.

822 Modern American literature.

Edited by Dorothy Nyren Curley. New York: Frederick
Ungar, 1969. 4th enl. ed. 3 vols. bibliog. (Library of
Literary Criticism).

A standard reference which includes an alphabetical list of American authors
from the early 1900s to the present. Each name is followed by excerpts of
significant criticism of the author's works, arranged in chronological sequence.

823 Modern American poetry: essays in criticism.

Edited by Jerome Mazzaro. New York: David McKay,
1970. 368p. bibliog.

An anthology of essays on fifteen American poets written by contemporary
American critics. It gives the student of modern American poetry a critical
insight into the work of the poets represented, as well as representing a variety of
critical techniques.

824 Modern black poets: a collection of critical essays.

Edited by Donald B. Gibson. Englewood Cliffs, New
Jersey: Prentice-Hall, 1973. 181p. (Twentieth Century
Views).

A collection of essays on black poetry, beginning with the 'Harlem renaissance' of
the 1920s, and continuing through to an analysis of the contemporary 'hate'
poetry of some modern black poets.

825 Naked and fiery forms: modern American poetry by women: a new tradition.

Suzanne Juhasz. New York: Octagon, 1976. 212p. bibliog.

An interesting study of the role of the 20th century woman poet and of the
development of what the author calls a 'new tradition': a feminine rather than a
masculine expression of the culture in which the poet lives. Juhasz discusses the
work of such poets as Emily Dickinson and Marianne Moore.

826 Native sons: a critical study of twentieth-century Negro American authors.

Edward Margolies. Philadelphia: J. B. Lippincott, 1968.
210p. bibliog.

A study of a number of black authors, concentrating mainly on works written
since 1940. Their work is discussed in terms of what it reveals about the quality
of American life. Some of the authors included are Richard Wright, James Baldwin and Langston Hughes.

827 The oblique light: studies in literary history and biography.

Robert Ernst Spiller. New York: Macmillan, 1968. 279p.

A collection of essays by a well-known scholar of American literature. In this
volume the author has gathered a number of his articles which he feels have
contributed to a reinterpretation of some major American writers. He discusses
such figures as James Fenimore Cooper, Henry Adams and Ralph Waldo Emer-

son. In an earlier volume, *The third dimension* (1965), he attempted to define the art of literary historiography.

828 Our literary heritage: a pictorial history of the writer in America.
Van Wyck Brooks, Otto L. Bettman. New York: E. P. Dutton, 1956. 241p.

This abridgment of *Makers and finders* (q.v.) retains some of the information contained in the original set, but the emphasis has been changed to include illustrations. The book will please those who enjoy pictorial Americana, and it preserves the main theme of Van Wyck Brooks' original work.

829 The Oxford companion to American literature.
James D. Hart. New York: Oxford University Press, 1965. 4th ed. 991p.

The latest edition of a standard reference which provides a guide to American authors and their writings. The author includes entries on non-literary aspects of the American scene which are reflected in American literature. Following the main alphabetical listing is a year-by-year outline of the social and literary history summarized in the book.

830 The Penguin companion to American literature.
Edited by Malcolm Bradbury, Eric Mottram, Jean Franco. New York: McGraw-Hill; Harmondsworth, England: Penguin, 1971. 384p. bibliog. (Penguin Companion to World Literature).

Another useful reference work which provides an alphabetical listing, concentrating mainly on critical biographies but with a few subject and title entries. The period covered ranges from colonial times to the present. The contributors come from both sides of the Atlantic, often lending a slightly different cultural or critical point of view.

831 The poetry of American women from 1632 to 1945.
Emily Stipes Watts. Austin, Texas: University of Texas Press, 1977. 218p. bibliog. (Dan Danciger Publication Series).

An attempt to define the poetic contributions of American women; it provides chronological surveys of the following periods: 1632-1758, 1735-1804, 1800-50, 1850-1900 and 1900-45. Professor Watts investigates the work of both major and minor poets, and examines the poetry for women's themes, as contrasted with traditional masculine concerns.

832 Proletarian writers of the thirties.
Edited by David Madden. Carbondale, Illinois: Southern Illinois University Press, 1968. 278p. (Crosscurrents: Modern Critiques).

A collection of essays by a variety of critics on the writings of such authors as John Dos Passos, Jack Conroy, B. Traven and others classified as 'proletarian'

writers. In his introduction, Madden discusses the meaning of the term 'proletarian', and the essays explore the portrayal of the 'bottom dog' in the poetry,
novels and criticism of the 1930s.

833 Prose and poetry of the revolution: the establishment of the nation, 1765-1789.
Edited by Frederick Clarke Prescott, John H. Nelson. Port
Washington, New York: Kennikat Press, 1969. 266p.

An anthology of prose and poetry written by American writers during the revolutionary period, and reflecting the spirit of the time. This is a reprint of the 1925
edition.

834 The pulps: fifty years of American pop culture.
Edited by Tony Goodstone. New York: Chelsea House,
1970. 239p. bibliog.

An interesting collection of stories, advertisements, covers and features from the
pulp magazines which flourished during the first half of this century. The magazines ranged from sports to science fiction, and included are stories from such
famous authors as Paul Gallico, Dashiell Hammett and Ray Bradbury. The
author provides some informative introductions and notes on the various areas
covered.

835 The reader's encyclopedia of American literature.
Max J. Herzberg. New York: Thomas Y. Crowell, 1962.
1,280p.

A useful one-volume quick-reference work on American literature. It includes
articles on authors, works, persons, places and events in literature; literary movements, groups and events; genealogical charts; and a glossary of literary terms.

836 Realism and naturalism in nineteenth-century American literature.
Donald Pizer. Carbondale, Illinois: Southern Illinois
University Press, 1966. 176p. bibliog. (Crosscurrents:
Modern Critiques).

A collection of essays, some of which appeared previously in literary magazines,
on 19th century American authors and literary criticism. A valuable study of
realism and naturalism in American literature.

837 The romance in America: studies in Cooper, Poe, Hawthorne, Melville, and James.
Joel Porter. Middletown, Connecticut: Wesleyan University
Press, 1969. 235p.

A scholary and highly readable work on the American romance, as shown in the
works of five writers of the 19th century. Porter studies individual works in great
detail and shows the authors' use of conventional figures, symbols, etc., to explore
human motivation, history, nature, and similar themes.

838 **The Saturday Review gallery; in which some of the outstanding writers of recent years present reminiscences and biographical portraits of important and striking figures who have appeared in or near the literary scene over the past century.**
New York: Simon & Schuster, 1959. 481p.

An interesting collection of biographical pieces which have appeared in the *Saturday Review* over the years. Portraits of such literary figures as William Faulkner, James Joyce, Edith Hamilton and James Thurber are included.

839 **A second flowering: works and days of the lost generation.**
Malcolm Cowley. New York: Viking Press, 1973. 276p.

Cowley discusses eight figures of the 'lost generation': F. Scott Fitzgerald, Ernest Hemingway, John Dos Passos, E. E. Cummings, Thornton Wilder, William Faulkner, Thomas Wolfe and Hart Crane. As a contemporary of these great literary figures, the author provides us with personal portraits of the men themselves as well as with long-range critical evaluations of their work.

840 **Selected essays.**
Robert Penn Warren. New York: Random House, 1958. 305p.

An interesting selection of essays by a well-known novelist who is also a gifted literary critic. Warren wrote most of these essays in the 1940s and they include analyses of the works of such writers as William Faulkner, Ernest Hemingway, Eudora Welty, Herman Melville, and many others.

841 **Seven American stylists from Poe to Mailer: an introduction.**
Edited by George Thaddeus Wright. Minneapolis, Minnesota: University of Minnesota Press, 1973. 318p. (Minnesota Library on American Writers).

The theme linking these seven essays on American writers is their use of language and style in a manner which might label them as 'poet'. The writers discussed are Edgar Allan Poe, George Santayana, Stephen Crane, Gertrude Stein, Vladimir Nabokov, Robert Penn Warren, and Norman Mailer.

842 **Seven modern American poets: an introduction.**
Edited by Leonard Unger. Minneapolis, Minnesota: University of Minnesota Press, 1967. 303p. (University of Minnesota Pamphlets on American Writers).

The poets discussed in this critical volume are Robert Frost, Wallace Stevens, William Carlos Williams, Ezra Pound, John Crowe Ransom, T. S. Eliot, and Allen Tate. It includes biographical material about the poets and critical discussions of their work. A useful addition to collections requiring material on modern American poetry.

843 **A short history of American poetry.**
Donald Barlow Stauffer. New York: E. P. Dutton, 1974.
459p. bibliog.
A survey of American poetry from colonial times to the present. The author has
provided biographical and historical information as well as samples of the poets'
work. A useful addition to any American literature collection.

844 **Six American novelists of the nineteenth century: an
introduction.**
Edited by Richard Foster. Minneapolis, Minnesota:
University of Minnesota Press, 1968. 270p. bibliog.
The essays in this volume on James Fenimore Cooper, Nathaniel Hawthorne,
Herman Melville, Mark Twain, William Dean Howells and Henry James are
based on material from the University of Minnesota Pamphlets on American
Writers series. The book includes biographical information about the writers and
critical discussions of their work.

845 **Southern fiction today: renascence and beyond.**
Edited by George Core. Athens, Georgia: University of
Georgia Press, 1969. 102p. (Reynolds Lectures, 1968).
A series of essays by three critics of Southern fiction, plus a lively symposium in
which the three exchange points of view. Some of the authors discussed are
William Faulkner, Thomas Wolfe, Robert Penn Warren, William Styron and
Flannery O'Connor.

846 **Southern renascence: the literature of the modern South.**
Edited by Louis Decimus Rubin, Robert D.
Jacobs. Baltimore, Maryland: Johns Hopkins Press, 1953.
450p.
A collection of essays on Southern culture and literature, most of which originally
appeared in the *Hopkins Review*. The book is divided into four parts: 'The mind
of the South'; 'The themes of Southern literature'; 'The novelists of the South';
and 'The poetry of the South'.

847 **The strenuous age in American literature.**
Grant Cochran Knight. Chapel Hill, North Carolina:
University of North Carolina Press, 1954. 270p. bibliog.
A sequel to the author's *The critical period in American literature* (1951) which
dealt with the period from 1890 to 1900. This volume covers 1900 to 1910 and
provides a scholarly survey of writing of the period, including best-selling fiction
and minor writers not covered elsewhere.

848 **Symbolism and American literature.**
Charles Feidelson. Chicago: University of Chicago Press,
1953. 355p. bibliog.
A study of the use of symbolism in American literature from the 17th to the 19th
century. The four symbolists discussed are Nathaniel Hawthorne, Walt Whitman,
Herman Melville and Edgar Allen Poe.

849 **The territory ahead: critical interpretations in American literature.**
Wright Morris.   New York: Harcourt, Brace, 1958. 231p.
Reprinted, Lincoln, Nebraska: University of Nebraska Press, 1978. 245p.
An interesting and very readable work of literary criticism on the works of authors such as Herman Melville, Mark Twain, Ernest Hemingway, F. Scott Fitzgerald, William Faulkner and many others.

850 **A time of harvest, American literature, 1910-1960.**
Edited by Robert Ernest Spiller.   New York: Hill & Wang, 1962. 173p. (American Century Series, AC50).
This small volume of fifteen essays by distinguished literary historians discusses the rise and fall of naturalism in American literature during the first half of the 20th century. All aspects of this period of writing are covered, including the novel, drama, humour, etc. An interesting analysis.

851 **Trials of the world: essays in American literature and the humanistic tradition.**
Richard Warrington Baldwin Lewis.   New Haven, Connecticut: Yale University Press, 1965. 239p.
An interesting collection of essays examining American literature of the 19th and early 20th century. Lewis examines the approaches to religion of the authors and also considers their personal consciousness. He discusses writers such as Walt Whitman, Henry James, and Edith Wharton, and explores their work in the context of cultural history.

852 **The twenties: American writing in the postwar decade.**
Frederick John Hoffman.   New York: Viking Press, 1955. 466p. bibliog.
A definitive guide to American writing in the 1920s. The author analyses the work of such writers as Ezra Pound, Ernest Hemingway, John Dos Passos, William Faulkner and Hart Crane, and provides a scholarly work for students of the period.

853 **The unwritten war: American writers and the Civil War.**
Daniel Aaron.   New York: Knopf, 1973. 385p. bibliog. (Impact of the Civil War).
An interesting and well-documented study of attitudes towards the American Civil War as represented by Northern and Southern writers. The author explores letters, diaries, essays, poems, novels and short stories, and explains how the Civil War influenced American literature.

854 **Vulnerable people: a view of American fiction since 1945.**
Josephine Hendin.   New York: Oxford University Press, 1978. 237p.
The author explores the fictional treatment of vulnerability in such areas as sexual mores, people's aspirations, and the desire for self-improvement. She dis-

cusses some two dozen contemporary novelists including Thomas Pynchon, John Barth, Joyce Carol Oates, John Updike, and Saul Bellow.

855 **The way of the new world: the black novel in America.**
Addison Gayle, Jr.   Garden City, New York: Anchor Press, 1975. 339p. bibliog.
This book, in contrast to Rosenblatt's *Black fiction* (q.v.), discusses black fiction in America in terms of its sociological orientation. The author discusses about thirty novels from the point of view of the writers' political, social and historical experiences.

856 **A world elsewhere: the place of style in American literature.**
Richard Poirier.   New York: Oxford University Press, 1966. 257p.
This book offers a different viewpoint for studying American literature: that of analysing style (language, grammar, literary form) rather than trends (realism, naturalism, etc.). The author cites examples from many familiar literary passages, but gives them an original interpretation.

857 **Writers and partisans: a history of literary radicalism in America.**
James Burkhart Gilbert.   New York: John Wiley & Sons, 1968. 303p. bibliog. (American Cultural History Series).
A history of the magazine *Partisan Review*, discussing its role in literary radicalism in the 20th century, from 1911 to the Second World War. The book examines the effect on writing of the various political 'isms', e.g. communism, pacifism, McCarthyism, etc.

858 **Writers on the left, episodes in American literary communism.**
Daniel Aaron.   New York: Harcourt, Brace & World, 1961. 460p.
The author reconstructs the milieu of the 1920s and 1930s in order to show why many American intellectuals of the time blended art and politics, and espoused the communist cause. He describes what caused some writers to resist the pull of radical politics, others to listen for a while and then become disillusioned, and the few to maintain their communist beliefs.

Folklore

859 **American folk medicine.**
Edited by Clarence Meyer. New York: Thomas Y. Crowell, 1973. 206p. bibliog.

An interesting collection in which to browse for the flavour of American folk medicine. The author has collected home remedies used since the pioneer days, and has listed them alphabetically by the complaint to be cured. An introductory chapter describes folk medicine tradition.

860 **American folklife.**
Edited by Don Yoder. Austin, Texas: University of Texas Press, 1976. 304p. bibliog.

A scholarly collection of essays on American traditions, intended to give an understanding of regional and ethnic differences and folk-ways. Various topics are explored, including folk religion, stories and beliefs.

861 **American folklore: a bibliography, 1950-1974.**
Cathleen C. Flanagan, John T. Flanagan. Metuchen, New Jersey: Scarecrow Press, 1974. 406p.

A useful bibliography containing over 3,500 entries, arranged alphabetically by author, and covering fourteen categories, including ballads, myths, superstitions, and folk heroes. Included is a list of obituaries of well-known folklorists.

862 **American folklore and legend.**
Pleasantville, New York: Reader's Digest, 1978. 448p.

A popular sampling of folk-tales and essays on American folk traditions and customs, designed to entertain and inform the reading public. Included in this richly illustrated volume is a state-by-state listing of folk events held annually in the United States, with information on the location, the event and where to obtain further details.

863 The American folklore reader: folklore in American literature.
Edited by John Theodore Flanagan, Arthur Palmer Hudson. New York: Barnes & Noble, 1958. 511p.

A rich collection of Americana, including selections of prose and verse containing superstition, tall tales, heroes and demigods, and folk wisdom. Included are little-known writings and work by such authors as Edgar Allen Poe, Washington Irving, Carl Sandburg and Stephen Vincent Benet.

864 Book of Negro folklore.
Edited by Langston Hughes, Arna Wendell Bontemps. New York: Dodd, Mead, 1958. 624p.

A rich collection of black folklore which covers a variety of material. Some of the topics represented are animal tales, ghost stories, spirituals, gospel, blues, recollections of slavery, work songs, jazz, and Harlem jive.

865 Buying the wind: regional folklore in the United States.
Richard Mercer Dorson. Chicago: University of Chicago Press, 1964. 573p. bibliog.

Folklore collected from coastal Maine, Pennsylvanian Germans, southern Appalachian mountaineers, Louisiana Cajuns, Illinois Egyptians, Southwest Mexicans, and the Utah Mormons; the tales are relayed in the oral traditions of the native storytellers. The author provides useful introductions to the various collections, and has gathered much material not easily found in print.

866 Davy Crockett, American comic legend.
Edited by Richard Mercer Dorson. Westport, Connecticut: Greenwood Press, 1977. 171p. bibliog.

Excerpts from a series of *Crockett almanacs* published from 1835 to 1856; they were first issued in Nashville but later imprints ranged from New York to Louisville. These almanacs contained a wide variety of frontier lore, and characterized the legend of Davy Crockett. This volume is a reprint of the 1939 edition which was published by Rockland Editions of New York.

867 The Eskimo storyteller: folktales from Noatak, Alaska.
Edwin S. Hall. Knoxville, Tennessee: University of Tennessee Press, 1975. 491p. bibliog.

A scholarly collection of 188 folk tales of the Noatak people in northwestern Alaska. The tales emphasize the beliefs and values of the Eskimos. The author has provided analyses of the tales, autobiographies of the native storytellers, a glossary, and a sketch of the land and people.

868 Folklore from the working folks of America.
Edited by Tristram Potter Coffin, Hennig Cohen. Garden City, New York: Anchor Press, 1973. 464p.

A fascinating collection of stories, songs, riddles, games, folk expressions, superstitions, customs and festivals deriving from the American workers. Occupations represented include farmers, hunters, trappers, prospectors, teamsters, cab drivers, soldiers, and cowboys. Selections are taken from folklore journals and archives, and the sources are specified.

Folklore

869 **Folklore in America: tales, songs, superstitions, proverbs, riddles, games, folk drama and folk festivals.**
Edited by Tristram Potter Coffin, Hennig Cohen. Garden City, New York: Doubleday, 1966. 256p.
A fine introductory collection of folklore selected from seventy years' issues of the *Journal of American Folklore*. The editors have arranged the material in topical sections: tales, songs, superstitions, proverbs, riddles, games, and drama and festivals. Includes comments on each type of material presented.

870 **Folklore on the American land.**
Duncan Emrich. Boston, Massachusetts: Little, Brown, 1972. 707p. bibliog.
An encyclopaedic work illustrated with forty photographs, this collection of American folklore includes legends, folk-songs and ballads, children's folklore, superstitions, and many other topics.

871 **Ghosts along the Cumberland: deathlore in the Kentucky foothills.**
William Lynwood Montell. Knoxville, Tennessee: University of Tennessee Press, 1975. 240p.
A specialized work suitable for large folklore collections seeking material on folk beliefs of southern central Kentucky. Included are ghost tales, beliefs and stories about warnings of death, and lore concerning the dead and burial.

872 **The *Life* treasury of American folklore.**
New York: Time-Life, 1961. 348p. maps.
An illustrated collection of more than 150 stories, legends and sayings, with interpretive paintings by James Lewicki. Also includes a glossary and index providing information on many persons, places and events of American folklore.

873 **The nonsense book of riddles, rhymes, tongue twisters, puzzles and jokes from American folklore.**
Edited by Duncan Emrich, illustrated by Ib Ohlsson. New York: Four Winds Press, 1970. 266p.
An attractively illustrated source book on American children's lore, including autograph verses, ball-bouncing chants, riddles, etc.

874 **One potato, two potato...the recent education of American children.**
Mary Knapp, Herbert Knapp. New York: Norton, 1976. 274p.
Shows the uses children make of folklore in their lives and in learning to become members of adult society. Includes the chants, sayings, games, jokes, rhymes, etc., which are part of the child's world in America. The items were collected during the 1960s and 1970s, and most were obtained from more than one state, making this representative and current material.

875 **The parade of heroes: legendary figures in American lore.**
Edited by Tristram Potter Coffin, Hennig Cohen. Garden
City, New York: Anchor Press, 1978. 630p. bibliog.
A collection of songs, ballads, stories, rhymes and sayings about American folk
heroes, gathered from folk tradition and popular lore. The material was selected
from journals and other folklore society publications as well as from archives.

876 **Sidewalks of America: folklore, legends, sagas, traditions,
customs, songs, stories and sayings of city folk.**
Edited by Benjamin Albert Botkin. Indianapolis, Indiana:
Bobbs-Merrill, 1954. 605p.
A treasury of American folklore, legends, songs and customs, based on the city in
America. The view of urban America covers life from 1880 to the 1950s, and
makes nostalgic reading for anyone who has grown up in one of these cities, or
who has heard stories from grandparents, etc.

877 **The silver bullet and other American witch stories.**
Edited by Hubert J. Davis. Middle Village, New York:
Jonathan David, 1975. 231p.
This collection of folk-tales draws heavily on a project during the Depression
years of the 1930s known as the Virginia WPA Writers Project. A group of
reporters and authors travelled through the Appalachian Mountains and recorded
beliefs and traditions of the mountain people, with the intention of publishing a
book on Virginia folklore. Many of the stories gathered appear in this book,
which emphasizes the role which belief in witches played in these people's lives.

878 **A treasury of American anecdotes.**
Edited by Benjamin Albert Botkin. New York: Random
House, 1957. 321p.
An anthology of American story-telling and jokes, arranged according to story-
telling types, which include cracker barrel tales, whopper wit and spun yarns. The
book is fully indexed by author, title, person, place, type of story and theme and
also contains a full section of footnotes.

879 **Treasury of American folk humor.**
Edited by James Nathan Tidwell. New York: Crown,
1956. 620p.
A delightful anthology of folk humour, ranging from puns, tall tales and anecdotes to practical jokes and word play.

880 **A treasury of railroad folklore: the stories, tall tales,
traditions, ballads and songs of the American railroad men.**
Edited by Benjamin Albert Botkin, Alvin F. Harlow. New
York: Bonanza, 1953. 530p.
A collection of American railway lore, including stories, tall tales, traditions and
songs. The editors have attempted to recreate the railroader's life as shown
through his stories and songs.

Folklore

881 **The voice of the folk: folklore and American literary theory.**
Gene Bluestein.   Amherst, Massachusetts: University of
Massachusetts Press, 1972. 170p.

An interesting series of essays discussing the effects of folk literature and cultural
values on literary development in the USA. Included are chapters on creators of
folk traditions as well as on musical forms and story-telling and their embodiment
in the works of such literary figures as Whitman and Emerson.

882 **Voices in the valley: mythmaking and folk belief in the
shaping of the Middle West.**
Frank R. Kramer.   Madison, Wisconsin: University of
Wisconsin Press, 1964. 300p. bibliog.

A scholarly work which analyses the relationship between the folklore of various
ethnic groups and the propaganda value of these myths in real life.

Philosophy

883 **American philosophy in the twentieth century: a sourcebook
from pragmatism to philosophical analysis.**
Edited by Paul W. Kurtz. New York: Macmillan, 1966.
573p. bibliog. (Classics in the History of Thought).
A companion volume to the editor's *American thought before 1900* (q.v.), this
book contains works by philosophers from the late 19th century to the present
day. Includes such philosophers as Alfred North Whitehead, George Santayana,
Paul Tillich and Ernest Nagel, and such movements as pragmatism, humanism and
existentialism.

884 **American philosophy today and tomorrow.**
Edited by Horrace Meyer Kallen, Sidney Hook. Freeport,
New York: Books for Libraries Press, 1968. 518p. (Essay
Index Reprint Series).
A reprint of a 1935 collection presenting the views of twenty-five American
scholars of that time on problems and solutions confronting the philosopher. The
contributors represent a wide range of viewpoints, and the editors indicate that
they chose for inclusion those who had not previously published their ideas.

885 **American thought before 1900: a sourcebook from puritanism
to Darwinism.**
Edited by Paul W. Kurtz. New York: Macmillan, 1966.
448p. bibliog.
A collection presenting the writings of twenty-two early Americans, including
Benjamin Franklin, Thomas Jefferson, Thomas Paine, Ralph Waldo Emerson,
Henry David Thoreau, Laurens P. Hickock, Josiah Royce and Chauncey Wright.
Includes a general introduction and individual introductory essays on the authors,
showing their place in history and philosophical thought.

Philosophy

886 **The golden age of American philosophy.**
Charles Frankel. New York: G. Braziller, 1960. 534p.
bibliog.
A picture of American philosophy between the Civil War and 1930, with selections from the works of nine philosophers: Chauncey Wright, James Mills Peirce, William James, Josiah Royce, George Santayana, John Dewey, Ralph Barton Perry, Clarence I. Lewis and Morris R. Cohen.

887 **A history of American philosophy.**
Herbert Wallace Schneider. New York: Columbia
University Press, 1963. 2nd ed. 590p. bibliog.
A revised edition of a work which first appeared in 1946, this is a survey of American philosophy from colonial times. The author discusses such schools of thought as transcendentalism, naturalism, and realism, and includes such philosophers as Ralph Waldo Emerson, Josiah Royce, William James and George Santayana.

888 **A history of philosophy in America.**
Elizabeth Flower, Murray Murphey. New York: G. P.
Putnam's Sons, 1976. 2 vols.
A scholarly study of American philosophy, tracing its European origins and providing a discussion of the role of philosophy and its relationship to science and religion. A comprehensive history of American philosophy.

889 **Pragmatism and the American mind: essays and reviews in philosophy and intellectual history.**
Morton Gabriel White. New York: Oxford University
Press, 1973. 265p.
Twenty-six essays and reviews, all previously published, covering pragmatism as well as other philosphical topics. A readable work which will be enjoyed by the general reader as well as the college student.

890 **Science and sentiment in America: philosophical thought from Jonathan Edwards to John Dewey.**
Morton Gabriel White. New York: Oxford University
Press, 1972. 358p. bibliog.
A historical study of American philosophy and of the views of various philosophers on science and the modern scientific method. The author offers critical analyses of the relevant schools of philosophy: transcendentalism, pragmatism, idealism, naturalism, etc.

891 **Seven sages; the story of American philosophy: Franklin, Emerson, James, Dewey, Santayana, Peirce and Whitehead.**
Hendrikus Boeve Van Wesep. New York: David McKay,
1960. 450p.
A study of seven important American philosophers, written for the general reader but presenting scholarly information. The author presents short biographies as

well as analyses of each man's philosophical concepts and places the philosophers in their historical contexts.

892 **The spirit of American philosophy.**
Edited by Gerald E. Myers. New York: G. P. Putnam's Sons, 1970. 350p. bibliog. (Spirit of Western Civilization, 8).
An anthology of the writings of American philosophers from colonial times to the present, exploring the relationship of the individual to the world through religion, morality, rationality, education, metaphysics and technology.

Art

893 **America as art.**
Joshua Charles Taylor.   Washington, D.C.: Smithsonian Institution Press, 1976. 320p.

This work was published to complement an exhibition at the National Collection of Fine Arts during the year of the American bicentennial. The study addresses itself to the question of what America is in terms of art. The author discusses American ideas and dreams as reflected in American art.

894 **American art.**
Joshua Charles Taylor.   New York: Penguin, 1976. 322p. bibliog. (Pelican History of Art).

A new look at American art, with emphasis on artistic development before the 20th century. The author stresses paintings, but also includes sculpture, prints and photography in his survey. He discusses the unique qualities of American art which reflect the growth of American society: in short, the attempt to cast off ties with tradition and to create an authentic American identity.

895 **American art of the 20th century.**
Sam Hunter.   New York: H. N. Abrams, 1972. 487p. bibliog.

An illustrated survey of 20th century American art, with emphasis on art since 1945. The author discusses the work of individual artists, and analyses such styles as pop art, earthworks, conceptual art, etc.

896 **American art since 1900; a critical history.**
Barbara Rose.   New York: Praeger, 1967. 320p. (Praeger World of Art Series).

A copiously illustrated survey of American art in the 20th century. The book examines in detail such topics as the 1913 Armory Show, the 1920s, the Works Progress Administration of the 1930s, and abstract expressionism. There are two separate chapters providing short histories of American sculpture and architecture. Useful for the general reader as well as the art student.

897 American art to 1900: painting, sculpture, architecture.
Milton Wolf Brown. New York: H. N. Abrams, 1977.
631p. bibliog.
Analyses and illustrates the art forms which flourished in America during its first
three centuries. It includes painting, sculpture and architecture, and is
documented by profuse illustrations, many in colour. A beautiful addition to any
art history collection.

898 American drawings: the 20th century.
Paul Cummings. New York: Viking Press, 1976. 207p.
bibliog.
An interesting collection of drawings by 20th century American artists. They are
arranged chronologically so that the reader may see how various influences have
affected the work over a period of time.

899 American folk painting.
Mary Black, Jean Lipman. New York: Clarkson N. Potter,
1966. 244p.
A richly illustrated discussion of a form of American art which flourished until
the development of photography at the time of the American Civil War.

900 American Negro art.
Cedric Dover. Greenwich, Connecticut: New York Graphic
Society, 1960. 186p. bibliog.
A survey, both in the text and through the many illustrations, of the work of
American black artists from early times to the present. The author, an anthropol-
ogist, has outlined the cultural development of the black in America.

901 The American tradition in the arts.
Richard B. K. McLanathan. New York: Harcourt, Brace
& World, 1968. 492p. bibliog.
A general survey of the arts in America, including architecture, painting, sculp-
ture, and the decorative arts. A very readable work, with an interesting emphasis
on the popular arts.

902 American views: prospects and vistas.
Gloria-Gilda Deak. New York: Viking Press, 1976. 134p.
A delight to the eye, this book is a collection of colour prints and drawings which
represent the work of a great many artists and engravers of the 16th to the 19th
centuries. The prints and drawings included are housed in the Prints Division of
the New York Public Library and they represent a panorama of American
growth over the years.

903 **Art and life in America.**
Oliver W. Larkin. New York: Holt, Rinehart & Winston, 1960. rev. and enl. ed. 559p.

A survey of the visual arts in America (architecture, sculpture, painting, etc.) and their relationship to the cultural development of the periods in which they appeared. This book blends history and art, beautifully illustrated by almost 500 reproductions, 30 in colour. Included are numerous interesting biographical sketches.

904 **Art and tradition.**
Emery Grossman. New York: T. Yoseloff, 1968. 176p.

Presents the work, backgrounds and philosophies of seventeen Jewish artists in America. Included are chapters on Jacques Lipchitz, Ben Shahn, Moses Soyer, George Segal and many other artists. The author based his material on personal interviews and provided recent photographs of the artists along with many illustrations of their work.

905 **Art for the millions: essays from the 1930s by artists and administrators of the WPA Federal Arts Project.**
Edited by Francis V. O'Connor. Greenwich, Connecticut: New York Graphic Society, 1973. 317p. bibliog.

Dr. O'Connor, an art historian specializing in the Depression, has selected a group of essays best reflecting the period from an anthology written between 1936 and 1940 but never published. The project was originally begun as an annual report for 1936 by the Works Progress Administration Federal Arts Project, but it grew to become a fascinating record - both verbal and visual - of the ideas and work of the artists of the time.

906 **Art in America.**
New York: Art in America, 1913- . bi-monthly. (Distributed by McGraw-Hill).

An excellent general art magazine dealing primarily with the visual arts. It features painting, sculpture, architecture, design and photography, and emphasizes contemporary art.

907 **Art in America.**
Suzanne La Follette. New York: Harper, 1929. 361p.

An early history of American art which is still found as a standard handbook in most library collections. This volume is a useful source for the layman who wishes to begin a study of American art.

908 **The artist in American society: the formative years, 1790-1860.**
Neil Harris. New York: G. Braziller, 1966. 432p. bibliog.

A study of art in relation to the society in which the artist lives. Harris discusses the role of the American artists of the 19th century from the point of view of their own ideals and achievements and also in the light of society's view of the visual arts at the time. A valuable discussion of social, religious, political and educational values, as well as a useful piece of art history.

909 **Artistic America, Tiffany glass, and art nouveau.**
Samuel Bing. Cambridge, Massachusetts: M.I.T. Press,
1970. 260p.
The author was a Parisian art dealer who made a trip to America in the early
1890s. He published a report to the French government and a number of essays
in which he comments with great enthusiasm on the American qualities which he
found revealed in its art. Bing was pivotal in the art nouveau movement, and
these translations of his essays are important contributions to the history of the
movement. The main translation is of 'La culture artistique en Amérique'. Also
included is a beautifully illustrated essay on Tiffany glass.

910 **Artists of the old West.**
John C. Ewers. Garden City, New York: Doubleday, 1965.
240p.
A magnificent visual record of the old West as portrayed by such artists as
George Catlin, Frederick Remington and Charles Russell. Some of the works
selected, such as those by several Indian artists, have seldom appeared in works
for the general reader. The author stresses the value of the artists' work as
documents of history rather than evaluating them solely for the quality of the art.

911 **Artists/U.S.A.**
Philadelphia: Artists/USA, 1970/71- . biennial.
A tool for the art buyer, presenting a visual and biographical directory of living
American professional artists. The information presented on each artist includes
the name and address, a reproduction of at least one work, plus gallery affilia-
tions, major exhibitions, awards and art positions.

912 **The artist's voice: talks with seventeen artists.**
Katharine Kuh. New York: Harper & Row, 1962. 248p.
Interesting interviews conducted by the author with a number of artists who chat
with her about their work and their impressions of the art world in general. This
book is illustrated with reproductions of work the artists have chosen as their
favourites.

913 **The art-makers of nineteenth-century America.**
Russell Lynes. New York: Atheneum, 1970. 514p.
A readable survey of artistic trends and events of the 19th century in America.
An attempt by a social historian to chronicle how society affected the American
artist and helped him to develop his own style.

914 **The arts in America: the colonial period.**
L. B. Wright, G. B. Tatum, J. W. McCoubrey, R. C.
Smith. New York: Charles Scribner's Sons, 1966. 368p.
bibliog.
A collection of essays appraising the various forms of art in colonial times. The
authors all draw attention to the aspects of architecture, painting and the decorative arts which were new and unique to American artists. while not neglecting to
call attention to the European models from which they drew inspiration. The
volume is well illustrated and of interest to the general reader.

915 **The arts in America: the nineteenth century.**
W. D. Garrett, P. F. Norton, A. Gowans, J. T.
Butler. New York: Charles Scribner's Sons, 1969. 412p.
bibliog.

An examination of 19th century American art, providing a useful and well-written work similar to the earlier volume on the colonial period (see preceding item).

916 **The arts in early American history.**
Walter Muir Whitehill. Chapel Hill, North Carolina:
University of North Carolina Press, 1965. 170p. bibliog.

This useful reference tool includes an introductory essay by Whitehill, followed by an annotated bibliography compiled by Jane and Wendell Garrett. The bibliography includes general works, works on architecture, painting, sculpture, graphic arts, etc.

917 **The arts in modern American civilization.**
John A. Kouwenhoven. New York: Norton, 1967. 259p.

Originally published in 1948 under the title *Made in America*, this work studies the various arts (architecture, painting, literature, etc.) and their relation to American life. The author suggests that a vernacular style evolved from America's need to respond to the challenge of a new and growing country.

918 **Arts of the United States: a pictorial survey.**
Edited by William H. Pierson, Martha Davidson. Athens,
Georgia: University of Georgia Press, 1960. 452p.

A useful reference tool in catalogue form which provides a survey of art forms developed in the United States from pre-colonial times to the present. This book grew out of a colour-slide project sponsored by the Carnegie Corporation of New York, through a grant to the University of Georgia. It includes introductory essays on the various topics, written by specialists in their respective fields. These are followed by the catalogue of slides.

919 **The Britannica encyclopedia of American art.**
Chicago: Encyclopaedia Britannica Educational, 1973. 669p.
bibliog. (Distributed by Simon & Schuster).

An invaluable reference tool, encompassing current trends in American art and biographies of new artists, as well as authoritative articles on historical aspects of painting, sculpture, architecture, photography and the decorative arts. An essential item for any collection on American art.

920 **Currier and Ives chronicles of America.**
Edited by John Lowell Pratt. Maplewood, New Jersey:
Hammond, 1968. 256p.

A chronological portrait of America as shown through the prints of Currier and Ives. The colourful reproductions are arranged under subject headings, and each section is introduced by a noted contributor. A fine addition to any collection of Americana.

921 **Depression modern: the thirties style in America.**
Martin Grief. New York: Universe, 1975. 192p.
A clarification of art deco and a description of design in America during the 1930s. The author discusses the influence of the founders of the style of Depression modern, with many illustrations of the work of such designers as Raymond Loewy, Norman Bel Geddes, Russell Wright and many others.

922 **A dictionary of contemporary American artists.**
Paul Cummings. New York: St. Martin's Press, 1971. 368p. bibliog.
A useful directory of American painters, sculptors and printmakers. Each entry gives biographical data on the artist and bibliographical references for more thorough research.

923 **The European vision of America: a special exhibition to honor the bicentennial of the United States.**
Hugh Honour. Kent, Ohio: Kent State University Press, 1975. 388p.
An interesting collection of European works of art which reflect what Europeans saw in America and how they felt about American traditions. The author does for the visual arts what many previous studies have done for the literary image of America in European minds.

924 **The federal presence: architecture, politics, and symbols in United States government buildings.**
Lois A. Craig. Cambridge, Massachusetts: M.I.T. Press, 1978. 580p. bibliog.
A fascinating pictorial history of the architecture of government buildings, providing a cultural as well as an architectural look at each era portrayed.

925 **The golden door: artist-immigrants of America, 1876-1976.**
Cynthia Jaffee McCabe. Washington, DC: Smithsonian Institution Press, 1976. 432p. bibliog.
A catalogue of the Hirshhorn Museum's bicentennial exhibition of works of major American artists who settled in America between 1876 and 1976. The interesting feature of this work is that it shows the influence on each artist of his experience as an immigrant.

926 **The great American nude.**
William H. Gerdts. New York: Praeger, 1974. 224p. bibliog.
An interesting and witty history of the nude in American painting and sculpture. The author relates the nude in art to the values and morals of each period, illustrating his text lavishly throughout.

927 **A guide to art museums in the United States.**
Erwin Ottomar Christensen. New York: Dodd, Mead, 1968. 303p.
A descriptive guide which contains information on opening hours and admission and descriptions of the collections. Includes a list of art museums connected with colleges and universities, as well as a list of museum directories and regional guides.

928 **A history of American art.**
Daniel Marcus Mendelowitz. New York: Holt, Rinehart & Winston, 1970. 2nd ed. 522p. bibliog.
A survey of all facets of the visual arts in the United States, beginning with the Indian cultures but emphasizing the modern period. Decorative arts and crafts are included in order to demonstrate how craftsmanship and use of technology have contributed to American culture.

929 **A history of the rise and progress of the arts of design in the United States.**
William Dunlap. New York: Dover, 1969. 3 vols.
A reprint of the original 1834 edition with a new introduction by James Thomas Flexner; newly edited by Rita Weiss. A classic for students of the arts in early America, this work covers painting, sculpture, architecture, etching and engraving, etc. The period covered ranges from the early 18th century to the 1830s, and the work is rich in source material. Many artists of the period are examined and the study includes much material that appears nowhere else.

930 **A pictorial history of architecture in America.**
George Everard Kidder Smith. New York: American Heritage, 1976. 2 vols.
A beautifully illustrated survey of American architecture. The author, an architect by profession, took the many excellent photographs included, and provides some critical commentary.

931 **Three centuries of American art.**
Lloyd Goodrich. New York: Praeger, 1966. 145p.
A pictorial survey of American art from colonial to modern times. This book is based on an exhibition, 'Art of the United States: 1670-1976', which took place at the Whitney Museum of Modern Art in 1966. The text concentrates on major artists of the past and present.

932 **Topics in American art since 1945.**
Lawrence Alloway. New York: Norton, 1975. 283p.
A collection of articles which have appeared previously in various publications and in which Alloway has recorded his views on visual arts of the past three decades. He discusses such topics as pop art (the coining of this term is credited to him), abstract expressionism, and the new realism in painting. He gives his views of such artists as Jackson Pollock, Barnett Newman, Jasper Johns, and many others. An important view of new styles in American art since 1945.

933 Traveler's guide to America's art.
Jane Norman, Theodore Norman. New York: Meredith Press, 1968. 436p.

A well-indexed guidebook for the traveller, giving a guided tour of museums, historic houses and art collections throughout the continental United States. The book is arranged by geographical region, and also includes examples of exceptional American architecture from early to contemporary times.

934 The triumph of American painting: a history of abstract expressionism.
Irving Sandler. New York: Praeger, 1970. 301p. bibliog.

A critical history of abstract expressionism, with chapters on individual artists such as Jackson Pollock, William de Kooning and Mark Rothko. Much of the material has been gathered from conversations and interviews with the artists, and the work includes 200 black-and-white plus 24 full-page colour illustrations. An important addition to any art history collection.

935 The USA: a history in art.
Bradley Smith. New York: Thomas Y. Crowell, 1975. 296p. bibliog.

This unusual and beautiful book chronicles the growth of the United States from prehistoric times to the end of the Second World War. It contains reproductions of paintings which mirror the times in which they were painted and which were made during the period of the event depicted. The work is a fine addition to any collection of Americana as well as of American art.

936 The way West: art of frontier America.
Peter H. Hassrick. New York: H. N. Abrams, 1977. 240p.

A pictorial history of the opening of America's Western frontier, this volume includes the work of many artists who made the West their theme. It includes works by George Catlin, Thomas Hart Benton and many others. Beautifully illustrated, this work presents a fine collection of essays on each artist as well as representative works.

937 What is American in American art.
Edited by Jean Lipman. New York: McGraw-Hill, 1963. 180p.

A series of articles gleaned from fifty years of the magazine *Art in America*. The contributors are distinguished critics and artists who offer their views on what gives American art its individual flavour. This attractive volume contains fifty colour plates, including the following colour portfolios: New England gravestone rubbings; American primitive watercolours; *The four seasons* by Andrew Wyeth; and lithographs by six American artists.

938 Who's Who in American Art.
New York: R. R. Bowker, 1936/37- . biennial.

Provides biographical data for Americans active in the field of art. Also included are a necrology section, a geographical index, and a brief description by each artist of the art form in which he or she works.

Music and Dance

939 **All the years of American popular music.**
David Ewen. Englewood Cliffs, New Jersey: Prentice-Hall,
1977. 850p.
Another of the author's fine musical histories, this work endeavours to trace in
one volume the entire world of popular music in America. The chapters are
arranged chronologically and cover the periods from 1620 to the present day. The
author discusses musical theatre, performers, the history of popular songs and
composers, and places where popular music has flourished such as Tin Pan Alley
or Preservation Hall in New Orleans. Also included are a variety of related
subjects such as discothèques and disc jockeys. A welcome addition to any music
collection.

940 **American composer speaks: a historical anthology,
1770-1965.**
Gilbert Chase. Baton Rouge, Louisiana: Louisiana State
University Press, 1966. 318p. bibliog.
A collection of essays by thirty composers, chosen to represent a cross-section of
musical ideas over the years. Each essay is preceded by a short biographical
sketch of the composer. The student of music will learn a great deal about
composers in early American history, as well as much about such contemporary
artists as Edgar Varese and John Cage.

941 **American music.**
Irving Sablosky. Chicago: University of Chicago Press,
1969. 228p. (Chicago History of American Civilization).
The Chicago History of American Civilization was a series dealing with two types
of books: those providing a chronological narrative of American history, and those
dealing with the history of significant aspects of American life. This book is an
example of the latter, providing a discussion of American music from a cultural
point of view and relating it to the time in which it evolved. A non-technical
survey and aimed at the general reader.

942 **American music since 1910.**
Virgil Thomson. New York: Holt, Rinehart & Winston, 1971. 204p. bibliog. (Twentieth-Century Composers, vol. 1).
The first of a two-volume work dealing with modern music (the second volume covers central European music). Thomson's work contains a series of general introductory chapters on American musical traits, etc.; these are followed by essays on individual composers such as Charles Ives and Aaron Copland. A final section of great reference value contains 106 biographies of modern American composers and their achievements.

943 **American popular songs: from the Revolutionary War to the present.**
Edited by David Ewen. New York: Random House, 1966. 507p.
A valuable reference tool in the form of a dictionary, providing basic information on the great American popular songs since 1776. The entries include information on the names of authors of lyrics and music, the names of the performers who have made the song famous, and material about how the song first became popular. There are over 4,000 entries arranged alphabetically by song title. A sampling of the many other works written and edited by David Ewen includes the following titles: *Panorama of American popular music* (Englewood Cliffs, New Jersey: Prentice-Hall, 1957. 365p.); *The life and death of Tin Pan Alley: the golden age of American popular music* (New York: Funk & Wagnalls, 1964. 380p. bibliog.); *Great men of American popular songs: the history of the American popular song told through the lives, careers, achievements and personalities of its foremost composers - from William Billings of the Revolutionary War to the 'folk-rock' of Bob Dylan* (Englewood Cliffs, New Jersey: Prentice-Hall, 1970. 3,870p.).

944 **American popular songs: the great innovators, 1900-1950.**
Alec Wilder. New York: Oxford University Press, 1972. 536p.
A witty and highly personal study of the musical comedy and the popular tune. The author analyses eleven major composers - Jerome D. Kern, Irving Berlin, George Gershwin, Richard Rodgers, Cole Porter, Harold Arlen, Vincent Youmans, Arthur Schwartz, Burton Lane, Hugh Martin and Vernon Duke - and mentions the work of a number of others. There are many musical examples cited throughout the book.

945 **America's music: from the pilgrims to the present.**
Gilbert Chase. New York: McGraw, 1955. 733p. bibliog.
A valuable reference source which traces the background and direction of American music from colonial times to the 20th century. Contains material on numerous subjects such as Puritan psalm singing, Negro spirituals, Indian tribal music, jazz, and Broadway musicals. An extensive bibliography enhances the value of this work as a reference tool. The second revised edition, published in 1966 (759p.), drops the chapter 'Indian tribal music' but adds one on music of the 1960s.

946 The art of ragtime: form and meaning of an original black American art.
William J. Schafer, Johannes Riedel. Baton Rouge, Louisiana: Louisiana State University Press, 1973. 249p.

A musicological analysis of ragtime which was written for the piano and merged black folk sources with white musical forms of the deep South in the mid-19th century. One section discusses the proponents of 'classic' ragtime such as Scott Joplin, James Scott and Joseph Lamb. Also included is an analysis of Joplin's folk opera *Treemonisha*. This work supplements the material in the basic work on ragtime, *They all played ragtime* (q.v.), by Rudi Blesh and Harriet Janis.

947 The ASCAP biographical dictionary of composers, authors and publishers.
New York: American Society of Composers, Authors and Publishers, 1966. 3rd ed. 845p.

A useful reference tool drawing its information primarily from questionnaires filled out by ASCAP members. Biographical works have also been consulted, as well as musical encyclopaedias. This dictionary does not attempt to be comprehensive but simply to give a representative sampling of the works of the personalities covered.

948 Ballads, blues, and the big beat.
Donald Myrus. New York: Macmillan, 1966. 136p.

A breezy, readable discussion of the various forms of folk-singing in America since 1950. The subjects include protest singers, folk-rock, hillbilly, old-time ballad and blues. The author emphasizes his own preferences, but is nevertheless quite informative.

949 The big bands.
George Thomas Simon. New York: Macmillan, 1967. 537p.

A recreation of the big band era in American music, from the mid-1930s to the mid-1940s. The book mentions 400 bands of the time, provides lengthy profiles of 72 top-rated groups. It discusses musical styles and arrangements, and relates marvellous humorous anecdotes. This book will be enjoyed by the big band enthusiast as well as by anyone researching the period.

950 Biographical dictionary of American music.
Charles Eugene Claghorn. West Nyack, New York: Parker, 1973. 491p.

A useful reference for identifying groups and individuals in the popular music business who are not easily found in other biographical sources. The information about individuals includes brief biographical data, main musical activities and important compositions in the case of composers. Group information includes the leader, chief musicians, places played and sometimes albums.

951 **Catalog of published concert music by American composers.**
Angelo Eagon. Metuchen, New Jersey: Scarecrow Press,
1969. 2nd ed. 348p. Suppls. to 2nd ed. 1971, 1974.
A reference catalogue of concert music by American composers suitable for
performance. American composers are defined as native-born composers, as well
as foreign-born composers who became naturalized American citizens before the
age of twenty-six and who have contributed to the American musical scene. The
different sections list music for solo voice, solo instruments, choral music, various
ensemble arrangements, etc. The supplements were planned to be issued about
every two years.

952 **The complete encyclopedia of popular music and jazz,
1900-1950.**
Roger D. Kinkle. New Rochelle, New York: Arlington
House, 1974. 4 vols.
A comprehensive work on all facets of popular American music (popular songs,
radio, television, show tunes, jazz, etc.). This set provides a definitive reference
which will be useful in any music collection. Vol. 1: is entitled *Music year by
year, 1900-1950*; vol. 2: *Biographies, A-K*; vol. 3: *Biographies, L-Z*; and vol. 4:
Indexes and appendices. Some of the useful appendixes include Academy Award
winners and nominees for music, 1934-73; a listing by artist and song of major
record labels from the mid-1920s to the early 1940s; and poll winners from *Down
Beat* and *Metronome*, 1937-73.

953 **Conversation with the blues.**
Paul Oliver. New York: Horizon Press, 1965. 217p.
Oliver made a research tour of the United States in the summer of 1960 and this
book is a record, with photographs, of the interviews which he taped. He relates
conversations with over sixty-five blues singers and their associates and success-
fully conveys how the blues were interwoven with the lives of the performers. A
beautiful book on American folk music.

954 **The country music encyclopedia.**
Melvin Shostack. New York: Thomas Y. Crowell, 1974.
410p.
A series of biographical sketches and essays on various aspects of country music -
honky-tonk, bluegrass, etc. These are arranged alphabetically and provide basic
information on the current country music scene. The articles are written in an
anecdotal style and are highly entertaining to read as well as providing current
material on the country and western music field.

955 **The country music story: a picture history of country and
western music.**
Robert Shelton. Indianapolis, Indiana: Bobbs-Merrill, 1966.
256p.
The history of country music as shown through numerous photographs and
memorabilia. The author includes material on country music stars, styles, origins,
etc. A fine nostalgic look at an area of American popular culture.

Music and Dance

956 Country music U.S.A.: a fifty-year history.
Bill C. Malone. Austin, Texas: University of Texas Press, 1968. 422p. bibliog. (Publication of the American Folklore Society. Memoir Series, vol. 54).

A scholarly account of the history of American country music from its early pre-commercial times to the 1960s. The author's writing style, the inclusion of all types of country music (honky-tonk, bluegrass, western swing, etc.) and the information on performers and musical instruments make this a useful work for all music and Americana collections.

957 Country roots: the origins of country music.
Douglas B. Green. New York: Hawthorn, 1976. 238p. bibliog.

Richly illustrated with photographs, this history of American country music traces the traditions of this unique musical form from early folk ballads to today's Nashville sound. The volume contains a useful chronology (including the top five records, 1923-75), plus a discography; both of these will be valuable to the collector and the student of this type of music.

958 The dance in America.
Walter Terry. New York: Harper & Row, 1956. 248p.

A readable survey of all types and periods of American dancing, from colonial times to the present. Included are discussions of the birth of American ballet, the influence of traditional dance, the use of dance in movies, stage shows and television, ballroom and recreational dancing, and even dance as a form of therapy. The author provides biographical sketches of a number of leading dance figures such as Isadora Duncan, Ted Shawn, Martha Graham. Numerous photographs illustrate the volume.

959 The encyclopedia of jazz in the sixties.
Leonard G. Feather. New York: Horizon Press, 1966. 312p.

An updated version of the 1955 and 1960 works. There are references in this edition to the fuller biographical entries in the 1960 edition, thus making both volumes sometimes necessary to obtain the most complete information. This encyclopaedia now contains over 2,000 biographies, over 200 photographs, a chronology, a historical survey of jazz, an explanation of jazz techniques, and many other features which, although not more current than 1966, make this work an invaluable reference for any music collection.

960 Flashes of merriment: a century of humorous songs in America, 1805-1905.
Lester S. Levy. Norman, Oklahoma: University of Oklahoma Press, 1971. 370p. bibliog.

Levy, a life-long collector of early American sheet music, has here provided a delightful volume of material for the student of popular culture in 19th century America. It contains the history of each song mentioned as well as facts about its composer, lyricist and the performers who made it famous. A useful book for amateur performers as well as social historians, because several verses of each song are included, as well as anecdotes about them.

961 The gospel sound: good news and bad times.

Tony Heilbut. New York: Simon & Schuster, 1971. 350p.

A study of gospel music, explaining its role in black America and showing its relationship to such forms of music as jazz and rhythm and blues. The author provides portraits of many major gospel figures such as Mahalia Jackson, Sam Cooke and Clara Ward, and discusses the stylistic aspects of this unique form of music. An important addition to any collection on American music.

962 Grace notes in American history: popular sheet music from 1820-1900.

Lester S. Levy. Norman, Oklahoma: University of Oklahoma Press, 1967. 410p.

A fascinating view of 19th century America, as shown through an examination of the popular sheet music of the day. The book is divided into two sections: one dealing with mores, the other with history. The topical chapters are profusely illustrated with sheet music covers and much of the music itself. The origins of the songs are discussed along with many of the song's subjects. An illuminating volume of Americana as well as music history.

963 The great American popular singers.

Henry Pleasants. New York: Simon & Schuster, 1974. 384p.

A collection of biographical chapters on a number of popular American singers: Al Jolson, Bing Crosby, Ella Fitzgerald, Frank Sinatra, Judy Garland, Barbara Streisand, and many others. The author analyses the vocal range and style of each of these singers, rather than concentrating on the usual biographical details of family, schooling, etc. Recommended for all American music collections.

964 An introduction to folk music in the United States.

Bruno Nettl. Detroit, Michigan: Wayne State University Press, 1962. rev. ed. 126p. bibliog.

A survey of American folk music presented in an elementary manner. A fine introduction for the layman distinguishes the variety of forms and cultures which are found in American folk music. The work includes chapters on the ethnic backgrounds of folk music, the professional folk-singer, and musical examples.

965 Jazz dance: the story of American vernacular dance.

Marshall Stearns, Jean Stearns. New York: Macmillan, 1968. 464p. bibliog.

A history of dancing performed to jazz rhythms, based on over 200 interviews with dancers, musicians, and choreographers of jazz. The authors begin the study with a section on 'Prehistory' which discusses backgrounds in Africa and the West Indies and traces Afro-American dances in the United States. The volume includes sections on Tin Pan Alley, Broadway shows, the Jitterbug, and many other topics. It also contains some valuable reference material in the appendixes which include a list of films in which jazz may be seen, and an analysis of basic jazz dance movements recorded in a system of movement-writing known as Labanotation (actually showing dance steps on paper). A valuable reference for any student of the dance.

Music and Dance

966 Jazz masters of New Orleans.
Martin Williams. New York: Macmillan, 1967. 287p.
bibliog. (Jazz Masters Series).

The fourth volume in the Jazz Masters Series, which includes *Jazz masters of the twenties*, *Jazz masters of the swing era*, *Jazz masters of the forties*, and *Jazz masters of the fifties*. The author deals here with the earliest period of jazz and focuses his attention on nine musicians and two bands of the era, devoting separate chapters to each. There is a discography and bibliography at the end of each chapter.

967 Jazz: the transition years, 1940-1960.
John S. Wilson. New York: Appleton-Century-Crofts,
1966. 185p. bibliog.

A compact analysis of a period when jazz made a come-back in popularity - the era following the Second World War. The author discusses the movements which developed in jazz during this time: 'bop', 'cool' jazz, West Coast jazz, and soul jazz. He mentions the performers and musical groups which emerged at this time and analyses the influence of the period on the musical world.

968 Music and musicians in early America.
Irving Lowens. New York: Norton, 1964. 328p.

A collection of articles which appeared over a fifteen-year period, discussing early American music from colonial times to the mid-19th century. This work contains some important essays on such subjects as early composers, the attitudes of transcendentalists like Emerson towards music, religious music, etc. It also presents a look at music as it relates to early sociological history. A worthwhile addition to any collection on Americana or musical history.

969 Music in a new found land: themes and developments in the history of American music.
Wilfred Mellers. New York: Knopf, 1965. 543p.

An interesting complement to Gilbert Chase's *America's music* (q.v.), written from the viewpoint of a British musicologist looking at American music. Mellers blends sociological and literary history with his musical themes, relating many literary works to musical compositions. The book is useful to the serious student of music as well as to the enthusiast.

970 Music in American life.
Jacques Barzun. Garden City, New York: Doubleday,
1956. 126p.

A short essay by a well-known writer on contemporary culture, discussing the impact of music on present-day American life. A thought-provoking work.

971 Music for patriots, politicians, and presidents: harmonies and discords of the first hundred years.
Vera Brodsky Lawrence. New York: Macmillan, 1975.
480p.

A unique look at the growth of the USA, this volume is a collection of 'patriotic tunes, political ballads, presidential campaign songs [and] a few songs of social protest'. It includes reproductions of sheet music, illustrated broadsides of the 18th and 19th centuries, and the author's interesting commentary on each song. A fascinating work for anyone interested in Americana.

972 The music merchants.
Milton Goldin.   New York: Macmillan, 1969. 242p. bibliog.

An interesting portrait of the music business in America, from opera houses to promoters. The author, who has been a member of the New York Symphony Orchestra and the Denver Symphony Orchestra and has also managed concerts and written musical articles, discusses the history and the future of American musical institutions.

973 The music of black Americans: a history.
Eileen Southern.   New York: Norton, 1971. 552p. bibliog.

A survey, written as a narrative history, which is an important item for any collection on American music, American history, or black studies. This scholarly work includes analyses of characteristic musical forms, definitions of terms, and a discography.

974 Our American music: a comprehensive history from 1620 to the present.
John Tasker Howard.   New York: Thomas Y. Crowell, 1965. 4th ed. 944p. bibliog.

A survey of American music which, although containing some material which should have been updated, presents a history complementing Gilbert Chase's *America's music* (q.v.). Together, these two works provide the student with much important material on the history of American music.

975 A pictorial history of jazz: people and places from New Orleans to modern jazz.
Orrin Keepnews, Bill Grauer, Jr.   New York: Crown, 1966. rev. ed. 297p.

A new revised version of the 1955 title which was a classic in the field. The book is an encyclopaedic picture-story of jazz and contains 725 illustrations accompanied by identifying captions. Unfortunately, some of the photographs are not reproduced very clearly, but the book is of value to all libraries in the field.

976 Portrait of Carnegie Hall: a nostalgic portrait in pictures and words of America's greatest stage and the artists who performed there.
Theodore O. Cron, Burt Goldblatt.   New York: Macmillan, 1966. 217p.

A worthwhile addition to any music and theatre collection, this illustrated volume provides a look at over seventy years of performances in the renowned Carnegie Hall. The book contains photographs, a discography, and descriptions of performances by a variety of artists such as Jascha Heifetz, Louis Armstrong, and Burl Ives.

Music and Dance

977 Quintet: five American dance companies.
Moira Hodgson. New York: William Morrow, 1976. 161p.

A history of the art of American dance as illustrated by descriptions of five leading dance companies: the Alvin Ailey City Center Dance Theater, Merce Cunningham and Dance Company, Dance Theater of Harlem, Eliot Field Ballet, and the Paul Taylor Dance Company. The author traces the common source from which they all spring - George Balanchine and Martha Graham. This lovely volume is enhanced by 200 black-and-white photographs.

978 The reluctant art: the growth of jazz.
Benny Green. New York: Horizon Press, 1963. 191p.

Green, a musician and jazz critic, analyses the work of five great jazz artists: Bix Beiderbecke, Benny Goodman, Lester Young, Charlie Parker, and Billie Holiday. This book is a worthwhile addition to jazz history collections.

979 Simon says: the sights and sounds of the swing era, 1934-1955.
George Thomas Simon. New Rochelle, New York: Arlington House, 1971. 491p.

A nostalgic look at the 'swing era' of American music as seen through a collection of articles written by the author for *Metronome*, a magazine of the music world which appeared from 1935 to 1955. There are some marvellous photographs, and the index makes this a useful reference work.

980 The social implications of early Negro music in the United States: with over 150 of the songs, many of them with their music.
Edited by Bernard Katz. New York: Arno Press, 1969. 146p. bibliog.

A collection of writings on the history of early Afro-American music, gathered together for use by the general reader or historian.

981 The sound of the city: the rise of rock and roll.
Charlie Gillett. New York: Outerbridge & Dienstfrey, 1970. 375p. bibliog. (Distributed by E. P. Dutton).

An analysis of rock and roll music, both historically and musically. The book discusses American popular music and the music industry from 1940 to 1970.

982 The story of the blues.
Paul Oliver. Philadelphia: Chilton, 1969. 176p. bibliog.

A well-illustrated reference work tracing the history of the blues from its origins among the African slaves in America through to the influence of blues in modern rock music. The book describes regional differences in music and includes musical examples and information on the great musicians such as Leadbelly, Jelly Roll Morton, Ray Charles and many others.

983 **They all played ragtime.**
Rudi Blesh, Harriet Janis.   New York: Oak, 1971. 347p.
This work, which first appeared in 1950, has remained a classic study of ragtime. The book was based on personal interviews and correspondence with important ragtime personalities, printed sources such as regional newspapers, and musical sources such as sheet music and records. Subsequent authors in the field have referred to Blesh and Janis as an invaluable reference source. Recommended for any collection on the subject.

984 **United States music: sources of bibliography and collective biography.**
Richard Jackson.   New York: Brooklyn Institute for Studies in American Music, Department of Music, Brooklyn College of the City University of New York, 1973. 80p. (I.S.A.M. Monographs, no. 1).
A short bibliography designed to aid students of American music. The author has included books which contribute most fruitfully to the subject areas under which they are listed, and he has eliminated books primarily concerned with historical or critical analysis.

985 **Variety music cavalcade, 1620-1969.**
Edited by Julius Mattfeld.   Englewood Cliffs, New Jersey: Prentice-Hall, 1971. 3rd ed. 766p.
A chronological checklist of music which was popular in the United States from 1620 to the present day. Only music still available in print is included. The information on each song includes its composer, lyricist, publisher, copyright, etc. An invaluable tool for anyone researching American music.

986 **The world of soul: black America's contribution to the pop music scene.**
Arnold Shaw.   New York: Cowles, 1970. 306p.
An important analysis of soul music - the blues of today - tracing its roots and showing it as a projection of the performers' and listeners' feelings about the world. The book includes a look at soul artists and provides a sociological approach to the development of soul as well as a musical analysis.

Theatre and Film

987 Academy Awards illustrated: a complete history of Hollywood's Academy Awards in words and pictures.
Robert Osborne. La Habra, California: Academy Awards Illustrated, 1972. 345p.

A complete record of Academy Award winners and nominees, spanning the years 1927-28, when the first awards were given, to 1972, when the 1971 awards were presented. This illustrated volume is very useful to any collection on American film history.

988 America in the movies: or Santa Maria, it had slipped my mind.
Michael Wood. New York: Basic Books, 1975. 206p.

A provocative and witty discussion of American films of the 1940s and 1950s and how they reflected America's self-image. The author focuses on several recurring themes in these films and includes material on film techniques and categories such as dance, Bible, etc.

989 American drama criticism: interpretations, 1890-1965 inclusive, of American drama since the first play produced in America.
Edited by Helen H. Palmer, Jane Anne Dyson. Hamden, Connecticut: Shoe String Press, 1967. 239p. Suppl. 1, 1970. 101p.; suppl. 2, 1976. 217p.

A bibliography of criticisms of American drama published between 1890 and 1965. A useful tool for anyone seeking criticism of individual plays. The second supplement was edited by Floyd Eugene Eddleman.

990 **American plays and playwrights of the contemporary theater.**
Allan Lewis. New York: Crown, 1970. rev. ed. 270p.
bibliog.
Examines American theatre of the 1950s and 1960s in the light of the new
freedom from conventions and as a reflection of the changing historical situation.
The book is an outgrowth of lectures given at the New School for Social
Research, and is of value to drama students.

991 **Anthology of the American Negro in the theater: a critical
approach.**
Edited by Lindsay Patterson. New York: Publishers Co.,
1969. 2nd rev. ed. 306p. bibliog. (International Library of
Negro Life and History, vol. 8).
An attempt to record the achievements of blacks in the American theatre, and to
analyse the lack of opportunity which has existed.

992 **The Best Plays Annual.**
Boston, Massachusetts: Small, 1920-25; New York: Dodd,
Mead, 1926- . annual.
This invaluable series was started in 1919 by Burns Mantle and it has appeared
every year since then. It contains the editors' choices of the best plays of each
New York season, and provides excerpts from the dialogue, plot summaries, and
critical comments. There have been a number of editors since the death of Burns
Mantle in 1968: John Arthur Chapman, Louis Kronenberger, Henry Hewes, and
Otis Guernsey. Recent volumes include details about all plays produced in New
York, the season around the United States, vital statistics of the theatre and a
wealth of related information. An indispensable companion pair of indexes are
available: *The index to the best plays series, 1899-1950* and *The index to the
best plays series, 1949-1960*. This is followed by a work entitled *Directory of the
American theater, 1894-1971: indexed to the complete series of Best Plays Theater
Yearbooks*, edited by Otis Guernsey (Dodd, Mead, 1971).

993 **The best remaining seats: the story of the golden age of the
movie palace.**
Bea M. Hall. New York: Bramhall House, 1961. 266p.
A wonderfully illustrated look at the glamorous heyday of the ornate and lavishly
decorated movie palaces of the 1920s and 1930s. The author's enthusiasm for his
subject infuses this pictorial history.

994 **The biographical encyclopedia and who's who of the
American theater.**
Edited by Walter Rigdon. New York: J. H. Heineman,
1966. 1,101p.
A comprehensive and authoritative work on the American theatre. As well as
biographies it includes sections on New York productions from 1900 to May
1964, theatre playbills, a production record of American plays which have pre-
miered abroad since 1946, awards presented to members of the American theatre,
and many other topics. A work useful to anyone interested in theatre history.

Theatre and Film

995 **Black drama: the story of the American Negro in the theater.**
Loften Mitchell. New York: Hawthorn, 1967. 248p.

A look at the American black in the theatre, tracing the image presented in early plays and how it has evolved, as well as discussing the careers of black actors and playwrights. The author examines Harlem theatre movements, off-Broadway productions and includes interviews with authors and stars. Mitchell himself is a native of Harlem and a well-known playwright.

996 **Broadway.**
Brooks Atkinson. New York: Macmillan, 1970. 484p.

An important addition to literature on the history of the New York theatre. The author, for thirty years a drama critic for the *New York Times*, is a witty and lucid chronicler of 20th century American theatre.

997 **The Citadel film series.**
Secaucus, New Jersey: Citadel Press, 1966- .

A series of works on Hollywood entertainers, reviewing the stars' careers and including a series of illustrations and descriptions of the films in which they appeared. These works provide a nostalgic look at film history for the enthusiast. The over fifty titles in this series include film histories of such stars as Bette Davis, Frank Sinatra, Cary Grant, Ingrid Bergman, John Wayne, and Katherine Hepburn.

998 **Curtain time: the story of the American theater.**
Lloyd R. Morris. New York: Random House, 1953. 380p.

A nostalgic history of the American theatre, written in an anecdotal and reminiscent style. Morris' book is brightened by many drawings, cartoons, and photographs, and it is a readable and informative work for the general reader.

999 **Dramas from the American theater, 1762-1909.**
Richard Moody. Boston, Massachusetts: Houghton Mifflin, 1969. 873p. bibliog.

An interesting collection of plays selected from America's early years, intended to reflect the prevailing tastes, attitudes, and morals of the times. Each play is introduced by an essay providing biographical and theatrical detail. Many of the plays have not previously been in print in the 20th century, and they range widely in form and subject matter.

1000 **The dramatic event, an American chronicle.**
Eric Russell Bentley. New York: Horizon Press, 1954. 278p.

A collection of essays on the American theatre, primarily concerned with Broadway. The author, a prominent theatre critic, provides an entertaining and knowledgeable book on living theatre.

1001 Dramatic soundings: evaluation and retractions culled from thirty years of dramatic criticism.
John Gassner. New York: Crown, 1968. 716p.
A collection of the author's many essays written during a long career as drama critic. All of Gassner's works will enhance theatre collections.

1002 Dramatis personae: a retrospective show.
John Mason Brown. New York: Viking Press, 1963. 563p.
A collection of the writings of John Mason Brown, a one-time drama critic and observer of the theatre. This volume contains sixty selections from eleven of his books and includes the complete text of his early book, *The modern theater in revolt*. Pleasurable reading for the theatre lover, the historian, and the student of drama.

1003 Dreams and dead ends: the American gangster crime film.
Jack Shadoian. Cambridge, Massachusetts: M.I.T. Press, 1977. 366p. bibliog.
An excellent analytical work on the gangster-crime film, tracing the gangster cycles from the early 1930s to the present in an attempt to show the relationship of these films to the mood of American society. Many individual films are examined in depth, including *High Sierra, White heat, Bonnie and Clyde, The godfather*, etc.

1004 Film: the democratic art.
Garth Jowett. Boston, Massachusetts: Little, Brown, 1976. 518p.
A scholarly study of the relationship of motion pictures to the social climate in which they are produced and shown. The book is packed with fascinating information and is very well documented.

1005 God on the gymnasium floor, and other theatrical adventures.
Walter Kerr. New York: Simon & Schuster, 1971. 320p.
A collection of Kerr's theatre commentaries, with analyses of such contemporary productions as *Butterflies are free, 1776*, and *Oh! Calcutta!*.

1006 The great movie serials; their sound and fury.
Jim Harmon, Donald F. Glut. Garden City, New York: Doubleday, 1972. 384p.
A nostalgic ramble back to Saturday afternoons spent at the cinema, this book offers accounts of most of the film serials. The authors include information on casting, production, and special effects. The film enthusiast will appreciate this title.

Theatre and Film

1007 History of the American theater, 1770-1950.
Glenn Hughes.   New York: Samuel French, 1951. 562p.
bibliog.
A high readable survey of the American theatre, providing much useful information on plays, theatres and actors of each period.

1008 Hollywood renaissance.
Diane Jacobs.   South Brunswick, New Jersey: A. S. Barnes,
1977. 192p. bibliog.
An interesting look at Hollywood movies of the late 1960s and early 1970s. The
author discusses the work of such directors as John Cassavetes, Robert Altman
and Francis Ford Coppola. The book includes many photographs and complete
filmographies of Altman, Cassavetes, Coppola, Scorsese and Mazursky.

1009 Hollywood, the haunted house.
Paul Mayersberg.   New York: Stein & Day, 1968. 188p.
bibliog.
A study of Hollywood from the point of view of the business side of film-making
in America. The author interviews film-makers and shows the role of the writer,
producer and director.

1010 The jumping-off place: American drama in the 1960s.
Gerald Weales.   New York: Macmillan, 1969. 306p.
The author considers this work to be an extension of his earlier work, *American
drama since World War II*. Here he discusses the change in American theatre
during the 1970s - primarily the emphasis on work written for and produced
off-Broadway. He discusses such departures as the disappearance of taboos on
subject matter and language, and experiments in ensemble playing.

**1011 King of the Bs: working within the Hollywood system: an
anthology of film history and criticism.**
Edited by Todd McCarthy, Charles Flynn.   New York: E.
P. Dutton, 1975. 561p.
An important addition to any American film study collection, this book describes
the 'B' movie and its place in the economy of the Hollywood system. A useful
inclusion is the final section containing filmographies for 325 directors.

1012 Matinee tomorrow: fifty years of our theater.
Ward Morehouse.   New York: McGraw, 1949. 340p.
A lively account of the New York stage from 1898 to 1948, well illustrated by
many photographs. Another film history for theatre enthusiasts.

214

1013 The modern American theater: a collection of critical essays.
Edited by Alvin B. Kernan. Englewood Cliffs, New Jersey: Prentice-Hall, 1967. 183p.
A fine collection of essays dealing with modern American drama. There is an attempt in the arrangement of the book and in the selection of the essays to analyse what makes great drama, and to identify the historical problems of the American theatre. Students of the theatre will find this book profitable reading.

1014 The movies.
Richard Griffith, Arthur Mayer. New York: Simon & Schuster, 1970. rev. ed. 494p.
An updated edition of a fine comprehensive guide to American films and the film industry; the revision brings it through the 1960s. This profusely illustrated volume is a worth-while addition to any general collection.

1015 Notable names in the American theater.
Clifton, New Jersey: James T. White, 1976. rev. ed. 1,250p.
The first edition of this work was published in 1966 under the title *The biographical encyclopedia and who's who of the American theater*. This new edition provides a collection of brief biographical sketches of today's leading theatrical figures, both Americans and other nationalities, who have contributed greatly to the American stage. The volume also includes a necrology section, a list of theatre groups and theatre buildings, chronologically arranged lists of awards, and much other information. A most useful reference tool.

1016 The off-Broadway experience.
Howard Greenberger. Englewood Cliffs, New Jersey: Prentice-Hall, 1971. 207p.
A series of interviews with well-known producers, writers and actors in the theatre world who have had experience with off-Broadway drama. A most readable and nostalgic collection of essays which conveys the flavour of this environment, but which, because of the lack of an index, loses some of its possible use as a reference source.

1017 A pictorial history of the American theater; 100 years: 1860-1970.
Daniel C. Blum. New York: Crown, 1969. 3rd ed. 416p.
A chronologically arranged pictorial record of the American stage. An important addition to any theatre collection.

1018 A pictorial history of the great comedians.
William Cahn. New York: Grosset & Dunlap, 1970. 221p.
A nostalgic, illustrated survey of American comedy from the time of George Washington to the present day. This work is an updated version of *The laughmakers*, 1957. The author examines the special brand of humour that allows people to laugh at themselves, and gives many examples of the comedy of many great comedians.

1019 **A pictorial history of westerns.**
   Michael Parkinson, Clyde Jeavons. London: Hamlyn, 1972.
   217p.
An illustrated look at the history of the western film, tracing its development from the early horse opera to the panoramic movies of today. The authors include the 'spaghetti western' and the television western series. They discuss the stars of these films and the directors such as John Ford who specialized in filming the wild West. The more than 380 photographs should provide pleasure to any enthusiast.

1020 **The political stage: American drama and theater of the Great Depression.**
   Malcolm Goldstein. New York: Oxford University Press,
   1974. 482p.
A discussion of American theatre during the 1930s, which dealt with social causes and issues. Goldstein includes material on cabaret theatre, Broadway productions, social protest productions, the Federal Theater sponsored by the Works Progress Administration, Orson Welles' Mercury Theater (which in 1938 broadcast the memorable *War of the worlds*), and many other topics. This book is filled with information useful to the student of the American theatre.

1021 **Popcorn Venus: women, movies and the American dream.**
   Marjorie Rosen. New York: Coward McCann &
   Geoghegan, 1973. 416p.
A chronicle of American films, showing the evolving role of women in America as portrayed in motion pictures. The author explores the question of whether art reflects life or life reflects art. She discusses the ways in which women have been encouraged to view themselves through the image presented on the screen.

1022 **Regional theater: the revolutionary stage.**
   Joseph Wesley Zeigler. Minneapolis, Minnesota: University
   of Minnesota, 1973. 277p.
The author, who worked in the regional theatre in the 1960s, traces the background of the movement since the Second World War and the histories of individual theatre companies. A useful study for the general reader as well as for the drama student.

1023 **Shakespeare on the American stage: from the Hallams to Edwin Booth.**
   Charles Harlen Shattuck. Washington, DC: Folger
   Shakespeare Library, 1976. 170p.
A beautifully illustrated work published during the bicentennial year on the history of Shakespeare in the American theatre. There is much information on actors who have performed Shakespeare, as well as on all aspects of the physical stage (costume, sets, etc.).

1024 Show biz: from vaude to video.

Abel Green, Joe Laurie, Jr.   Port Washington, New York:
Kennikat Press, 1971. reprint. 2 vols.

A breezy chronicle, first published in 1951, of fifty years of American show business, written in the style of *Variety*, the show business newspaper. The casual style makes it no less an important reference work, and it includes a useful index and glossary of show business terms.

1025 Simon's directory of theatrical materials, services and information.

New York: B. Simon, 1955- .

A directory that has been updated every few years, listing 'where and how to get what' in the theatre. The sections include: plays and actors, costumes, lighting, scenery, film-makers' supplies, advertising, etc. There is an alphabetical table of contents and an index of advertisements. This catalogue is essential for any collection used by people in the performing arts.

1026 Stages: the fifty-year childhood of the American theater.

Emory Lewis.   Englewood Cliffs, New Jersey:
Prentice-Hall, 1969. 290p.

Examines the American theatre from the point of view, which the author espouses, that all theatre has a message of one kind or another and that by examining the works of any period we can gain a mirror of the times. This book analyses many periods of American drama from early Greenwich Village days to the 1960s.

1027 Theater at the crossroads.

John Gassner.   New York: Holt Rinehart & Winston, 1960.
327p.

A series of essays on the theatre in general and on particular theatrical productions during the 1950s. The author, who has written a great deal on the theatre and edited many noted anthologies, provides us with a witty and enthusiastic work.

1028 The theater in colonial America.

Hugh F. Rankin.   Chapel Hill, North Carolina: University
of North Carolina Press, 1965. 328p.

A definitive study of early American theatre, approached from the point of view of the historian rather than the dramatist.

1029 The theater in our times: a survey of the men, materials and movements in the modern theatre.

John Gassner.   New York: Crown, 1954. 609p.

A series of essays which originally appeared in other publications, evaluating trends, works, and dramatists in the modern theatre. The book discusses both European and American works, but it is an important contribution from an American perspective.

1030 The theater in spite of itself.
Walter Kerr.   New York: Simon & Schuster, 1963. 319p.
A witty and stimulating collection of play reviews and magazine articles written by a well-known theatre critic. Kerr discusses contemporary theatre and puts it into historical perspective.

1031 Theater, U.S.A., 1668 to 1957.
Barnard Wolcott Hewitt.   New York: McGraw-Hill, 1959. 528p.
A fascinating history of 300 years in the American theatre, told through contemporary accounts and amplified by commentary. Interesting reading for the layman as well as for the student of the theatre.

1032 The theatrical 20s.
Allen Churchill.   New York: McGraw-Hill, 1975. 362p. bibliog.
The high point of this book on Broadway in the 1920s is its collection of photographs illustrating each chapter. The book is arranged chronologically and presents an interesting panorama of this period of American theatre.

1033 There must be a Lone Ranger: the American West in film and in reality.
Jenni Calder.   London: Hamilton, 1974. 241p.
Relates the realities of Western life to films and fictional works which have attempted to reflect those realities. The work has several interesting chapters, including one on 'Women in the West' which focuses on literary works rather than film.

1034 Thirty plays hath November: pain and pleasure in the contemporary theater.
Walter Kerr.   New York: Simon & Schuster, 1969. 343p.
Another enertaining collection of Kerr's pieces on contemporary plays, playwrights, actors, directors, repertory theatre, and even on such topics as the price of theatre tickets.

1035 Toms, coons, mulattoes, mammies, and bucks: an interpretive history of blacks in American films.
Donald Bogle.   New York: Viking Press, 1973. 260p.
An interesting film history tracing the role of blacks in American films, beginning in 1905 and following the changes to the 1970s.

1036 Trouping: how the show came to town.
Philip C. Lewis.   New York: Harper & Row, 1973. 266p.
An enjoyable account of the touring road shows in the United States between 1850 and 1905. There is no attempt at completeness, but this is an informative work for the theatre enthusiast.

1037 Up against the fourth wall, essays on modern theater.
John Lahr. New York: Grove Press, 1970. 305p.
An articulate chronicle and interpretation of American drama of the 1960s. Lahr, a drama critic who emerged in the field at the same time as the modern theatre of which he writes, gives a useful historical record of the period.

1038 Voices of the black theater.
Loften Mitchell. Clifton, New Jersey: James T. White, 1975. 238p.
A record of taped sessions with artists in the black theatre, illustrating their struggles during the first half of this century. The author adds explanatory comments. Such artists as Abram Hill and Ruby Dee are represented. An important addition to theatre history collections.

1039 We're in the money: Depression America and its films.
Andrew Bergman. New York: New York University Press, 1971. 200p. bibliog.
An interesting study of the films of the 1930s, written from the point of view of the Hollywood producers, the theatre-owners and the press of the time. The author analyses about 100 films to find out what made them successful.

1040 Words with music.
Lehman Engel. New York: Macmillan, 1972. 358p.
The author, a composer, conductor and writer, examines musical theatre, tracing its origins and assessing its future growth. This work is of interest both to the general reader and to the aspiring writer and composer trying to learn what succeeds and why in the unique art form of the American musical.

1041 Yankee theater: the image of America on the stage, 1825-1850.
Francis Hodge. Austin, Texas: University of Texas Press, 1964. 320p. bibliog.
A scholarly analysis of the 'stage Yankee' who performed before audiences between 1825 and 1850. These actors, with their New England dialect comedy, presented the American as they saw him and set the stage for the realistic American 'character' plays of the later 19th century. A worthwhile addition to any American drama collection.

Fashion

1042 American denim: a new folk art.
Peter Beagle. New York: H. N. Abrams, 1975. 156p.
A collection of colour photographs of garments submitted in a contest sponsored by Levi Strauss and Company in 1973 for the best-decorated denims. Included is a social history of 'Levis' as well as captions describing the method of decoration.

1043 American fashion: the life and lines of Adrian, Mainbocher, McCardell, Norell and Trigere.
Edited by Sarah Tomerlin Lee. New York: Quadrangle and New York Times Book Co., 1975. 509p.
A lavishly illustrated record of fifty years of fashion, sponsored by the Fashion Institute of Technology. It concentrates on the work of the five designers of the title.

1044 Early American costume.
Estelle Ansley Worrell. Harrisburg, Pennsylvania: Stackpole, 1975. 183p.
A beautifully illustrated chronological look at American costume between 1680 and 1850. The book is very useful for people designing theatrical costumes, since it includes instructions on drafting patterns and constructing costumes.

1045 Early American dress: the colonial and revolutionary periods.
Edward Warwick, Henry C. Pitz, Alexander Wyckoff. New York: Benjamin Blom, 1965. 428p. (History of American Dress, vol. 2).
This illustrated volume on American costume from 1607 to 1800 is a revised version of an earlier work by Warwick and Pitz, *Early American costume*, 1930. A useful addition to all costume collections.

1046 **Five centuries of American costume.**
R. Turner Wilcox. New York: Charles Scribner's Sons,
1963. 207p. bibliog.
A survey of American dress, beginning with pre-colonial peoples such as Indians,
Vikings, Eskimos, etc., and covering modern times up to the space suits of 1962
astronauts. The chapters are well illustrated with detailed line drawings, and this
book is very useful to students, artists, etc. who want to accurately reproduce
American costume.

1047 **Historic dress in America, 1607-1870.**
Elisabeth McClellan. New York: Arno Press, 1977. 454p.
A reissue of a long-out-of-print classic in the field of historic costume, this is an
invaluable addition to any collection on American fashion history. This work was
first published in two separate parts in 1904 and 1910 under the titles *Historic
dress in America, 1607-1800* and *Historic dress in America, 1800-1870*. It
includes illustrations and documentation of men's, women's and children's dress,
and covers all walks of life and occasions.

1048 **Ready-made miracle: the American story of fashion for the
millions.**
Jessica Daves. New York: G. P. Putnam's Sons, 1967.
256p.
An illustrated history of the American fashion industry, written by a former
editor of *Vogue*, the noted fashion magazine. The book tells the story of the
ready-made fashion business, from the designer to the buyer, and its impact on
American women.

1049 **Suiting everyone: the democratization of clothing in
America.**
Claudia B. Kidwell, Margaret C. Christman. Washington,
DC: Smithsonian Institution Press, 1974. 208p. bibliog.
This book is the result of an exhibition at the National Museum of History and
Technology on the subject of the democratization of clothing in America - the
birth of ready-made quality clothing which could provide what people needed at
moderate prices. This well-illustrated work covers the period from the 18th cen-
tury to the present.

1050 **Women's Wear Daily.**
New York: Fairchild Publications, 1910- . 5 issues per week.
The trade newspaper of the retail fashion industry. Included is information on
fashion and buying trends as well as other news of interest to those in the fashion
business.

Fashion

1051 **Working dress in colonial and revolutionary America.**
Peter F. Copeland.   Westport, Connecticut; London:
Greenwood Press, 1977. 223p. bibliog. (Contributions in
American History, no. 58).

An illustrated history of the costumes of the various types of workers (farmers,
fishermen, tradesmen, pedlars, soldiers, etc.) during the period 1710-1810. The
sketches are all in black-and-white, and useful annotations are included along
with the text.

Food

1052 American cooking.
Dale Brown. New York: Time-Life, 1968. 2 vols. map. (Foods of the World).
This beautifully illustrated work includes its own accompanying small volume of recipes. It attempts to represent the regions of America and includes recipes as well as text tracing regional culinary history and describing the variety of food available in America.

1053 American food: the gastronomic story.
Evan Jones. New York: E. P. Dutton, 1975. 387p.
A collection of original recipes representing the ethnic influences on American cookery. The author discusses these influences and traces regional cooking traditions from colonial times to the present.

1054 The American regional cookbook: recipes from yesterday and today for the modern cook.
Nancy Hawkins, Arthur Hawkins. Englewood Cliffs, New Jersey: Prentice-Hall, 1976. 301p.
A cookery book which includes recipes from nine regions of the United States: New England, the East, the South, the Gulf coast, the Midwest, the Prairie states, the Northwest, the Southwest, and the Pacific coast. Each section contains an introduction to the region and includes excerpts from documents such as old diaries and journals.

1055 Colonial cooking: a treasury of colonial recipes.
Rebecca Caruba. Maplewood, New Jersey: Hammond, 1975. 128p.
A basic, easy-to-follow collection of colonial recipes adapted for the cooking methods of today. Most of the recipes can be prepared in an hour or less, and this should make them popular in today's busy world.

Food

1056 **Foods from harvest festivals and folk fairs: the best recipes from and a guide to food happenings across the nation.**
Anita Borghese. New York: Thomas Y. Crowell, 1977. 270p.
A unique book on American harvest festivals, describing the features of the fairs, emphasizing the food events, and including many recipes gathered from participants in the fairs.

1057 **Grandmother in the kitchen: a cook's tour of American household recipes from the early 1800s to the late 1890s.**
Helen Lyon Adamson. New York: Crown, 1965. 308p.
An interesting collection of recipes which reflect 19th century America and the conditions under which housewives of the time worked to provide their families with meals.

1058 **James Beard's American cookery.**
James Andrews Beard. Boston, Massachusetts: Little, Brown, 1972. 877p. bibliog.
An excellent cookery book which contains recipes for cooks of all levels, from the novice to the experienced chef. It includes discussions of American food and of the adaptation by immigrants of their cooking to the resources found in a new country.

1059 **The New York Times heritage cook book.**
Jean Hewitt. New York: G. P. Putnam's Sons, 1972. 804p.
A regional cookery book, offering recipes from six regions of the United States: the Northeast, the South, the Midwest, the mountain states, the northern plains, the Southwest, and the Northwest (including Hawaii and Alaska). The colour illustrations enhance this well-indexed guide to traditional American cookery of all varieties.

1060 **The Old Farmer's Almanac colonial cookbook.**
Edited by Clarissa M. Silitch. Dublin, New Hampshire: Yankee, 1976. 64p.
A collection of recipes for authentic colonial foods which were gathered from the files of the *Old Farmer's Almanac* and updated for preparation by modern cooks.

1061 **The presidents' cookbook: practical recipes from George Washington to the present.**
Poppy Cannon, Patricia Brooks. New York: Funk & Wagnalls, 1968. 545p.
An enjoyable glimpse of the presidents of the United States as shown through menus and recipes chosen throughout their stays in the White House. Included are anecdotes which reflect the regional origins of the presidents as well as the manners of their times.

Sports

1062 The all-American dollar: the big business of sports.
Joseph Durso. Boston, Massachusetts: Houghton Mifflin, 1971. 294p.
An interesting book describing the sports boom of the 1960s and showing the events that have turned professional sport into a money-making business. The author covers expensive television competition for sporting events, extravagant rewards for athletes (and their organization into labour unions), and the advent of such new institutions as off-track betting.

1063 The armchair referee - 500 questions and answers about football.
Jerry Markbreit. Garden City, New York: Doubleday, 1973. 218p. bibliog.
Written for the enthusiast who needs explanations of the complicated rules of professional and college football. The author presents an indexed question-and-answer format, arranging his chapters by topics such as fouls and penalties, scoring, etc. Some colourful football anecdotes are also included.

1064 The baseball encyclopedia: the complete and official record of major league baseball.
New York: Macmillan, 1976. 2,142p.
A comprehensive reference source on baseball, providing such information as the yearly performances of every player in the major leagues; a chronological listing of the teams, with their batting, running and pitching leaders for each year; a register of all major league managers with their records, and much more. The statistics cover baseball history from 1876 to 1975.

1065 The baseball handbook for coaches and players.
Jim Depel. New York: Charles Scribner's Sons, 1976. 96p.
A simple guide which contains tips on playing techniques, diagrams for players, information on constructing and maintaining playing equipment and the field, lists of baseball associations, and directions for computing baseball statistics.

1066 Basketball's Hall of Fame.
Sandy Padwe. Englewood Cliffs, New Jersey: Prentice-Hall, 1970. 193p.

This history of basketball was published in cooperation with the Basketball Hall of Fame which was established in Springfield, Massachusetts in 1968. It contains the story of the founding of the Hall of Fame, tells of the players and coaches who were renowned in the sport, and is illustrated with many photographs of the Hall of Fame members.

1067 The Book of Baseball Records.
Edited by Seymour Siwoff. New York: Seymour Siwoff. annual.

An authoritative, exhaustive baseball record book covering all official major league baseball records, including World Series and All-Star games.

1068 A carnival of sports: spectacles, stunts, crazes, and unusual sports events.
William Severn. New York: David McKay, 1974. 182p.

Explores some of the American sports fads outside of the main area of the major sports such as baseball and basketball. In this illustrated work Severn has captured such diverse crazes and stunts as flag-pole sitting, frisbee flinging, skateboard riding, and skating in the Roller Derby.

1069 The complete book of running.
James P. Fixx. New York: Random House, 1977. 314p. bibliog.

Running, or jogging, has been an increasingly popular American sport, and the author provides a virtual encyclopaedia on this activity. He includes chapters on gear, diet, psychology, running after a heart attack, preparing for a marathon, etc. The advice offered is practical and the appendixes give useful information for the novice as well as for the experienced runner.

1070 The complete jogger.
Jack Batten. New York: Harcourt Brace Jovanovich, 1977. 145p. bibliog.

A practical guide for the jogger, giving information on its effects on health, what to wear, where to run, diet, etc. A useful handbook for a popular sport.

1071 The encyclopedia of football.
Roger L. Treat, edited by Peter Palmer. South Brunswick, New Jersey: A. S. Barnes, 1977. 15th ed. 702p.

A continually revised reference which brings up to date the history and records of football. Included is information on such topics as the World Football League, Hall of Fame selections, and Super Bowls. A useful source in any general reference collection.

1072 Family games America plays.
Walter Brown Gibson. Garden City, New York:
Doubleday, 1970. 275p.

A marvellous illustrated collection of games. It includes the basic rules of the
games and explains intricate plays. The book is divided into nine chapters: group
games, games for two persons, board games, special board games, card games,
special card games, dominoes, games with varied equipment, and mah-jongg.

1073 Five seasons: a baseball companion.
Roger Angell. New York: Simon & Schuster, 1977. 413p.

A collection of articles, most of which first appeared in the *New Yorker*, giving
the author's impressions of modern baseball of the 1970s. It provides accounts of
the heroes and top stars of today's baseball world - such as Catfish Hunter, Pete
Rose, and Tom Seaver - and covers such diverse topics as Angell's times with a
baseball scout. A fascinating book for the baseball fan.

1074 The modern encyclopedia of basketball.
Edited by Zander Hollander. New York: Four Winds,
1973. rev. ed. 547p. bibliog.

A comprehensive, illustrated record of a most popular American sport: basketball.
Included are sketches of players and coaches, a history of the game, detailed
statistics, rules of the game, and much more. A welcome addition to any reference collection on sports.

1075 The New York Times guide to spectator sports.
Leonard Koppett. New York: Quadrangle, 1971. 259p.

A much-needed book for the enthusiast who watches sport on television and
wishes to understand the rules of play, patterns of competition, inside strategies,
and how to calculate sports records and team standings. The book covers baseball,
football, basketball, hockey, boxing, golf, tennis, track and field, swimming and
diving, racing, soccer, lacrosse, fencing, bowling, winter sports, court games, boat
racing, gymnastics, wrestling, weight-lifting, and the Olympic games.

1076 The NFL's official encylopedic history of professional
football.
National Football League. New York: Macmillan, 1973.
392p.

A comprehensive fact-book containing records, statistics, names and data relating
to the history of professional football in the United States. Included are the
histories of the teams of the National Football League as well as descriptions of
many historic games. Essential for any football fan.

1077 Ski down the years.
John Clarkson Jay, Frankie O'Rear. New York: Award
House, 1966. 268p.

A nostalgic picture history of thirty years of skiing in America. The book is
crammed with photographs from the files of *Ski Magazine* and provides anecdotes and memorabilia dating back to the 1930s. Certain to delight the skiing
enthusiast.

1078 Skiing U.S.A.: a guide to the nation's ski areas.
Lucy M. Fehr.   New York: William Morrow, 1977. 211p.
(Americans Discover America Series).

A list of skiing areas in thirty-eight American states, including information on the snow season, mailing address, telephone number, number and types of lifts, ski jumps, nearest lodging, and much more. Although much of the information will have changed by the time of this publication, as a general guide this volume will be useful to anyone planning a skiing trip.

1079 Soccer for Americans.
John Allen.   New York: Grossett & Dunlap, 1967. 256p.

Soccer, which is a basically British game, has become increasingly popular in the United States. This book was written to give Americans some knowledge of the history, rules, and personalities that have been famous in the sport.

1080 Sportsworld: an American dreamland.
Robert Lipsyte.   New York: Quadrangle and New York Times Book Co., 1975. 292p.

The author, who for fourteen years was a sports writer for the *New York Times*, discusses professional sports in America and gives his view of what is wrong with the big-business aspect of promotion and distortion of sports. He calls this structure of attitudes and ethics that has been built up over the past fifty years 'Sportsworld', and gives many examples of the danger of this emphasis to spectators and athletes alike.

1081 A thinking man's guide to pro football.
Paul Lionel Zimmerman.   New York: E. P. Dutton, 1970. 383p.

Written by a sports writer, this book on professional football is aimed at the football fan. Using anecdotes and quotes from players, coaches, etc., Zimmerman discusses technique, how coaches rate referees, broadcasters, the minor leagues, and other assorted topics.

1082 200 years of sport in America.
Wells Twombly.   New York: McGraw-Hill, 1976. 287p.

A beautifully illustrated history of sports in America from 1776 to 1976. This volume is divided into four sections: 'The pastoral age' (1776-1865); 'The passionate age' (1866-1919); 'The golden age' (1920-45); and 'The electronic age' (1946-76). The illustrations include the work of great artists, such as Thomas Eakins and Winslow Homer, and also memorable photographs.

1083 Who was who in American sports.
Ralph Hickok.   New York: Hawthorn, 1971. 338p.

The major sports included are baseball, football, basketball, boxing, golf, tennis, and track. The book contains almost 1,500 entries and provides biographical information, records, and career highlights for America's most important past sports figures. Sports reporters, broadcasters and managers are covered as well as great athletes.

1084 **The World Series: a complete pictorial history.**
John Devaney, Burt Goldblatt. Chicago: Rand McNally,
1972. 352p.
Gives a capsule history of baseball as shown through black-and-white illustrations
covering the World Series games from 1903 to 1973. The authors use photographs, newsreel frames, and other illustrations to tell the story of some seventy
years of baseball in America.

Print Media

1085 American Book Trade Directory.
Edited and compiled by Jacques Cattell Press. New York: R. R. Bowker, 1915- . biennial.

A current listing of American and Canadian booksellers, wholesalers and publishers. Section 1 provides data on retail outlets; section 2 on wholesalers, jobbers and distributors of books and magazines; section 3 on dealers in foreign books, exporters, importers and rental library chains; section 4 on book publishers; and section 5 is an alphabetical index to all outlets in sections 1 and 2.

1086 The American magazine: a compact history.
John William Tebbel. New York: Hawthorn, 1969. 279p. bibliog.

A short survey of American magazine history from 1741 to 1969. The material about the magazines since 1930 is especially important, since this continues where Mott leaves off in his *History of American magazines* (q.v.). The author discusses the successes and failures of modern publishing empires and the current trend towards specialized audiences.

1087 Ayer Directory of Publications.
Philadelphia: Ayer Press, 1880- . annual.

The title varies; *N. W. Ayer and Son's American Newspaper Annual* and other variations have been used. The subtitle reads: 'The professional's directory of print media published in the United States; Puerto Rico; Virgin Islands; Canada; Bahamas; Bermuda; the Republic of Panama and the Philippines. Economic descriptions of the states, provinces, cities and towns in which all listees are published; fifteen separate, classified lists; sixty-nine custom-made maps on which all publication cities and towns are indicated'.

1088 The book in America: a history of the making and selling of books in the U.S.
Helmut Lehmann-Haupt. New York: R. R. Bowker, 1951.
2nd rev. and enl. ed. 493p.
First published in Leipzig in 1937 under the title *Das amerikanische Buchwesen*, this volume is a classic on all aspects of the book trade in the United States. It should be included in any library collection on the subject.

1089 The compact history of the American newspaper.
John William Tebbel. New York: Hawthorn, 1969. new
rev. ed. 286p. bibliog.
A survey of the American newspaper from colonial times to the present. The author describes the earliest newspapers as propaganda; those of the late 19th and early 20th centuries as personal instruments; and those since the First World War as business institutions.

1090 Forthcoming Books.
New York: R. R. Bowker, 1961- . bimonthly.
Lists books published since the most recent *Books in Print*, and those to be published in the succeeding five months.

1091 A history of American magazines.
Frank Luther Mott. Cambridge, Massachusetts: Harvard
University Press, 1938-68. 5 vols. bibliog.
Vol. 1: 1741-1850; vol. 2: 1850-65; vol. 3: 1865-85; vol. 4: 1885-1905; vol. 5: sketches of twenty-one magazines, 1905-30, with a cumulative index to the five volumes. A scholarly history of the American magazine from 1741 to 1930. The author died in 1964, having almost completed five of a projected six-volume work. Three of these volumes earned him a Pulitzer prize and the Bancroft prize for history. This set has become a standard reference source on the history of the American magazine.

1092 A history of book publishing in the United States.
John William Tebbel. New York: R. R. Bowker, 1972- .
Vol. 1: *The creation of an industry, 1630-1865*; vol. 2: *The expansion of an industry, 1865-1919*; vol. 3: *The golden age between two wars, 1920-1940*. This work aims to provide a definitive study of American book publishing, comparable to Mott's *History of American magazines*. The author began his undertaking as an outgrowth of a course which he taught at New York University on American publishing. He found a dearth of material on this topic, and decided to begin the project. A wealth of material can be found here.

1093 Literary Market Place, with Names and Numbers: the Directory of American Book Publishing.
New York: R. R. Bowker, 1940- . annual.
This indispensable reference provides a history of personnel in publishing and related fields and a buyers' guide for those who purchase materials in the book publishing area. Includes sections on book trade events, services and suppliers, radio, television and motion pictures, book manufacturing, magazine and news-

paper publishing and many other areas. Names, addresses and telephone numbers make this a working tool.

1094 Magazines in the twentieth century.
Theodore Bernard Peterson. Urbana, Illinois: University of Illinois Press, 1964. 2nd ed. 484p. bibliog.

A history of the modern magazine, tracing it from its origins in the late 19th century to 1964. The first edition was published in 1956, but so many changes took place in such a short time that a second edition was prepared in 1964 to include a discussion of them. The general scope of the book covers commercial magazines intended for the lay public.

1095 The printed book in America.
Joseph Blumenthal. Boston, Massachusetts: D. R. Godine, 1977. 250p. bibliog.

A survey of printing in America from its origins in colonial times. Included are discussions of the greatest typographers - Daniel Updike, Frederic Goudy, William Dwiggins, etc. - and of the special presses noted for their achievements in typography. The book is beautifully illustrated with plates duplicating pages from books; these were chosen to illustrate letterpress printing and typography.

1096 The Publishers' Trade List Annual.
New York: R. R. Bowker, 1873- . annual.

A list of active and forthcoming publications from about 2,000 US and from a number of Canadian trade publishers. Included are some university presses, religious denominations and learned societies. The bibliographical information is supplied by each publisher. Two indexes are also produced: *Books in Print: an Author-Title Series Index to the Publishers' Trade List Annual* (New York: R. R. Bowker, 1948-); *Subject Guide to Books in Print: an Index to the Publishers' Trade List Annual* (New York: R. R. Bowker, 1957-).

1097 Publishers' Weekly, the Book Industry Journal.
New York: R. R. Bowker, 1872- . weekly.

An alphabetical listing of current American book publications, providing brief annotations, published prices and the addresses of the publishers.

1098 What happens in book publishing.
Edited by Chandler B. Grannis. New York: Columbia University Press, 1967. 2nd ed. 467p. bibliog.

A collection of essays by experts in many areas of book publishing. This revised edition of a work originally published in 1957 provides a picture of what happens in publishing a book for general retail sale. It covers book design, advertising, distribution, legal aspects of publishing and special areas such as children's books and religious books, etc.

1099 Writer's Market.
Cincinnati, Ohio: Writer's Digest, 1930- . annual.

A reference for the writer, leading the writer to the editor who will read and hopefully publish his or her work. It includes information on submitting the manuscript; copyright data; taxation; descriptive lists of book publishers; a variety of publications, opportunities and services such as literary agents; writer's clubs; and a wealth of related information.

Broadcasting

1100 The complete encyclopedia of television programs, 1947-1976.
Vincent Terrace.   New Brunswick, New Jersey: A. S. Barnes, 1976. 2 vols.
An alphabetical anthology, tracing thirty years of American television programming. This work includes more than 2,700 network and syndicated programmes of all types: comedy, adventure, children's, documentary, etc. The brief profiles of the shows contain descriptions of content, cast lists, and dates of airing.

1101 The golden age of television.
Max Wilk.   New York: Delacorte Press, 1976. 274p.
A look at the early years of television, as shown through the recollections of writers, performers, technicians and executives who have worked in the medium.

1102 A history of broadcasting in the United States.
Erik Barnouw.   New York: Oxford University Press, 1966-70. 3 vols. bibliog.
Vol. 1: *A tower in Babel, to 1933*; vol. 2: *The golden web, 1933-1953*; vol. 3: *The image empire, from 1953*. A comprehensive history of American broadcasting from the earliest days of radio to television and its impact on our lives. A valuable addition to any collection on communications.

1103 How sweet it was; television: a pictorial commentary.
Arthur Shulman, Roger Youman.   New York: Shorecrest, 1966. 447p.
A nostalgic pictorial look at 20 years of television. The authors, long-time staff members of *TV Guide* magazine, have collected and reproduced 1,435 photographs, which they have arranged into twelve chapters on the various types of television programming: comedy, panel shows, news shows, children's programming, etc.

1104 I looked and I listened: informal recollections of radio and TV.
Ben Gross. New Rochelle, New York: Arlington House, 1970. 373p.

A reminiscent account of forty-five years of broadcasting as set down by a well-known columnist in the field. This book provides an interesting record of radio and television through their birth and development.

1105 In search of light: the broadcasts of Edward R. Murrow, 1938-1961.
Edward R. Murrow, edited by Edward Bliss, Jr. New York: Knopf, 1967. 364p.

A selection of broadcasts by a prominent journalist. When read, they provide a fascinating historical record from the Second World War to Kennedy's inauguration. Murrow covered many issues which are relevant today, such as censorship, national security, etc., and his style and technique of reporting should be studied as important examples of fine broadcasting journalism.

1106 Living room war.
Michael J. Arlen. New York: Viking Press, 1969. 242p.

A collection of almost forty of Arlen's essays, originally published in the *New Yorker*, on the role of television in people's lives. A witty and thought-provoking book which makes fascinating reading.

1107 The New York Times encyclopedia of television.
Les Brown. New York: Times Books, 1977. 492p.

A comprehensive work covering television from its inception in 1948, with entries arranged alphabetically to facilitate use as a reference. The book includes programmes and personalities which would be judged important because of their prominence or reference value. There is also much useful information on networks, unions, advertising agencies, rating systems, etc. An important source book on television.

1108 The Today show: an inside look at twenty-five tumultuous years.
Robert Metz. Chicago: Playboy Press, 1977. 264p.

An interesting look at one of the longest-running and most influential of all television shows. The author concentrates on personalities, and the book will interest the general reader and television viewer.

1109 Tube of plenty: the evolution of American television.
Erik Barnouw. New York: Oxford University Press, 1975. 518p. bibliog.

A history of broadcasting in the United States. This work condenses and updates the author's three-volume *History of broadcasting in the United States* (q.v.), 1966-70.

Reference Works

1110 **American bibliography: a chronological dictionary of all books, pamphlets, and periodical publications printed in the United States of America from the genesis of printing in 1639 down to and including the year 1800; with bibliographical and biographical notes.**
Charles Evans. Chicago: printed for the author, 1903-59. 14 vols.

A general list of early American publications - including books, pamphlets and periodicals - arranged chronologically by publication date. Important for the large reference collection.

1111 **Concise dictionary of American biography.**
New York: Charles Scribner's Sons, 1964. 1,273p.

An alphabetically arranged condensed version of the *Dictionary of American biography* (see the following entry). No individuals who died later than 1940 are included, as in the original work, but the original articles have been revised when new information has been found.

1112 **Dictionary of American biography.**
New York: Charles Scribner's Sons, 1928-37. 20 vols. suppl. 1-6, 1944-60. Reprinted, New York: Charles Scribner's Sons, 1943. 21 vols.; 1946. 11 vols.

A scholarly reference source containing signed articles and bibliographies. Living persons are not included. The dictionary contains an index which is most useful for finding prominent members of various occupations, as well as states' leading citizens. The reprinted editions contain lists of errata found in the original.

236

1113 Dictionary of books relating to America, from its discovery to the present time.
Joseph Sabin. New York: Sabin, 1868-92; Bibliographical Society of America, 1928-36. 29 vols. Reprinted, Amsterdam: N. Israel, 1961-62.
A classic reference work listing books, pamphlets, and periodicals pertaining to America. The works are listed by author, and in many cases the bibliographical information includes the names of libraries possessing copies.

1114 Encyclopedia Americana.
New York: Americana Corporation. 30 vols.
An excellent general encyclopaedia, continuously revised, with good information on American towns and cities. Many of the articles are signed and include bibliographies, maps, illustrations and pronunciation. A must for every reference collection.

1115 Monthly Catalog of United States Government Publications.
US Superintendent of Documents. Washington, DC: US Government Printing Office, 1895- . monthly.
Lists the publications of all branches of government, and includes information for ordering the documents. The publications are listed alphabetically by department and bureau, and there are monthly and annual indexes as well as decennial indexes.

1116 National cyclopedia of American biography.
New York: White, 1892- .
Much more comprehensive than the *Dictionary of American biography* (q.v.), this work includes many more names of people of local as well as national prominence. Articles are unsigned and are prepared from questionnaires filled out by families of those listed. Some photographs are included, but there is no bibliography and the indexes must be used since this work is not arranged alphabetically.

1117 Notable American women, 1607-1950: a biographical dictionary.
Cambridge, Massachusetts: Belknap Press of Harvard University Press, 1971. 3 vols. bibliog.
Contains biographical sketches of over 1,350 women and provides an important supplement to the *Dictionary of American biography* (q.v.) since most of the women included here were not included in the earlier work. The only women entered in this work on the basis of their husbands' credentials were wives of United States presidents; all others have been included for work which took them before the public and gained them distinction beyond the local level.

1118 **Notable American women: the modern period.**
Barbara Sicherman (and others). Cambridge,
Massachusetts: Harvard University Press, 1980. 773p.

This supplement to the original *Notable American women, 1607-1950* (see the preceding item) extends the coverage to 1975 with the biographies of 442 additional subjects. The articles are well written and signed.

1119 **Readers' Guide to Periodical Literature.**
New York: H. W. Wilson, 1905- . bimonthly, with annual
cumulations.

Indexes a large number of United States periodicals of general, non-technical character. The volumes are arranged alphabetically by author, subject and title (when necessary) and provide full information with each article: date, volume, inclusive paging, indication of illustrations, bibliographies, etc. An invaluable reference tool for every library.

1120 **Statistical Abstracts of the United States, 1878- .**
US Bureau of the Census. Washington, DC: US
Government Printing Office, 1899- . annual.

Provides statistics of national importance in the areas of politics, economics and social sciences and includes a subject guide to statistical services.

1121 **Vertical File Index: Subject and Title Index to Selected
Pamphlet Material.**
New York: H. W. Wilson, 1935- . monthly (except August),
with annual cumulations.

A list, arranged by subject, of free and inexpensive pamphlets and mimeographs useful to general and school libraries. Contains complete bibliographical information, including prices and descriptions.

1122 **White's conspectus of American biography.**
New York: David White, 1937. 2nd ed. 455p.

A revised and enlarged edition of the conspectus section of the conspectus and index volume of the *National cyclopedia of American biography* (q.v.). This work is useful as a source book of information: chronological lists of many types of office-holders, lists of prize winners, pseudonyms, etc. It may also be used as a classified index to the *National cyclopedia.*

1123 **Who was who in America: a companion biographical
reference work to Who's who in America.**
Chicago: Marquis, 1942-68. 4 vols.

Includes articles removed from *Who's Who in America* (q.v.) because the people have died. The dates of death and sometimes burial locations, plus some revisions, are appended to the entries. Vol. 4 contains a cumulated index.

1124 **Who was who in America: historical volume, 1607-1896.**
Chicago: Marquis, 1963. 670p.
Together with *Who was who in America*, volumes 1-4, this work forms a series
entitled *Who's who in American history.*

1125 **Who's Who in America, a Biographical Dictionary of
Notable Living Men and Women.**
Chicago: Marquis, 1899- . semi-annual.
A standard reference source with information supplied by those listed. Included
are prominent individuals notable for particular achievements or official positions.
Sectional publications supplement the work; these are: *Who's who in the East: a
biographical dictionary of noteworthy men and women of the middle Atlantic
and northeastern states and eastern Canada* (1942-43-); *Who's who in the
Midwest: a biographical dictionary of noteworthy men and women of the central
and midwestern states* (1949-); *Who's who in the South and Southwest: a
biographical dictionary of noteworthy men and women of the southern and
southwestern states* (1950-); *Who's who in the West: a biographical dictionary
of noteworthy men and women of the Pacific coastal and western states* (1949-).

1126 **Who's Who of American Women: a Biographical Dictionary
of Notable Living American Women.**
Chicago: Maquis, 1958/59- . semi-annual.
Includes many names not found in *Who's who in America*; the information is
supplied by the women listed. An earlier work covering 1935-40 is *American
women* (Los Angeles: American, 1935-39. 3 vols.).

Index

The index is a single alphabetical sequence of authors (personal and corporate), titles of publications and subjects. Index entries refer both to the main items and to other works mentioned in the notes to each item. Title entries are in italics. Numeration refers to the items as numbered.

244

C

Cabaret theatre
  Depression era 1020
Cabinet
  lists of members 415
Cady, Edwin Harrison 803
Cage, John 940
Cahn, W. 657, 1018
Cajuns
  folklore 865
Calder, J. 56, 1033
California
  Amerindians 239
  archaeology 58
  settlement 140
Cambodia
  US intervention 543, 545
Cambon, G. 811
Cambridge history of American
  literature 784
Camera, spade and pen: an inside view
  of Southwestern archaeology 57
Campaign spending 401
  congressional 419, 421
  presidential 449
Campbell, C. S. 544
Campbell, Rita Ricardo 376
Camping 46
Canals 626
Canby, Henry Seidel 815
Cannon, P. 1061
Canoeing 43, 46, 52
Cantor, M. 396
Capitalism 554
Capote, Truman 795
Carnegie, Andrew 595
Carnegie Corporation 918
Carnegie Council on Children 338
Carnegie Endowment for International
    Peace 649
Carnegie Hall 976
Carnival of sports: spectacles, stunts,
    crazes, and unusual sports
    events 1068
Carroll, J. W. 322
Carruth, G. 75
Carter, D. 212
Carter, Jimmy 434
  foreign policy 523
Cartograms 22
Caruba, R. 1055
Case, K. 49
Cassavetes, John 1008

Casta, Beverly da 50
Castells, M. 554
Catalog of published concert music by
    American composers 951
Cather, Willa 798
Catholic America 297
Catholic church 298, 324, 333
  history 297, 311
  philosophy 290, 293
  role in society 297
Catlin, George 910, 936
Catton, B. 103, 149
Catton, W. B. 103
Causes of the American Revolution 90
Cavalcade of the American novel:
    from the birth of the nation to
    the middle of the twentieth
    century 785
Ceaser, J. W. 446
Centennial history of the Civil
    War 149
Center for Independent Education 734
Central America
  relations with 547
Century of struggle: the woman's
    rights movement in the United
    States 253
Certain morbidness: a view of
    American literature 786
Chafe, W. H. 247
Chambers, C. D. 344
Chambers, John Whiteclay 179
Chambers of commerce
  directories 598
Chandler, L. V. 572
Changing world of the American
    military 190
Chapin, F. S. 695
Chapman, J. A. 992
Chapman, J. D. 30
Charles, Ray 982
Charleston, South Carolina
  segregation 227
Chase, G. 940, 945
Cheape, C. W. 630
Chemical and Engineering News 756
Chemical coping: a report on legal
    drug use in the United States 344
Chemical engineering
  periodicals 755
Chemical industry
  health and safety 606
Chemical pollution 686
Chemistry
  periodicals 756

252

259

264

H

270

History *contd.*
  segregation 212, 227, 231
  slavery 145, 213—214, 228—230
  Southern states 41—42, 77, 128, 142, 165, 172
  state governors 71
  Supreme Court 484, 489
  teaching 101
  towns 93—94
  urban 93
  utopianism 72
  Vietnam War 189
  War of 1812 134
  Western states 83, 129
  women 247—249, 252—256, 258—260, 262—263, 265, 268, 270—273
  World War I 175
  World War II 186—187
History, Cultural 5, 7—8, 11—12, 14—15, 86, 88, 188, 820
  Amerindians 242
  colonial period 107
  popular 80
  role of art 903, 908, 917, 928
  role of music 941
History of accounting in America: an historical interpretation of the cultural significance of accounting 578
History of American archaeology 61
History of American art 928
History of American economic life 560
History of American law 459
History of American magazines 1091
History of American philosophy 887
History of American presidential elections, 1789-1968 439
History of the American Revolution 119
History of American technology 743
History of the American theater, 1770-1950 1007
History of book publishing in the United States 1092
History of broadcasting in the United States 1102
History of the Catholic church in the United States 311
History of education in American culture 720
History of the Indians of the United States 240

History of the labor movement in the United States 650
History of philosophy in America 888
History of the rise and progress of the arts of design in the United States 929
History of social welfare and social work in the United States 357
History of the South 165, 172
History of the Southern Confederacy 153
History of the United States of America, from the discovery of the continent 104
History of violence in America: historical and comparative perspectives 358
History of women in America 259
Hochman, S. 84
Hockey 1075
Hodge, C. 17
Hodge, F. 1041
Hodge, F. W. 239
Hodgson, G. 436
Hodgson, M. 977
Hoffman, D. N. 412
Hoffman, F. J. 776, 803, 852
Hofstadter, R. 8, 112, 162, 167, 392
Holiday, Billie 978
Holiness-Pentecostal church 298
Hollander, Z. 1074
Hollowell, J. 795
Hollywood
  Depression era 1039
  film industry 1009
  film stars 997
  films 1008
  role of 'B' movies 1011
Hollywood, the haunted house 1009
Hollywood renaissance 1008
Home health services 371
Homemade world: the American modernist writers 807
Homer, Winslow 1082
Honky-tonk music 954, 956
Honour, H. 923
Hook, S. 884
Hooker, Thomas 125
  bibliographies 794
Hooks, W. H. 366
Hoover, J. Edgar 387
Hopkins, Harry Lloyd 184
Hopkins Review 846
Horan, J. R. 494
Hornung, Clarence Pearson 635

N

National health insurance: benefits, costs, and consequences 365
National interest and the human interest 535
National Labor Union
attitude to Afro-Americans 218
National parks 51—52
National party conventions, 1831-1976 429
National party platforms 430
National Welfare Rights Organization 368
National Woman Suffrage Association 256
National wonders of America 50
Nationalism 135
colonial period 113
Southern 142, 152
Nationalities 10, 202—204, 206—208, 210
encyclopaedias 201
folklore 865
Native sons: a critical study of twentieth-century Negro American authors 826
Natives and strangers: ethnic groups and the building of America 204
NATO - North Atlantic Treaty Organization 510
Natural resources 20
Natural Resources Defense Council 670
Naturalism 887, 890
Naturalist literature 766
Naturalists 32
Navy
history 98—100
Neal, H. E. 741
Needleman, Carolyn Emerson 691
Needleman, M. L. 691
Negro almanac: a reference work on the Afro-American 224
Negro Collection, Howard University 225
Negro in the United States: a selected bibliography 225
Neier, A. 474
Nelson, John H. 833
Neoconservatives: the men who are changing America's politics 403
Netherlands
colonies 106
Nettl, B. 964
Neustadt, R. E. 445
Nevins, A. 157

New age now begins: a people's history of the American Revolution 120
New American dream machine: toward a simpler lifestyle in an environmental age 673
New American political system 404
New American world: a documentary history of North America to 1612 82
New America's wonderland: our national parks 51
New careers and roles in the American school 723
New commonwealth, 1877-1890 164
'New communities' movement 689
New Deal 162, 168, 181—184, 660
city planning programme 693
New deal for blacks: the emergence of civil rights as a national issue 226
New Deal in the suburbs; a history of the greenbelt town program, 1935-1954 693
New England
archaeology 62
New England: Indian summer 820
New extended family: day care that works 366
New Freedom 176
New gods in America: an informal investigation into the new religions of American youth today 317
New heavens and new earth; political religion in America 318
New Mexico
'dust bowl' 182
settlement 140
New Orleans, Louisiana
segregation 227
New realist painting 932
New School for Social Research 990
New Senate: liberal influence on a conservative institution 422
New trends in the schools 724
New York
transport 630
urban design 690
New York Public Library. Prints Division 902
New York state
environmental management 682
laws on race 461

New York Stock Exchange 567, 570, 577, 579
  1929 crash 176, 571
  investment bankers 575
New York Times encyclopedia of television 1107
New York Times guide to business and finance: the American economy and how it works 581
New York Times guide to spectator sports 1075
New York Times heritage cook book 1059
Newman, Barnett 932
Newspapers
  history 1089
  Jewish 315
  role in presidential elections 448
NFL's official encylopedic history of professional football 1076
Niagara Falls 53
Nichiren Shoshu 303
Nichols, R. L. 204
Nicholson, M. 280
Nigro, F. A. 497
Nixon, Richard M. 405, 407
  Cambodia policy 543
  foreign policy 519, 545, 550
  impeachment 444
Noatak Eskimos
  folk-tales 867
Nobel prizes 748
Noise pollution 686
Nongraded schools in action: bold new venture 725
Nonsense book of riddles, rhymes, tongue twisters, puzzles and jokes from American folklore 873
Nootka 243
Norell, N. 1043
Norman, J. 933
Norman, T. 933
Norris, Frank 799
North America from earliest discovery to first settlements: the Norse voyages to 1612 34
North Atlantic Treaty Organization - NATO 510
Northeastern states
  Amerindians 239
  prehistory 64
Northwestern states
  Amerindians 243
Norton, M. B. 262, 273
Norton, P. F. 915

Notable American women, 1607-1950: a biographical dictionary 1117
Notable American women: the modern period 1118
Notable names in the American theater 1015
Novak, M. 295
Novelists 768, 783, 785, 797, 799
  19th century 844
  20th century 793
  Afro-American 781, 855
  Southern 776
Novels
  19th century 760
  20th century 814, 854
  Afro-American 855
  non-fiction 795
  progressive era 799
  Southern 776
Nowell, C. E. 106
Nuclear pollution 674
Nuclear question: the United States and nuclear weapons, 1946-1976 536
Nuclear weapons 536
  limitation talks 541
Nursery schools 381
Nursing homes 386
Nutrition 346
Nutrition programmes
  aged people 371
Nyren, D. 813

O

O strange new world: American culture: the formative years 14
Oates, Joyce Carol 854
O'Ballance, E. 189
Obituaries
  folklorists 861
Oblique light: studies in literary history and biography 827
O'Brien, D. 295
O'Brien, D. M. 485
Occupations
  health and safety 639
O'Connor, F. V. 905
O'Connor, Flannery 776, 845
Odyssey of the American right 405
Off-Broadway experience 1016
Office of Economic Opportunity 723
Official Congressional Directory 423
Oge, K. A. 523

288

Puns 879
Puritanism 3, 12
Puritans
  literature 770, 794
  psalms 945
*Pursuit of dignity: new living
  alternatives for the elderly* 371
*Pursuit of knowledge in the early
  American republic: American
  scientific and learned societies
  from colonial times to the Civil
  War* 746
Puzzles 873
Pynchon, Thomas 854

Q

Quaker church 298
Quality of the environment 681
Quinn, D. B. 34, 82
*Quintet: five American dance
  companies* 977
Quotations 772

R

Rabinowitz, H. N. 227
Rabushka, A. 200
*Race for the presidency: the media
  and the nominating process* 448
*Race relations in the urban South,
  1865-1890* 227
Races and racism 12, 15, 202−204,
  206, 208, 213−216, 220,
  222−225, 228−230, 554
  civil rights 226
  employment 217−219
  encyclopaedias 201
  law 461
  segregation 212, 227, 231
  Supreme Court rulings 482
  violence 358−359
Racing 1075
Radicalism
  left wing 396, 410
  right wing 408
Radio
  history 1102, 1104
Ragtime music 946, 983
Railways 626
  economics 553
  folklore 880
  history 622, 629, 632, 635

Raimo, J. 71
*Raising children in modern America:
  problems and prospective
  solutions* 372
Ramsay, W. 672
Randall, J. 150
*Random House guide to natural areas
  of the eastern United States* 52
Rankin, H. F. 1028
Ranney, A. 442
Ransom, John Crowe 842
Ratner, S. 559
Rawick, G. P. 213
Rawlins, Nolan Omri 619
*Reader's encyclopedia of American
  literature* 835
*Reader's encyclopedia of the American
  West* 83
*Readers' Guide to Periodical
  Literature* 1119
*Ready-made miracle: the American
  story of fashion for the
  millions* 1048
Real world of the public schools 726
Realism 887
*Realism and naturalism in
  nineteenth-century American
  literature* 836
Recipes 1053, 1056, 1058, 1061
  19th century 1057
  colonial period 1055, 1060
  regional 1052, 1054, 1059
Reconstruction 150, 155, 158−160
Reconstruction Act, 1867 154
*Reconstruction: after the Civil
  War* 158
*Reconstruction: ending of the Civil
  War* 159
Reed, E. 64
*Reference encyclopedia of the
  American Indian* 244
*Reform and regulation: American
  politics, 1900-1916* 177
*Reforming American education: the
  innovative approach to improving
  our schools and colleges* 727
Reforms
  19th century 162, 168
  20th century 162, 168, 177
  city government 498
  congressional 419
  congressional budget 414
  industrial regulation 606
  judicial 463
  prisons 347, 360, 370

role of the press 123
women 262
Rhymes 873—875
Rhythm and blues
influence of gospel music 961
Richey, R. E. 291
Rickenbacker, W. F. 734
Riddles 868—869, 873
Rideout, W. B. 769
Riedel, J. 946
Riesman, D. 13
Rigdon, W. 994
Righteous empire: the Protestant
experience in America 331
Rise of Adventism: religion and
society in mid-nineteenth century
America 332
Rise of American civilization 91
Rise of the West, 1754-1830 129
Rivers
canoeing 46
Rix, S. E. 353
Road show theatre 1036
Road to the White House: the politics
of presidential elections 449
'Roaring twenties' 174
Robbins, Roland Wells 60
Robinson, E. A. 798, 811
Robinson, J. 669
Robinson, J. K. 769
Rock and roll music 981
influence of blues music 982
Rockefeller Brothers Fund 683
Rodgers, D. T. 646
Rodgers, H. R. 563
Rodgers, Richard 944
Roebuck, J. 465
Rohrbough, M. J. 131
Roll Jordan roll 228
Roller, D. C. 77
Roman Catholic church 297—298, 311
philosophy 290
Romance in America: studies in
Cooper, Poe, Hawthorne, Melville,
and James 837
Romance of American
communism 433
Romero, P. W. 223
Roosevelt, Eleanor
role in civil rights 226
Roosevelt, Franklin Delano 162, 181,
184, 193, 195, 660
foreign policy 530
Supreme Court 'packing' 481

Roosevelt: soldier of freedom 530
Roosevelt, Theodore 173, 195
foreign policy 549
Roots of involvement: the U.S. in Asia,
1784-1971 540
Rose, B. 896
Rose, Pete 1073
Rosen, M. 1021
Rosenbaum, W. A. 675
Rosenblatt, R. 781
Rosenbloom, D. H. 393
Rosenthal, G. S. 305
Ross, H. 379
Rossiter, C. L. 125, 127, 438
Rosten, Leo Calvin 325
Roth, Philip 788
Rothchild, D. 523
Rothko, Mark 934
Rothman, D. J. 347
Rothman, S. M. 270
Rowley, P. 317
Royce, Josiah 885—887
Rubin, B. 538
Rubin, L. D. 6, 846
Rural life 349
poverty 349
Rush, Theressa Gunnels 780
Russell, Charles 910

S

Sabato, L. 495
Sabin, J. 1113
Sabloff, J. 61
Sablosky, I. 941
Safety, Industrial 639
Sagan, Carl 754
Sagas 875—876
Salamon, L. M. 565
Saldich, Anne Rawley 398
Salinger, J. D. 786, 793
SALT experience 541
SALT - Strategic Arms Limitation
Talks 541
Saltonstall, R. Jr. 686
Sampson, T. J. 382
San Francisco, California
urban design 690
Sandburg, Carl 863
Sandler, I. 934
Sansom, R. L. 673
Santayana, George 841, 883,
886—887, 891

293

297

U.S. Naval Academy 99
US Naval Academy 99
U.S. Navy: an illustrated history 100
US Office of Business Economics 609
US Superintendent of Documents 1115
USA: a history in art 935
USSR
  relations with 196, 515, 517, 521,
    530, 532, 537, 541—542
Utah
  Mormon folklore 865
  settlement 140
Utley, R. M. 234
Utopianism
  history 72

V

Van Buren, Martin 143
Vanderbilt, Cornelius 570
Varese, Edgar 940
Varg, P. A. 528, 548
Variety music cavalcade,
  1620-1969 985
Vegetation 19—21, 32
Velvet on iron: the diplomacy of
  Theodore Roosevelt 549
Verba, S. 642
Vermont
  environmental management 682
  guidebooks 52
Vertical File Index: Subject and Title
  Index to Selected Pamphlet
  Material 1121
Vietnam War 15, 189, 514, 540
  chronologies 75
  Paris agreement 534
  peace negotiations 534
  political impact 451
Vikings
  costume 1046
Violence
  history 358
Violence, Urban 192
  19th century 146
Viorst, M. 192
Virginia
  Appalachian folklore 877
  laws on race 461
Virginia WPA Writers Project 877
Visher, Stephen Sargent 23
Visible scientists 754
Vivelo, F. R. 765
Vivelo, J. J. 765

Vogel, D. 602
Vogelgesang, S. 508
Voice of black America 233
Voice of the folk: folklore and
  American literary theory 881
Voices in the valley: mythmaking and
  folk belief in the shaping of the
  Middle West 882
Voices of the black theater 1038
Volunteer Personal Service
  Program 501
Volunteer work
  role in community life 381
Vonnegut, Kurt 788
Voting 399
  unemployed 642
  urban 491
Vulnerable people: a view of American
  fiction since 1945 854

W

Wage-earning women: industrial work
  and family life in the United
  States, 1900-1930 269
Wagenknecht, E. C. 785
Wages 643
  government controls 553
Wagon and the star: a study of
  American community
  initiative 381
Wagons, Conestoga 624
Wakelyn, J. L. 148
Walden, D. 689
Walker, C. E. 568
Walker, S. E. 466
Walking: a guide to beautiful walks
  and trails in America 56
Walking trails 56
Wall Street 567, 570, 577, 579
  1929 crash 176, 571
  investment bankers 575
Walton, C. C. 562
War of 1812 134
War of 1812 134
War Powers Act, 1973 419
Ward, Clara 961
Warren, Robert Penn 840—841, 845
Warwick, E. 1045
Wasby, S. L. 487
Washburn, W. E. 234
Washington, DC
  segregation 227
  transport 628

Washington, George 124, 132
Washington state
environmental management 682
Waste
disposal 675
pollution 674
Watch Tower Bible and Tract
Society 298
Water pollution 675, 677, 686
Watercolours, Primitive 937
Watergate scandal 15
chronologies 75
Waterways, Inland 631
Watts, Emily Stipes 831
Watts, W. 378
*Way of the new world: the black novel
in America* 855
*Way West: art of frontier
America* 936
Wayne, John 997
Wayne, S. J. 449
We who built America 207
Weales, G. 1010
Weaponry, Military 527
nuclear arms 536
Weather 19—20, 54
maps 23
Wedel, W. R. 64—65
Weeber, S. C. 465
Weight-lifting 1075
Weingartner, C. 286, 728
Weinreb, L. L. 458
Weinstein, J. 396
Weisband, E. 529
Weisberger, B. A. 335
Weiss, I. 762
Weiss, Rita 929
Weissman, M. 259
Welch, J. 326
*Welfare: a handbook for friend and
foe* 382
*Welfare: the elusive consensus: where
we are, how we got there, and
what's ahead* 565
Welfare system 340, 367, 565
handbooks 382
history 357, 373
Welty, Eudora 776, 809, 840
Wentworth, H. 282
*We're in the money: Depression
America and its films* 1039
Werge, T. 794

Wesep, Hendrikus Boeve Van 891
Wesley, C. H. 223
West coast
prehistory 64
West Point atlas of American wars 31
West Virginia
guidebooks 52
Western films 1019, 1033
Western states
19th century 129
encyclopaedias 83
frontier art 910, 936
geography 21
history 83, 140
prehistory 66
settlement 235
Western swing 956
*Westward expansion: a history of the
American frontier* 147
Wharton, Edith 851
*What happens in book
publishing* 1098
*What is American in American
art* 937
What schools can do 735
*What we save now: an Audobon
primer of defense* 685
*What's the difference? A
British/American dictionary* 289
*Wheels across America: a pictorial
cavalcade illustrating the early
development of vehicular
transportation* 635
Wheels for a nation 636
*When your parents grow old:
information and resources to help
the adult son or daughter cope
with the problems of aging
parents* 383
*Where have all the voters gone? The
fracturing of America's political
parties* 435
*Whereby we thrive: a history of
American farming, 1607-1972* 620
Whitaker, Jennifer Seymour 506
White heat 1003
White House Conference for the
Aging 337
White House years 550
White, Jon Manchip 238
White, M. G. 122, 889—890
*White man's Indian: images of the
American Indian from Columbus
to the present* 246
White, T. H. 440

304

Map of the USA

This map shows the more important towns and other features.

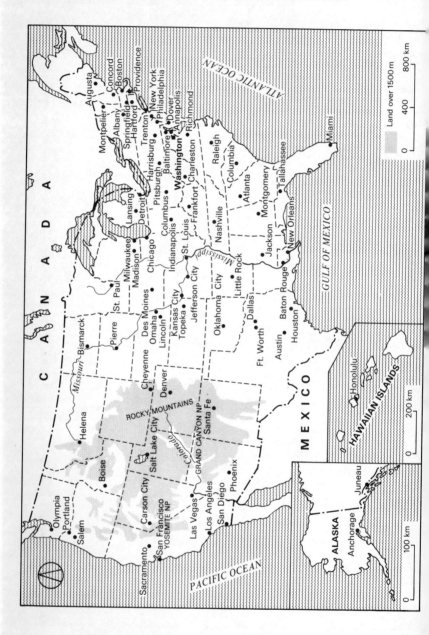